How to Read the
NEW TESTAMENT

How to Read the
NEW TESTAMENT

*An Introduction to Linguistic and
Historical-Critical Methodology*

WILHELM EGGER

Edited and with an Introduction by

HENDRIKUS BOERS

HENDRICKSON
PUBLISHERS

Translated from the German by Peter Heinegg
Methodenlehre zum Neuen Testament: Einführung in linguistische und historisch-kritische Methoden, by Wilhelm Egger. Freiburg: Verlag Herder, 1987.

ISBN 1–56563–149–8

First printing — October 1996

Library of Congress Cataloging-in-Publication Data

Egger, Wilhelm
  Methodenlehre zum Neuen Testament.   English]
  How to read the New Testament: an introduction to linguistic and
historical-critical methodology / Wilhelm Egger: translated by
Peter Heinegg.
    Includes bibliographical references and index.
    ISBN 1–56563–149–8 (pbk.)
    1. Bible—Hermeneutics.   I. Title.
  BS476.E4413   1996
  225.6′01—dc20   95–42126
                                                                          CIP

Table of Contents ❧

PART 2: PREPARATORY STEPS IN ANALYSIS

PART 3: SYNCHRONIC READING

PART 4: DIACHRONIC READING

PART 5: READING HISTORICALLY

Foreword ❖

THE METHODOLOGY PRESENTED HERE IS MEANT AS A GUIDE TO scholarly work on New Testament texts. A peculiar feature of this methodology is the attempt to link a sampling of recent methods derived from linguistics with the analytical procedures of historical critical exegesis. The interconnection of the methods is established primarily through the theoretical model of "communication through texts" as well as by reflection on the act of reading and understanding.

The selection and order of the individual methodical steps, which occasionally deviate from those generally accepted, and which make no claim to being the last word on the subject, have grown out of my teaching in Brixen, Innsbruck, and Erfurt.

I would especially like to thank two partners in dialogue: my brother Kurt and my colleague Claus-Peter März in Erfurt. I must also thank my colleagues Jacob Kremer in Vienna and Hubert Frankemölle in Paderborn for checking the manuscript and making a series of suggestions to improve it.

The manuscript was finished in July, 1986. My appointment as bishop of Bozen-Brixen made it my special mission to do what Heinrich Zimmermann describes in the introduction to *his* methodology as the task of New Testament scholarship: " . . . to bring the reader to a deeper understanding of the word of God, as presented in the historically bound form of the New Testament, to grasp its theological content and to let its message for today's men and women be heard." In so doing we cannot dispense with the scholarly treatment of the word of God.

Brixen

List of Diagrams ❀

Bibliography and Short Titles

Achtemeier, *Hermeneutic*   Achtemeier, P. J. *An Introduction to the New Hermeneutic.* Philadelphia: Westminster, 1969.

Akmajian, Demers, Harnish, *Linguistics*   Akmajian, A., R. Demers, R. M. Harnish. *Linguistics: An Introduction to Language and Communication.* Cambridge: MIT Press. 1979.

Akmajian, Demers, Harnish, "Pragmatics"   Akmajian, A., R. Demers, R. M. Harnish. "Pragmatics: The Study of Language Use and Linguistic Communication." Pages 267–302. In Akmajian, Demers, Harnisch, *Linguistics.*

Aland, *Konkordanz*   Aland, K. ed. *Vollständige Konkordanz zum griechischen Neuen Testament.* Berlin, 1978.

Aland, K. & B., *Text*   Aland, K., B. Aland. *The Text of the New Testament.* 2d. ed. Trans. E. F. Rhodes. Grand Rapids: Eerdmans, 1989.

Albertz, "Antrittsrede"   Albertz, R. "Die 'Antrittsrede' Jesu im Lukasevangelium auf ihrem alttestamentlichen Hintergrund." *ZNW* 74 (1983) 182–206.

Aletti, "Jésus"   Aletti, J. N. "Jésus à Nazareth (Lc 4, 16–30). Prophétie, Ecriture et typologie." Pages 431–51. In *Festschrift für Jacques Dupont.* Paris, 1985.

Aletti, *Miracles*   Aletti, J. N. et al. *Les miracles de Jésus.* Paris, 1977.

Alonso Schökel, *Alte Testament*   Alonso Schökel, L. *Das Alte Testament als sprachliches Kunstwerk.* Cologne, 1971; from the Spanish.

Alter, *Narrative*   Alter, R. *The Art of Biblical Narrative.* New York: Basic Books, 1981.

Altpeter, *Exegese*   Altpeter, G. *Textlinguistische Exegese alttestamentlicher Literatur. Eine Dekodierung.* Bern, 1978.

AnBib   Analecta biblica

Anderegg, *Fiktion*   Anderegg, J. *Fiktion und Kommunikation.* Göttingen, 1977.

Anderegg, *Stiltheorie*   Anderegg, J. *Literaturwissenschaftliche Stiltheorie.* Göttingen, 1977.

ANRW   *Aufstieg und Niedergang der römischer Welt.* Ed. H. Temporini and W. Haase. Berlin, 1972.

Arens, *Logic*   Arens, E. *The Logic of Pragmatic Thinking.* Trans. D. Smith. Atlantic Highlands, N.J.: Humanities Press, 1994.

Arens, "Theologie"   Arens, E. "Narrative Theologie und theologische Theorie des Erzählens." *KBl* 110 (1985) 868–71.

Asher, *Encyclopedia of Linguistics*   Asher, R. E. ed. *Encyclopedia of Language and Linguistics*. 10 vols. Oxford: Pergamon, 1994.

Assmann, Hardmeier, *Schrift*   Assmann, A. and J., C. Hardmeier. *Schrift und Gedächtnis. Beiträge zur Archäologie der literarischen Kommunikation.* Munich, 1983.

Austin, *Words*   Austin, J. L. *How to Do Things with Words.* Cambridge, Mass.: Harvard University Press, 1975.

Baarlink, "Jahr"   Baarlink, H. "Ein gnädiges Jahr des Herrn und ein Tag der Vergeltung (Lk 4,18–19)." *ZNW* 73 (1982) 204–20.

Babilas, *Tradition*   Babilas, W. *Tradition und Interpretation.* Munich, 1971.

Baldinger, *Semantic Theory*   Baldinger, K. *Semantic Theory: Towards a Modern Semantics.* Trans. William C. Brown. Ed. Roger Wright. New York: St. Martin's Press, 1980.

Baltensweiler, *Geschichte*   Baltensweiler, H. ed. *Neues Testament und Geschichte. Historisches Geschehen und Deutung im Neuen Testament. Festschrift für O. Cullmann.* Tubingen: J. C. B. Mohr, 1972.

Barnwell, *Semantics and Translation*   Barnwell, K. G. *Introduction to Semantics and Translation: With Special Reference to Bible Translation.* 2d. ed. Summer Institute of Linguistics, 1980.

Barr, *Semantics*   Barr, J. *The Semantics of Biblical Language.* Oxford, 1961.

Barth, Schramm, *Bibel*   Barth, H., T. Schramm. *Selbsterfahrung mit der Bibel. Ein Schlüssel zum Lesen und Verstehen.* Munich, 1977.

Barthes, *Exégèse*   Barthes R. et al. *Exégèse et herméneutique.* Paris, 1971.

Barthes, "Introduction"   Barthes, R. "Introduction à l'analyse structurale des récits." *Communication* 8 (1966) 1–27.

Barthes, "L'analyse"   Barthes, R. "L'analyse structurale du récit. A propos d'Actes 10–11." In Barthes, *Exégèse.*

Barthes, *Semiology*   Barthes, R. *Elements of Semiology.* Trans. A. Lavers and C. Smith. New York: Noonday Press, 1988.

BAGD   Bauer, W. *A Greek-English Lexicon of the New Testament and Other Early Christian Literature.* 2d ed. Trans. W. F. Arndt and F. W. Gingrich. Revised and edited F. W. Danker. Chicago: University of Chicago Press, 1979.

Baumert, *Ehelosigkeit*   Baumert, N. *Ehelosigkeit und Ehe im Herrn. Eine neue Interpretation von 1 Kor 7.* FB 47. Würzburg, 1984.

BBB   Bonner biblische Beiträge

BDF   Blass, F., A. Debrunner, and R. Funk. *A Greek Grammar of the New Testament and Other Early Christian Literature.* Chicago: University of Chicago, 1961.

Beardslee, *Criticism*   Beardslee, W. A. *Literary Criticism and the New Testament.* Guides to Biblical Scholarship. Philadelphia: Fortress, 1970.

Becker, "Literatur"   Becker, J. "Aus der Literatur zum Johannesevangelium (1978–80)." *ThR* 47 (1982) 294–301.

Beekman, Callow, *Translating*   Beekman, J., J. Callow. *Translating the Word of God.* Grand Rapids: Zondervan Publishing House, 1974.

Berger, *Exegese*   Berger, K. *Exegese des Neuen Testaments. Neue Wege vom Text zur Auslegung.* UTB 658. Heidelberg 1977.

Berger, *Formgeschichte*   Berger, K. *Formgeschichte des Neuen Testaments.* Heidelberg, 1984.

Berger, "Hellenistische"   Berger, K. "Hellenistische Gattungen und Neues Testament." Pages 1031–42, 1831–85. In *ANRW* II, 25, 2.
Berger, "Methode"   Berger, K. "Die impliziten Gegner: Zur Methode des Erschließens von 'Gegnern' in neutestamentlichen Texten." Pages 373–400. In *Festschrift für G. Bornkamm.* Tübingen, 1980.
Berger, Preuß, *Bibelkunde*   Berger, K., H. D. Preuß, *Bibelkunde des Alten und Neuen Testaments,* II. Heidelberg, 1980. 475–502.
Berger, P.-R., "Aramäisch"   Berger, P.-R. "Zum Aramäisch der Evangelien und der Apostelgeschichte." *ThRev* 82 (1986) 1–18.
Berruto, *Semantica*   Berruto, G. *La semantica.* Bologna, n.d.
Betti, *Allgemeine*   Betti, E. *Allgemeine Auslegungslehre als Methodik der Geisteswissenschaften.* Tübingen, 1967.
Betz, "Composition"   Betz, H.-D. "The Literary Composition and Function of Paul's Letter to the Galatians." *NTS* 21 (1975) 353–79.
Betz, "Defense"   Betz, H.-D. "In Defense of the Spirit: Paul's Letter to the Galatians as a Document of Early Christian Apologetics." Pages 99–114. In Fiorenza, *Propaganda.*
Betz, *Galatians*   Betz, H.-D. *Galatians: A Commentary on Paul's Letter to the Churches in Galatia.* Philadelphia: Fortress, 1979.
BEvT   Beiträge zur evangelischen Theologie
Beyer, *Syntax*   Beyer, K. *Semitische Syntax in Neuen Testament.* SUNT 1. Göttingen, 1962.
Bib   Biblica
BibLeb   Bibel und Leben
Black, "Erwiderung"   Black, M. "Erwiderung." *ThRev* 82 (1986) 18–22.
Blanke, *Einführung*   Blanke, G.-H. *Einführung in die semantische Analyse.* Munich, 1973.
Boers, *"Mountain"*   Boers, H. *"Neither on This Mountain, Nor in Jerusalem":* *A Study of John 4.* SBLMS 34. Atlanta: Scholars Press, 1988.
Boers, "Theologie"   Boers, H. "Die Theologie des Paulus im Lichte der Philosophie Platons." Pages 57–77. In H.-D. Betz and L. Schottroff, eds. *Neues Testament und christlich Existenz. Festschrift für Herbert Braun zum 70. Geburtstag am 4. Mai 1973.* Tübingen: J.C.B. Mohr (Paul Siebeck) 1973.
Boers, "Thessalonians."   Boers, H. "The Form Critical Study of Paul's Letters: I Thessalonians as a Case Study." *NTS* 22 (1976) 140–58.
Boers, "Usage"   Boers, H. "Language Usage and the Production of Matthew 1:18–2:23." Pages 217–34. In Spencer, R. ed. *Orientation by Disorientation: Studies in Literary Criticism and Biblical Literary Criticism in Honor of William A. Beardslee.* Pittsburgh: Pickwick Press, 1980.
Boismard, Lamouille, *Werkstatt*   Boismard, M. E., A. Lamouille. *Aus der Werkstatt der Evangelisten. Einführung in die Literarkritik.* Munich, 1980.
Bornkamm, *Paul*   Bornkamm, G. *Paul.* Trans. D. M. G. Stalker. New York: Harper & Row, 1971.
Bornkamm, Barth, Held, *Tradition*   Bornkamm, G., G. Barth, H. J. Held. *Tradition and Interpretation in Matthew.* Trans. P. Scott. Philadelphia: Westminster, 1963.
Breimeyer, "Propp"   Breimeyer, R. "Vladimir Jakovlevic Propp (1895–1970): Leben, Wirken und Bedeutsamkeit." *LingBibl* 15/16 (1972) 32–66.
Brekle, *Semantik*   Brekle, H. *Semantik.* UTB 102. 2d ed. Munich 1972.

Bremond, *Longique*   Bremond, C. *Longique du récit*. Paris, 1973.

Breuer, *Texttheorie*   Breuer, D. *Einführung in die pragmatische Texttheorie*. UTB 106. Munich, 1974.

Breytenbach, "Erzählung"   Breytenbach, C. "Das Markusevangelium als episodische Erzählung. Mitüberlegungen zum 'Aufbau' des zweiten Evangeliums." Pages 137–69. In F. Hahn, ed., *Erzähler*.

Bright, *International Encyclopedia*   Bright, W. ed. *International Encyclopedia of Linguistics*. 4 vols. New York: Oxford, 1992.

Brown, *Community*   Brown, R. E. *The Community of the Beloved Disciple*. New York: Paulist, 1979.

Brown, *John*   Brown, R. E. *The Gospel according to John*. 2 vols. Anchor Bible 28, 28A. Garden City, N.Y.: Doubleday, 1966–70.

Bruce, *History*   Bruce, F. F. *History of the Bible in English*. Oxford: Oxford, 1978.

Bryson, *Ideas*   Bryson, L. ed. *The Communication of Ideas*. n.p., 1948.

Bühler, *Sprachtheorie*   Bühler, K. *Sprachtheorie. Die Darstellungsfunktion der Sprache. Mit einem Geleitwort von Friedrich Kainz*. Stuttgart: G. Fischer, 1965.

Bühlmann, Scherer, *Stilfiguren*   Bühlmann, W., K. Scherer. *Stilfiguren der Bibel. Ein kleines Nachschlagwerk*. Fribourg, 1973.

Bultmann, "Mythologie"   Bultmann, R. "Neues Testament und Mythologie." Pages 15–48. In Bartsch, H.-W. ed. *Kerygma und Mythos*. Hamburg: Herbert Reich. Vol. 1. 1948. 2d ed. 1951. ET: "The New Testament and Mythology." Pages 1–44. In *Kerygma and Myth*. Trans. R. Fuller. London: SPCK, 1953.

Bultmann, *Stil*   Bultmann, R. *Der Stil der paulinischen Predigt und die kynisch-stoische Diatribe*. FRLANT 13. Göttingen, 1910.

Bultmann, *Synoptic*   Bultmann, R. *The History of the Synoptic Tradition*. Trans. J. Marsh. 1963. Reprint. Peabody, Mass.: Hendrickson Publishers, 1992.

Busseman, Van der Sluis, *Bibel*   Busseman, C., D. Van der Sluis. *Die Bibel studieren. Einführung in die Methoden der Exegese*. Munich, 1982.

Buzzetti, "Parola"   Buzzetti, C. "Parola del Signore. Una traduzione 'popolare' della Bibbia in Italia." Pages 120–26. In C. Mesters, *Lettura popolare della Bibbia*. Bologna, 1978.

Buzzetti, *Tradotta*   Buzzetti, C. *La parola tradotta. Aspetti linguistici, erme-neutici e teologici della traduzione della sacra Scrittura*. Brescia: Morcelliana, 1973.

BZ   *Biblische Zeitschrift*

BZNW   Beihefte zur *ZNW*

Calloud, *Analysis*   Calloud, J. *Structural Analysis of the Narrative*. Trans. D. Patte. Philadelphia: Fortress Press, 1976.

Calloud, "L'analyse"   Calloud, J. "L'analyse structurale du récit. Quel-ques éléments d'une méthode." *FoiVie* 73 (1974) 2–65.

Cancik, *Markus-Philologie*   Cancik, Hubert ed. *Markus-Philologie: Histo-rische, literaturgeschichtliche und stilistische Untersuchungen zum zweiten Evan-gelium*. WUNT 33. Tübingen, 1984.

Cancik, *Senecas*   Cancik, Hildegard. *Untersuchungen zu Senecas Epistulae Morales*. Hildesheim: Olms, 1969.

Carmignac, "Mc 9, 23"   Carmignac, J. "Ah, si tu peux! . . . 'Tout est possible en faveur de celui qui croit' (Mc 9, 23)." Pages 83-86. In *Festschrift for Bo Reicke*. Macon: Mercer, 1984.

CBibNT   Coniectanea biblica. New Testament series

CBQ   Catholic Biblical Quarterly

Chomsky, *Structures*   Chomsky, N. *Syntactic Structures*. The Hague: Mouton, 1957.

Church, "Structure"   Church, F. F. "Rhetorical Structure and Design in Paul's Letter to Philemon." *HTR* 71 (1978) 17–33.

CivCatt   Civilta Cattolica

Conzelmann, *Theology*   Conzelmann, H. *The Theology of St. Luke*. Trans. G. Buswell. Philadelphia: Fortress Press, 1982.

Conzelmann, Lindemann, *Interpreting*   Conzelmann, H., A. Lindemann. *Interpreting the New Testament: An Introduction to the Principles and Methods of New Testament Exegesis*. Trans. S. S. Schatzmann. Peabody, Mass.: Hendrickson Publishers, 1988.

Coreth, *Hermeneutik*   Coreth, E. *Grundfragen der Hermeneutik*. Freiburg, 1969.

Courtés, *Introduction*   Courtés, J. *Introduction à la sémiotique narrative et discursive*. Preface by A. J. Greimas. Paris, 1976.

de Beaugrande, Dressler, *Linguistics*   de Beaugrande, R.-A., W. U. Dressler. *Introduction to Text Linguistics*. London/New York: Longman, 1981.

de Gaulmyn, "Réflection"   de Gaulmyn, M. M. "Réflection sur l'Epître de Paul à Philemon." Pages 18–23. In Group de Montpellier, "Epître."

de la Potterie, "Compositione"   de la Potterie, I. "De compositione evangelii Marci." *VD* 44 (1966) 135–41.

de la Potterie, "Impostare"   de la Potterie, I. "Come impostare il problema del Gesù istorico." *CivCatt* 120 (1969) 2855, 447–63.

de Lubac, *Exégèse*   de Lubac, H. *Exégèse médiévale. Les quatre sens de l'Ecriture*. Paris, 1959.

de Pomero, *Analisi*   de Pomero, P. J. *Il vangelo come racconto. Analisi morfologica del vangelo di Matteo*. Turin, 1983; from the French, *Quand un évangile nous est conté*. Brussels, 1983.

de Saussure, *Course*   de Saussure, F. *Course in General Linguistics*. Trans. Wade Baskin. New York: Philosophical Library, 1959; from the French, *Cours de linguistique générale*. Posthumously collected and published by his students, Charles Bally and Charles Albert Sechehaye. Paris: Payot 1916.

de Waard, "Prinzipien"   de Waard, J. "Die heremeutischen Prinzipien der 'Bibel in heutigem Deutsch.' " Pages 169–79. In Gnilka, Rüger, *Bibel.*

Detweiler, "Reader"   Detweiler, R. ed. "Reader Response Approaches to Biblical and Secular Texts." *Semeia* 31 (1985).

Dewey, *Orality*   Dewey, J. ed. *Orality and Textuality in Early Christian Literature*. Semeia 65. Atlanta: Scholars Press, 1995.

Di Marco, "Chiasmus"   Di Marco, A. "Der Chiasmus in der Bibel III and IV." *LingBibl* 39 (1976) 37–85 and 44 (1979) 3–70.

Dibelius, *ThR*   Dibelius M. *ThR* New Series 1 (1929) 214.

Dibelius, *Tradition*   Dibelius, M. *From Tradition to Gospel*. Trans. B. L. Wolf. 1935. Reprint. James Clarke & Co., 1991.

Dodd, "Framework"   Dodd, C. H. "The Framework of the Gospel Narrative." *ExpT* 43 (1931–32) 396–400.

Donfried, *Romans*   Donfried, K. P. ed. *The Romans Debate*. Minneapolis: Augsburg, 1977.

Dormeyer, *Leidens*   Dormeyer, D. *Der Sinn des Leidens Jesu. Historisch-kritische und textpragmatische Analyse der Markuspassion*. SBS 96. Stuttgart, 1979.

Dressler, *Einführung*   Dressler, W. U. *Einführung in die Textliguistik*. Tübingen: Niemeyer, 1973.

Drewermann, *Exegese*   Drewermann, E. *Tiefenpsychologie und Exegese*. Olten, 1984.

Dschulnigg, *Sprache*   Dschulnigg, P. *Sprache, Redaktion, und Intention des Markus-Evangeliums. Eigentümlichkeiten der Sprache des Markus-Evangeliums und ihre Bedeutung für der Redaktionskritik*. SBB 11. Stuttgart, 1984.

Dupont, *Jésus*   Dupont, J. ed. *Jésus aux origines de la christologie*. Gembloux, 1975.

Ebeling, *Auslegung*   Ebeling, G. *Kirchengeschichte als Auslegung der Heiligen Schriften*. Tübingen, 1947.

Eco, *Lector*   Eco, U. *Lector in Fabula*. Milan, 1979.

Eco, *Semiotics*   Eco, U. *A Theory of Semiotics*. Bloomington: Indiana University Press, 1976.

Eco, *Trattato*   Eco, U. *Trattato di semiotica generale*. Milan: Bompiani, 1975.

EDNT   Balz, H. R., G. Schneider eds. *Exegetical Dictionary of the New Testament*. 3 vols. Grand Rapids: Eerdmans, 1978–80.

Egger, "1 Kor 7"   Egger, W. "Ehe und Jungfräulichkeit. 1 Kor 7 als Beispiel ethischer Argumentation des Apostels Paulus." *Conference Proceedings (Brixen)* 90 (1979) 89–97.

Egger, *Alternative*   Egger, W. *Franz von Assisi. Das Evangelium als Alternative*. Innsbruck, 1981.

Egger, "Auslegung"   Egger, W. "Handlungsorientierte Auslegung der Antithesen Mt 5, 21–48." Pages 119–44. In Kertelge, *Rückfrage*.

Egger, "Bergpredigt"   Egger, W. "Faktoren der Textkonstitution in der Bergpredigt." *Laurentianum* 19 (1978) 177–98.

Egger, *Bibelkunde*   Egger, W. *Kleine Bibelkunde zum neuen Testament*. 2d ed. Innsbruck, 1984.

Egger, "Bibellesens"   Egger, W. "Die zweite Unbefangenheit des Bibellesens." *BibLit* 50 (1976) 247–55.

Egger, *Galaterbrief*   Egger, W. *Galaterbrief, Philipperbrief, Philemonbrief*. Echter Bibel. Würzburg: Echter, 1985.

Egger, *Gemeinsam*   Egger, W. *Gemeinsam Bibel lesen. Eine Handreichung zur Rundenarbeit mit der Bibel*. Innsbruck, 1987.

Egger, *Lehre*   Egger, W. *Frohbotschaft und Lehre. Die Sammelberichte des Wirkens Jesu im Markusevangelium*. Frankfurt am Main, 1976.

Egger, "Mitarbeiter"   Egger, W. "Die Mitarbeiter des Paulus. Hinweise auf die Ordnung der Gemeinden in den Briefen des Apostels Paulus." *Conference Proceedings (Brixen)* 92 (1981) 12–17.

Egger, "Nachfolge"   Egger, W. "Der Ruf in die Nachfolge als Impuls für das Ordensleben." *Ordensnachrichten* 21 (1982) 215–26.

Egger, *Nachfolge*   Egger, W. *Nachfolge als Weg zum Leben. Chancen neurer exegetischer Methoden dargelegt an Mk 10, 17–31.* ÖBS 1. Klosterneuburg, 1979.

Egger, *Programm*   Egger, W. *Das Programm Jesu. Ein Arbeitsheft zum Lukasevangelium.* Klosterneuburg, 1976.

Ehlich, "Alltägliches"   Ehlich, K. "Alltägliches Erzählen." In K. Wegenast, ed. *Erzählen für Kinder. Erzählen von Gott.* Stuttgart, 1980.

Ehlich, "Textbegriff"   Ehlich, K. "Zum Textbegriff." Pages 9–25. In A. Rothkegel, B. Sandig, eds. *Texte-Textsorten-Semantik. Linguistische Modelle und maschinelle Verfahren.* Paper on Textual Linguistics 52. Hamburg, 1984.

EKK   Evangelisch-Katholischer Kommentar zum Neuen Testament. Edited by J. Blank, R. Schnackenburg, E. Schweizer, U. Wilckens.

Epp, Fee, *Theory and Method*   Epp, E., G. D. Fee. *Studies in the Theory and Method of New Testament Textual Criticsm.* Grand Rapids: Eerdmans, 1993.

Erl, Gaiser, *Methoden*   Erl, W., F. Gaiser. *Neue Methoden der Bibelarbeit.* Tübingen, 1969.

ETL   Ephemerides Theologicae Lovanienses

ExpT   Expository Times

Fages, *Structuralisme*   Fages. J.-B. *Comprendre la structuralisme.* Toulouse, 1968. German: *Den Strukturalismus verstehen. Einführung in das strukturale Denken.* Gießen 1974.

FB   Forschung zur Bibel

Fee, *Exegesis*   Fee, G. D. *New Testament Exegesis: A Handbook for Students and Pastors.* Revised edition. Louisville: Westminster John Knox, 1993.

Fillmore, "Case"   Fillmore, C. J. "The Case for Case." Pages 1–88. In Bach, E., and R. T. Harms eds. *Universals in Linguistic Theory.* New York: Holt, Rinehart and Winston, 1968.

Fiorenza, *Propaganda*   Fiorenza, E. S. ed. *Aspects of Religious Propaganda in Judaism and Early Christianity.* Notre Dame: University of Notre Dame, 1976.

Fleischer, Michel, *Stilistik*   Fleischer, W., G. Michel. *Stilistik der deutschen Gegenwartssprache.* Leipzig, 1975.

Fohrer, *Exegese AT*   Fohrer, G. *Exegese des Alten Testaments. Einführung in die Methodik* UTB 267. Heidelberg, 1979.

FoiVie   Foi et Vie

Fossion, *Leggere*   Fossion, A. *Leggere le Scritture.* Teoria e practica della lettura strutturale. Torino 1982. From the French. *Lire les Ecritures.* Brussels, 1980.

Fowler, "Reader"   Fowler, R. M. "Who Is the 'Reader' of Mark's Gospel?" Pages 31–53. In *SBLSP 22.* Scholars, 1983.

Frankemölle, "Bibel"   Frankemölle, H. "Die Bibel und der heutige Leser. Zur neuen Übersetzung 'Die Bibel in heutigem Deutsch'—Würdigung und Kritik." *Diakonia* 15 (1984) 119–32.

Frankemölle, "Bibelübersetzungen"   Frankemölle, H. "Bibelübersetzungen—für wen?" *Diakonia* 16 (1985) 338–45.

Frankemölle, "Evangelist"   Frankemölle, H. "Evangelist und Gemeinde. Eine methodenkritische Besinnung (mit Beispielen aus dem Matthäusevangelium)." *Bib* 60 (1977) 153–90.

Frankemölle, *Handlungsanweisungen*   Frankemölle, H. *Biblische Handlungsanweisungen. Beispiele pragmatischer Exegese.* Mainz, 1983.

Frankemölle, *Kirche*   Frankemölle, H. *Jahwe-Bund und Kirche Christi. Studien zur Form- und Traditionsgeschichte des "Evangeliums" nach Matthäus.* Münster, 1984.

Frankemölle, "Kommunikatives"   Frankemölle, H. "Kommunikatives Handeln in Gleichnissen Jesu. Historisch-kritische und pragmatische Exegese. Eine kritische Sichtung." *NTS* 28 (1982) 61–90.

Frankemölle, "Sozialethik"   Frankemölle, H. "Sozialethik im Neuen Testament. Neuere Forschungstendenzen, offene Fragen und hermeneutische Anmerkungen." ThBerichte 14. Zurich, 1985.

Friedrich, "Struktur"   Friedrich, G. "Die formale Struktur von Mt 28:18–20." *ZthK* (1983) 137–83.

Friedrich, "Prehistory"   Friedrich, G. "Prehistory of the Theological Dictionary of the New Testament." *TDNT* (1976) 10.613–61.

Friedrich, "Problem"   Friedrich, G. "Zum Problem der Semantik." *KerDogma* 16 (1970) 41–57.

Friedrich, "Wortstatistik"   Friedrich, J. H. "Wortstatistik als Methode am Beispiel der Frage einer Sonderquelle im Matthäusevangelium." *ZNW* 76 (1985) 29–42.

FRLANT   Forschungen zur Religion und Literatur des Alten und Neuen Testaments

Funk, *Status*   Funk, A. *Status und Rollen in den Paulusbriefen. Eine inhaltsanalytische Untersuchung zur Religionssoziologie.* Innsbruck, 1981.

Funk-Kolleg Literatur   Brackert H., E. Lammert eds. *Funk-Kolleg Literatur.* 2 vols. Fischer-Bücherei 6326f. Frankfurt am Main, 1972.

Funk-Kolleg Sprache   *Funk-Kolleg Sprache. Eine Einführung in die moderne Linguistik.* 2 vols. Fischer-Bücherei 6111/2. Frankfurt am Main, 1973.

Gadamer, *Problema*   Gadamer, H.-G. *Il problema della coscienza storica.* Naples, 1969.

Gadamer, *Truth*   Gadamer, H.-G. *Truth and Method.* Trans. W. Glen-Doepel. London: Sheed and Ward, 1979.

Gayer, *Stellung*   Gayer, R. *Die Stellung der Sklaven in den paulinischen Gemeinden. Zugleich ein sozialgeschichtlich vergleichender Beitrag zur Wertung der Sklaven in der Antike.* Bern, 1976.

Gerhart, Williams, *Narrativity*   Gerhart, M., J. G. Williams eds. *Genre, Narrativity, and Theology.* Semeia 43. Atlanta: Scholars Press, 1988.

Glinz, *Textanalyse*   Glinz, H. *Textanalyse und Verstehen.* 2 vols. Vol. 1: Frankfurt am Main, 1973. Vol. 2.: Wiesbaden, 1978.

Gnilka, *Epheserbrief*   Gnilka, J. *Der Epheserbrief.* HTK 10. Freiburg, 1971.

Gnilka, *Markusevangelium*   Gnilka, J. *Markusevangelium.* EKK 2. Zürich: Benzinger/Neukirchen. Vluyn: Neukirchen, 1978.

Gnilka, *Philemonbrief*   Gnilka, J. ed. *Philemonbrief.* HTK 10/4. Freiburg im Breisgau: Herder, 1982.

Gnilka, Rüger, *Bibel*   Gnilka, J., H. P. Rüger, eds. *Die Übersetzung der Bibel—Aufgabe der Theologie.* Stuttgart Symposium, 1984. Bielefeld, 1985.

GNT   *The Greek New Testament*

Grant, *Translating the Bible*   Grant, F. C. *Translating the Bible.* Greenwich, 1971.

Grässer, "Jesus"   Grässer, E. ed. "Jesus in Nazareth." BZNW 40. Berlin, 1972.

Greenlee, *Text Criticism*   Greenlee, J. H. *Introduction to New Testament Textual Criticism*. Revised edition. Peabody, Mass.: Hendrickson, 1995.

Greimas, *Maupassant*   Greimas, A. J. *Maupassant, la sémiotique du texte*. Exercises pratiques. Paris: Éditions du Seuil, 1976.

Greimas, *Meaning*   Greimas, A. J. *On Meaning: Selected Writings in Semiotic Theory*. Trans. P. J. Perron, F. H. Collins. London: F. Pinter, 1987. Minneapolis: University of Minnesota Press, 1987.

Greimas, *Semantics*   Greimas, A. J. *Structural Semantics: An Attempt at a Method*. Trans. D. McDowell, R. Schleifer, A. Velie. Lincoln: University of Nebraska Press, 1983.

Greimas, *Sémantique.*   Greimas, A. J., *Sémantique structurale*. Paris: Librairie Larousse, 1966

Greimas, *Sens*   Greimas, A. J. *Du sens: Essais sémiotiques*. Paris: Editions du Seuil, 1970.

Greimas, *Sens II*   Greimas, A. J. *Du sens II: Essais sémiotiques*. Paris: Editions du Seuil, 1983.

Greimas, Courtés, *Semiotics*   Greimas, A. J., J. Courtés. *Semiotics and Language. An Analytical Dictionary*. Trans. L. Crist, D. Patte, et al. Bloomington: Indiana University Press, 1982.

Greimas, Courtés, *Sémiotique*   Greimas, A. J., J. Courtés. *Sémiotique. Dictionnaire raisonné de la théorie du langage*. Langue, linguistique, communication. Paris: Hachette, 1979.

Grimm, *Literatur*   Grimm, G. ed. *Literatur und Leser: Theorien und Modelle zur Rezeption literarischer Texte*. Stuttgart, 1975.

Grimminger, "Kommunikation"   Grimminger, n.i. "Literarische Kommunikation." In *Funk-Kolleg Literatur*. I, 104–6.

Große, "Semiotik"   Große, E. U. "Was ist Semiotik?" *LingBibl* 52 (1982) 87–113; 54 (1983) 27–52.

Groupe d'Entrevernes, *Analyse*   Groupe d'Entrevernes. *Analyse sémiotique des textes*. Introduction–Théorie–Pratique. Lyon, 1977.

Groupe d'Entrevernes, *Signes*   Groupe d'Entrevernes. *Signes et paraboles. Sémiotique et texte évangelique*. Paris, 1977.

Groupe de Montpellier, "Epître"   Groupe de Montpellier. "L'Epître de Paul à Philemon." *SémBible* 11 (1978) 7–17.

Guiraud, Kuentz, *La stylistique*   Guiraud P., P. Kuentz. *La stylistique*. Initiation à la linguistique A1. Paris, 1975.

Guiraud, Kuentz, *Lectures*   Guiraud, P., P. Kuentz. *La stylistique: Lectures [par] Pierre Guiraud et Pierre Kuentz*. Paris: Klincksieck, 1970.

Gülich, Raible, "Textanalyse"   Gülich, E., W. Raible. "Überlegungen zu einer makrostrukturellen Textanalyse." Pages 73–126. In E. Gülich, K. Heger, W. Raible, *Linguistische Textanalyse. Überlegungen zur Gliederung von Texten*. Papiere zur Textlinguistik. Hamburg, 1974.

Gülich, Raible, *Textmodelle*   Gülich, E., W. Raible. *Linguistische Textmodelle: Grundlage und Möglichkeiten*. UTB 130. Munich, 1977.

Gülich, Raible, *Textsorten*   Gülich, E., W. Raible. *Textsorten. Differenzierungskriterien aus linguistischer Sicht*. 2d ed. Wiesbaden, 1972.

Gülich, Raible, "Textsortenprobleme"   Gülich, E., W. Raible. "Text-sortenprobleme." Pages 144–97. In *Linguistische Probleme der Textanalyse*. Sprache der Gegenwart 35. Düsseldorf: Schwann, 1975.

Gumpers, Hymes, *Ethnography*   Gumpers, J. J., D. Hymes eds. *The Ethnography of Communication*. Washington: American Anthropological Association, 1964.

Güttgemanns, "Analyse"   Güttgemanns, E. "Narrative Analyse synoptischer Texte." *LingBibl* 25/26 (1973) 50–73.

Güttgemanns, "Einleitende"   Güttgemanns, E. "Einleitende Bemerkungen zur strukturalen Erzählforschung." *LingBibl* 23/24 (1973) 2–47.

Güttgemanns, *Linguistik*   Güttgemanns, E. *Einführung in die Linguistik für Textwissenschaftler*. Forum Theologiae Linguisticae 2. Bonn: Linguistica Biblica, 1978.

Güttgemanns, *Questions*   Güttgemanns, E. *Candid Questions Concerning Gospel Form Criticism*. Trans. W. G. Doty. Pittsburgh: Pickwick Press, 1979.

Güttgemanns, "Texttheorie"   Güttgemanns, E. "Elementare semiotische Texttheorie." *LingBib* 52 (1982) 87–113.

Hahn, *Erzähler*   Hahn, F. ed. *Der Erzähler des Evangeliums. Methodische Neuansätze in der Markusforschung*. SBS 118/119. Stuttgart, 1985.

Hahn, "Jesus"   Hahn, F. "Methodische Überlegungen zur Rückfrage nach Jesus." Pages 11–77. In Kertelge, *Rückfrage*.

Hahn, "John 1,35–51"   Hahn, F. "Die Jüngerberufung John 1,35–51: Neues Testament und Kirche." In *Festschrift für R. Schnackenburg*. Freiburg im Breisgau, 1974.

Hahn, "Matthäus 28, 16–20"   Hahn, F. "Der Sendungsauftrag des Auferstandenen. Matthäus 28, 16–20." Pages 28–43. In *Fides pro mundi vita. Festschrift für H.-W. Gensichen*. Gütersloh: Gütersloher Verlagshaus, 1980.

Hahn, "Methodologische"   Hahn, F. "Methodologische Überlegungen." Pages 11–77. In Kertelge, *Rückfrage*.

Halliday, *Explorations*   Halliday, M. A. K. *Explorations in the Functions of Language*. London: Edward Arnold, 1973.

Halliday, *Language*   Halliday, M. A. K. *Spoken and Written Language*. Oxford: Oxford University Press, 1985.

Hardmeier, *Texttheorie*   Hardmeier, C. *Texttheorie und biblische Exegese. Zur rhetorischen Funktion der Trauermetaphorik in der Prophetic*. BEvT 79. Munich, 1978.

Harris, "Discourse"   Harris, Z. S. "Discourse Analysis." *Language* 28 (1952) 1–30.

Haubrich, *Theorien*   Haubrich, W. ed. *Erzählforschung. Theorien, Modelle, und Methoden der Narrativik*. Göttingen, 1976.

Hauser, *Initiation*   Hauser, H. J. *Initiation à l'analyse structurale*. Cahiers Evangile. Paris, 1976.

Hauser, *Strukturen*   Hauser, H. J. *Strukturen der Abschlußerzählung der Apostelgeschichte (Apg 28, 16-31)*. AnBib 86. Rome, 1979.

Hawkins, *Horae*   Hawkins, J. C. *Horae Synopticae*. 2d ed. Oxford, 1909.

Hayes, Holladay, *Biblical Exegesis*   Hayes, J. H., C. R. Holladay. *Biblical Exegesis: A Beginner's Handbook*. Atlanta: John Knox, 1982.

Heger, *Monem*   Heger, K. *Monem, Wort, Satz und Text*. Tübingen: Max Niemeyer Verlag, 1971; 2d expanded edition, 1976.

Hellholm, *Hermas*   Hellholm, D. *Das Visionenbuch des Hermas als Apokalypse. Formgeschichte und texttheoretische Studien zu einer literarischen Gattung, I: Methodologische Vorüberlegungen und makrostrukturelle Textanalyse.* CBibNT. Lund, 1980.

Hempfer, *Gattungstheorie*   Hempfer, K. W. *Gattungstheorie. Information und Synthese.* UTB 133. Munich, 1973.

Hengel, *Leader*   Hengel, M. *The Charismatic Leader and His Followers.* Trans. J. Greig. New York: Crossroad, 1981.

Hengstel, *Papyri*   Hengstel, J. ed. *Papyri als Zeugnis des öffentlichen und privaten Lebens. Griechisch-Deutsch.* Darmstadt, 1978.

Hennig, Huth, *Kommunikation*   Hennig J., L. Huth. *Kommunikation als Problem der Linguistik.* Göttingen, 1975.

HerderKorr   *Herder–Korrespondenz*

Holz, "Bibel"   Holz, T. "Die deutsche Bibel: Erbe Luthers und Auftrag." *TLZ* 108 (1983) 785–801.

HTK   *Herders theologischer Kommentar zum Neuen Testament,* ed. A. Wikenhauser, A. Vögtle, R. Schnackenburg.

HTR   *Harvard Theological Review*

Initiation   *Initiation à l'analyse structurale.* Cahiers Evangile 16. Paris: 1976.

Isenberg, "Grundfragen"   Isenberg, H. "Grundfragen der Texttypologie." Pages 303–42. In F. Daneš, D. Viehweger eds. *Ebenen der Textstruktur.* Akademie der Wissenschaften der DDR, Zentralinstitut für Sprachwissenschaft, Linguistische Studien Series A, 112. East Berlin, 1983.

Isenberg, "Texttypen"   Isenberg, H. "Texttypen also Interaktionstypen." *Zeitschrift für Germanistik* (Leipzig) 5 (1984) 261–70.

Iser, *Reading*   Iser, W. *The Act of Reading: A Theory of Aesthetic Response.* Baltimore: Johns Hopkins University Press, 1978.

Jakobson, "Statements"   Jakobson, R. "Closing Statements: Linguistics and Poetics." Pages 350–77. In Sebeok, *Style.*

JBL   *Journal of Biblical Literature*

Jeremias, *Parables*   Jeremias, J. *The Parables of Jesus.* Trans. S. H. Hooke. New York: Scribners, 1972.

Jeremias, *Theology NT*   Jeremias, J. *Theology of the New Testament.* New York: Scribners, 1971.

Kahrmann, *Erzähltextanalyse*   Kahrmann C. et al. *Erzähltextanalyse. Einführung in Grundlagen und Verfahren.* Kronberg, 1977.

Kallmeyer, *Lektürekolleg*   Kallmeyer, W. et al. *Lektürekolleg zur Textlinguistik.* 2 vols. Frankfurt am Main 1974.

Kalverkämpfer, *Orientierung*   Kalverkämpfer, H. *Orientierung zur Textlinguistik.* Linguistische Arbeiten 100. Tübingen: Niemeyer, 1981.

Kanzog, *Einführung*   Kanzog, K. *Erzählstrategie. Eine Einführung in die Normeinübungen des Erzählens.* UTB 495. Heidelberg, 1976.

Käsemann, "Alleys"   Käsemann, E. "Blind Alleys in the 'Jesus of History' Research." Pages 23–68. In Käsemann, *Questions.*

Käsemann, *Essays*   Käsemann, E. *Essays on New Testament Themes.* Philadelphia: Fortress, 1982.

Käsemann, "Problem"   Käsemann, E. "The Problem of the Historical Jesus." Pages 15–47. In Käsemann, *Essays.*

Käsemann, *Questions*   Käsemann, E. *New Testament Questions of Today.*
London: SCM, 1969.

Käsemann, *Romans*   Käsemann, E. *Commentary on Romans.* Trans. and ed.
G. Bromiley. Grand Rapids: Eerdmans, 1980.

Kassel, *Auslegung*   Kassel, M. *Biblische Urbilder. Tiefenpsychologische Auslegung nach C.G. Jung.* 2d ed. Munich, 1982.

Kassel, "Urbilder"   Kassel, M. "Biblische Urbilder—Begegnung mit ver-
gessenen Menschheitserfahrungen in der Bibel." *Bibel und Kirche* 38
(1983) 105–12.

Kassülke, "Übersetzung"   Kassülke, R. "Übersetzung—das Unmögliche
möglich machen." Pages 19–62. In Meurer, *Bibel.*

Keck, "Mark 3:7–12"   Keck, L. E. "Mark 3:7–12 and Mark's Christology."
JBL 84 (1965) 341–58.

Kedar, *Semantik*   Kedar, B. *Biblische Semantik. Eine Einführung.* Stuttgart,
1981.

Kelber, *Oral*   Kelber, W. *Oral and Written Gospel.* Philadelphia: Fortress,
1983.

KEK   Kritisch-exegetischer Kommentar zum Neuen Testament

KerDogma   Kerygma und Dogma

Kermode, *Secrecy*   Kermode, F. *The Genesis of Secrecy. On the Interpretation
of Narrative.* Cambridge, Mass./London: Harvard, 1979.

Kertelge, *Rückfrage*   Kertelge, K. ed. *Rückfrage nach Jesus. Zur Methodik
und Bedeutung der Frage nach dem historischen Jesus.* QD 63. Freiburg:
Herder, 1974.

Kintsch, "Stories"   Kintsch, W., "On Comprehending Stories." Pages
33–62. In Just, M. J., P. A. Carpenter eds. *Cognitive Processes in Comprehension.* Hillsdale, N.J.: Lawrence Erlbaum, 1977.

Kintsch, van Dijk, "Histoires"   Kintsch, W., T. A. van Dijk. "Comment on
se rapelle et on résume des histoires." *Langages* 40 (1975) 98–116.

Klauck, "Frage"   Klauck, H.-J. "Die Frage der Sündenvergebung in der
Perikope von der Heilung des Gelahmten (Mk 2, 1–12)." *BZ* 25 (1981)
223–48.

Kloppenberg, *Formation*   Kloppenberg, J. S. *The Formation of Q: Trajecto-
ries in Ancient Wisdom Collections.* Studies in Antiquity and Christianity.
Philadelphia: Fortress, 1987.

Kloppenberg, Vaage, *Q*   Kloppenberg, J. S., L. E. Vaage eds. *Early
Christianity, Q and Jesus.* Semeia 55. Atlanta: Scholars Press, 1992.

Koch, *Growth*   Koch, K. *The Growth of the Biblical Tradition: The Form-
Critical Method.* Trans. S. M. Cupitt. New York: Scribners, 1969.

Koester, *Literature*   Koester, H. *Introduction to the New Testament.* Volume
2. *History and Literature of Early Christianity.* Philadelphia: Fortress/Berlin;
New York: de Gruyter, 1982.

Koller, *Übersetzungswissenschaft*   Koller, W. *Einführung in die Übersetzungswissenschaft.* UTB. 2d ed. Heidelberg, 1983.

Kremer, "Alte"   Kremer, J. "Alte, neuere und neueste Methoden der
Exegese." *LPThQ* 128 (1980) 3–12.

Kremer, "Bibel"   Kremer, J. "Die Bibel einfach lesen. Bibelwissenschaft-
liche Erwägungen zum nichtwissentschaftlichen Umgang mit der Heiligen Schrift." Pages 327–61. In *Festschrift für Cardinal König.* Vienna, 1980.

Kremer, *Buch*   Kremer, J. *Die Bibel—ein Buch für alle. Berechtigung und Grenzen einfacher Schriftlesung.* Stuttgart, 1986.

Kremer, *Lazarus*   Kremer, J. *Lazarus. Die Geschichte einer Auferstehung. Text, Wirkungsgeschichte und Botschaft von Joh 11, 1–46.* Stuttgart, 1985.

Kremer, *Österevangelien*   Kremer, J. *Die Österevangelien—Geschichten um Geschichte.* 2d ed. Stuttgart, 1981.

Kümmel, *Introduction*   Kümmel, W. G. *Introduction to the New Testament.* Rev. ed. Trans. H. C. Kee. Nashville: Abingdon Press, 1975.

Kümmel, *Jahre*   Kümmel, W. G. *30 Jahre Jesusforschung (1950–1980).* Königstein, 1985.

Kümmel, *Neue Testament*   Kümmel, W. G. *Das Neue Testament in 20. Jahrhundert. Ein Forschungsbericht.* SBS 50. Stuttgart, 1970.

Lack, *Letture*   Lack, R. *Letture strutturaliste dell'antico testamento. "Universo semantico" (on Hos. 4:1–14).* Rome: Borla, 1978.

Lähnemann, Böhm, *Philemonbrief*   Lähnemann, J., G. Böhm, *Der Philemonbrief. Zur didaktischen Erschließung eines Paulusbriefes.* Gütersloh, 1973.

Lambiasi, *L'autenticità*   Lambiasi, F. *L'autenticità storica dei Vangeli.* Studio di criteriologia. Bologna, 1976.

Lämmert, *Symposium*   Lämmert, E. ed. *Erzählforschung. Ein Symposium.* Stuttgart, 1982.

Lampe, Luz, "Overview"   Lampe, P., U. Luz. "Overview of the Discussion." Pages 387–404. In Stuhlmacher, *Gospel.*

Lang, "Gratia"   Lang, F. G. "Sola gratia in Markusevangelium. Die Soteriologie des Markus nach 9, 14–29 und 10, 17–31." Pages 321–37. In *Rechtfertigung: Festschrift für E. Käsemann.* Tübingen, 1976.

Lange, *Verzeichnis*   Lange, J. ed. *Ökumenisches Verzeichnis der biblischen Eigennamen nach den Loccumer Richtlinien.* 2d ed. Stuttgart, 1981.

Latourelle, *Gesù*   Latourelle, R. *A Gesù attraverso i vangeli. Storia e ermeneutica.* Assisi, 1979.

Laub, "Falsche"   Laub, F. "Falsche Verfasserangaben in neutestamentlichen Schriften. Aspekte der gegenwärtigen Diskussion um die neutestamentliche Pseudoepigraphie." *TTZ* (1980) 228–42.

Lausberg, *Elemente*   Lausberg, H. *Elemente der literarischen Rhetorik: Eine Einführung für Studierende.* 7th ed. Munich, 1982.

Lausberg, *Handbuch*   Lausberg, H. *Handbuch der literarischen Rhetorik: Eine Grundlegung der Literaturwissenschaft.* Munich, 1973.

Leech, *Semantics*   Leech, G. *Semantics.* Harmondsworth: Penguin, 1974.

Lentzen-Deis, "Bestimmung"   Lentzen-Deis, F. "Methodischeüberlegungen zur Bestimmung literarischer Gattungen im Neuen Testament." *Bib* 62 (1981) 1–20.

Lentzen-Deis, "Kriterien"   Lentzen-Deis, F. "Kriterien für die historische Beurteilung der Jesusüberlieferung." Pages 78–117. In Kertelge, *Rückfrage.*

Léon-Dufour, *Dictionary*   Léon-Dufour, X. *Dictionary of the New Testament.* Trans. T. Prendergast. San Francisco: Harper & Row, 1980.

Léon-Dufour, "Structure"   Léon-Dufour, X. "Structure et fonction du récit de miracle." Pages 289–353. In Aletti, *Miracles.*

Leoni, Pigliaccio, *Retorica*   Leoni, F. A., M. R. Pigliaccio, eds. *Retorica e scienze del linguaggio.* Rome, 1979.

Lévi-Strauss, "Myth"   Lévi-Strauss, C. "The Structural Study of Myth."
Myth, A Symposium. *Journal of American Folklore* 78 (1955) 428–44.
Translated with some additions and modifications as "La structure des
mythes." Pages 225–55. In *Anthropologie Structurale*. Vol. 1. Paris: Plon,
1958. English: Pages 206–31. In *Structural Anthropology*. Vol 1. Trans. C.
Jacobson, and B. G. Schoeps. New York: Basic Books, 1963. Also in
paperback: Pages 202–28. Harper Torchbook TB 5017, 1966.

Lévi-Strauss, "Structure"   Lévi-Strauss, C. "La Structure et la forme.
Réflexions sur un ouvrage de Vladimir Propp." *Cahiers de l'Institut de
science économique appliquée* 9 (1960) 3–36. Simultaneously under the title
"L'analyse morphologique des contes russes." *International Journal of
Slavic Linguistics and Poetics* 3 (1960). Reprint. Pages 139–73. In *Anthopolo-
gie structurale*. Vol. 2. Paris: Plon, 1973. English, "Structure and Form:
Reflections on a Work by Vladimir Propp." Pages 115–45. In *Structural
Anthropology*. Vol 2. Trans. M. Layton. New York: Basic Books, 1976.

Lewandowski, *Linguistisches*   Lewandowski, T. *Linguistisches Wörterbuch
1–3*. UTB 200.201.300. Heidelberg 1979/1980.

Lindemann, "Bemerkungen"   Lindemann, A. "Bemerkungen zu den
Adressaten und zum Anlaß des Epheserbriefes." *ZNW* 67 (1976) 235–51.

LingBibl   Linguistica Biblica

Link, *Rezeptionsforschung*   Link, H. *Rezeptionsforschung: Ein Einführung in
Methoden und Probleme*. Stuttgart: Kohlhammer, 1976.

Lohfink, *Bible*   Lohfink, G. *The Bible: Now I Get It!* Trans. D. Coogan.
Garden City, N.J.: Doubleday, 1979.

Lohfink, "Kommentar"   Lohfink, G. "Kommentar als Gattung." *BibLeb*
15 (1974) 7–16.

Lohse, *Colossians*   Lohse, E. *Colossians and Philemon: A Commentary on the
Epistles to the Colossians and to Philemon*. Trans. W. R. Poehlman and R. J.
Karris. Ed. H. Koester. Philadelphia: Fortress Press, 1971.

Lohse, "Prinzipien"   Lohse, B. "Entstehungsgeschichte und hermeneutische Prinzipien der Lutherbibel." Pages 133–48. In Gnilka, Rüger,
Bibel.

Louw, *Lexicography*   Louw, J. P. ed. *Lexicography and Translation*. Cape
Town: Bible Society of South Africa, 1985.

Louw, *Semantics*   Louw, J. P. *Semantics of New Testament Greek*. Philadel-
phia/Chico: Fortress/Scholars Press, 1982.

Louw, Nida, *Lexicon*   Louw, J. P., E. A. Nida. *Greek-English Lexicon of the
New Testament based on Semantic Domains*. 2 vols. New York: United Bible
Societies, 1988.

Luz, *Matthew*   Luz, U. *Matthew 1–7: A Commentary*. Trans. W. C. Linss.
Edinburgh: T. & T. Clark, 1990.

Lyons, *Semantics*   Lyons, J. *Semantics*. 2 vols. Cambridge/New York: Cambridge University Press, 1977.

Magaß, "Thesen"   Magaß, W. "Elf Thesen zum Bibellesen und zum
'Suchen' in der Schrift (Joh 5: 39)." *LingBibl* 47 (1980) 5–20.

Maier, *Temple Scroll*   Maier, J. *The Temple Scroll: An Introduction, Translation
and Commentary*. Sheffield: JSOT Press, 1985.

Malherbe, "Gentle"   Malherbe, A. J., " 'Gentle as a Nurse': The Cynic
Background to I Thess ii." *NovT* 12 (1970) 203–17.

Marguerat, *Strukturale*   Marguerat, D. *Strukturale Textlektüren der Evangelien.* ThBerichte 13. Zurich, 1983.

Martini, *Il testo*   Martini, C. M. *Il testo biblico: I libri di Dio. Introduzione generale alla Sacra Scrittura.* Turin, 1975.

Marxsen, *Mark*   Marxsen, W. *Mark the Evangelist: Studies on the Redaction History of the Gospel.* Trans. J. Boyce. Nashville: Abingdon Press, 1969.

März, "Traditionsgeschichte"   März, C.-P. " . . . mich habt ihr nicht allezeit': Zur Traditionsgeschichte von Mk 14, 3–9 und Parallelen." *Studien zum Neuen Testament und seiner Umwelt* 6–7 (1981) 89–112.

McKnight, *Form*   McKnight, E. *What Is Form Criticism?* Philadelphia: Fortress Press, 1969.

McKnight, *Meaning*   McKnight, E. V. *Meaning in Texts: The Historical Shaping of a Narrative Hermeneutics.* Philadelphia: Fortress, 1978.

McKnight, *Reader*   McKnight, E. V. ed. *Reader Perspectives on the New Testament.* Semeia 48. Atlanta: Scholars Press, 1989.

Meletinskij, "Strukturell"   Meletinskij, E. "Zur strukturell-typologischen Erzählforschung des Volksmärchens." Pages 179–214. In Propp, *Morphologie.*

Merklein, "Einheitlichkeit"   Merklein, H. "Die Einheitlichkeit des 1. Korintherbriefes." *ZNW* 75 (1984) 153–83.

Merklein, *Jesu*   Merklein, H. *Jesu Botschaft von der Gottesherrschaft. Eine Skizze.* SBS 111. Stuttgart, 1983.

Mesters, *Incontrici*   Mesters, C. *Incontrici biblici.* Assisi, 1974.

Metz, "Apologie"   Metz, J. B. "Kleine Apologie des Erzählens." *Concilium* 9 (1973) 334–41.

Metzger, *Commentary*   Metzger, B. M. *A Textual Commentary on the Greek New Testament.* London: United Bible Societies, 1971.

Metzger, *Text*   Metzger, B. M. *The Text of the New Testament.* 3d ed. New York: Oxford University Press, 1992.

Meurer, *Bibel*   Meurer, S. ed. *Eine Bibel—viele Übersetzungen. Not oder Notwendigkeit?* Stuttgart: Deutsche Bibelstiftung, 1978.

Meurer, "Weltbundes"   Meurer, S. "Die Übersetzungsstrategien des Weltbundes der Bibelgesellschaften." Pages 173–89. In Meurer, *Bibel.*

Meyer, *Commentary*   Meyer, H. A. W. *Critical and Exegetical Commentary on the New Testament.* Rev. and ed. W. P. Dickson, W. Stewart, and F. Crombie. Edinburgh: T. & T. Clark, 1873–83.

Meynet, *Initiation*   Meynet, R. *Initiation à la rhétorique biblique.* Paris, 1982.

Michel, *Methodik*   Michel, G. *Einführung in die Methodik der Stiluntersuchung. Ein Lehr- und Übungsbuch.* Berlin, 1972.

Michel, *Römer*   Michel, O. *Der Brief an die Römer.* Göttingen: Vandenhoeck & Ruprecht, 1978.

Minguez, *Pentecostés*   Minguez, D. *Pentecostés: Ensayo de Semiotica Narrativa en Hch 2.* Rome: Biblical Institute Press, 1976.

Moore, *Criticism*   Moore, S. D. *Literary Criticism and the Gospels. The Theoretical Challenge.* New Haven/London: Yale, 1989.

Morgan, *Nature*   Morgan, R. *The Nature of New Testament Theology.* London: SCM Press/Naperville, Ill.: Alec R. Allenson, 1973.

Morgenthaler, *Statistik*   Morgenthaler, R. *Statistik des neutestamentlichen Wortschatzes.* Zurich, 1958.

Morgenthaler, *Synopse*   Morgenthaler, R. *Statistische Synopse.* Zurich, 1971.

Mounin, *Introduction*   Mounin, G. *Introduction à la sémiologie.* Paris: Minuit, 1970.

Müller, "Funktion"   Müller, P. G. "Zur Funktion der Bibel-übersetzung 'Die Gute Nachricht.'" *Una Sancta* 38 (1983) 243–49.

Müller, "Methode"   Müller, K. "Die religionsgeschichtliche Methode. Erwägungen zu ihrem Verständnis und zur Praxis ihrer Vollzüge." *BZ* 29 (1985) 161–92.

Murphy-O'Connor, "Interpolations"   Murphy-O'Connor, J. "Interpolations in 1 Corinthians." *CBQ* 48 (1986) 81–94.

Mußner, *Epheser*   Mußner, F. *Brief an die Epheser.* ÖTK. Gütersloh, 1982.

Mußner, *Hermeneutik*   Mußner, F. *Geschichte der Hermeneutik. Von Schleiermacher bis zur Gegenwart.* 2d ed. Freiburg, 1976.

Mußner, "Methodologie"   Mußner, F. "Methodologie der Frage nach dem historischen Jesus." Pages 118–47. In Kertelge, *Rückfrage.*

Neirynck, *Duality*   Neirynck, F. *Duality in Mark: Contributions to the Study of Markan Redaction.* Louvain: Louvain University Press, 1988.

Neirynck, van Segbroeck, *Vocabulary*   Neirynck, F., F. van Segbroeck. *New Testament Vocabulary: A Companion Volume to the Concordance.* Louvain: Louvain University Press, 1984.

Nida, *Analysis*   Nida, E. A. *Componential Analysis of Meaning: An Introduction to Semantic Structures.* The Hague: Mouton, 1975.

Nida, "Einige Grundsätze"   Nida, E. A. "Einige Grundsätze heutiger Bibel—Bibelübersetzung." Pages 11–18. In Meurer, *Bibel.*

Nida, *Science of Translating*   Nida, E. *Toward a Science of Translating.* Leiden: E. J. Brill, 1964.

Nida, *Semantic*   Nida, E. A. *Exploring Semantic Structures.* Munich: Fink, 1975.

Nida, "Signs"   Nida, E. A. "Signs—Sense—Translation." Unpublished typescript for lectures in Pretoria. 1981.

Nida, Louw, *Semantics*   Nida, E. A., J. P. Louw. *Lexical Semantics of the Greek New Testament: A Supplement to the Greek-English Lexicon of the New Testament Based on Semantic Domains.* SBL Resources for Biblical Study 25. Atlanta: Scholars Press, 1992.

Nida, Taber, *Theory*   Nida, E. A., C. R. Taber. *The Theory and Practice of Translation.* Leiden: E. J. Brill, 1974.

Niederwimmer, "Unmittelbarkeit"   Niederwimmer, K. "Unmittelbarkeit und Vermittlung als hermeneutisches Problem." *KerDogma* 17 (1971) 97–112.

NovT   *Novum Testamentum*

NTS   *New Testament Studies*

OBO   *Orbis biblicus et orientalis*

ÖBS   *Österreichische biblische Studien*

Odelain, Seguineau, *Dictionary*   Odelain, O., R. Seguineau. *Dictionary of Proper Names and Places in the Bible.* Trans. M. J. O'Connell. London: R. Hale, 1982.

Ogden, Richards, *Meaning*   Ogden, C. K., I. A. Richards. *The Meaning of Meaning*. n.p., 1923.

Ollrog, *Paulus*   Ollrog, W.-H. *Paulus und seine Mitarbeiter. Untersuchungen zur Theorie und Praxis der paulinischen Mission*. WMANT 50. Neukirchen, 1979.

Olsson, *Structure*   Olsson, B. *Structure and Meaning in the Fourth Gospel. A Text Linguistic Analysis of John 2:1–11 and 4:1–42*. Lund: Gleerup, 1974.

Ossege, "Aspekte"   Ossege, M. "Aspekte zur Gliederung des neutestamentlichen Wortschatzes (am Beispiel von dikaiosyne bei Mt)." *LingBibl* 34 (1975) 37–101.

ÖTK   Ökumenischer Taschenbuchkommentar zum Neuen Testament. Edited by E. Gräßer, K. Kertelge.

Palmer, *Hermeneutics*   Palmer, R. E. *Hermeneutics: Interpretation Theory in Schleiermacher, Dilthey, Heidegger and Gadamer.* Evanston: Northwestern University Press, 1969.

Panier, "Commentaire"   Panier, L. "Le Commentaire: Expansion figurative et sélection sémiotque." *SémBib* 31 (1983) 43–74

Panier, "Introduction"   Panier, L. ed. "Petite introduction à l'analyse des textes. . . ." *SémBib* 38 (1985) 3–31.

Panier, "Kommentar"   Panier, L. "Was ist ein Kommentar?" *BZ* 24 (1980) 1–20.

Parisi, Castelfranchi, "Comprensione"   Parisi, D., C. Castelfranchi. "La comprensione dei brani come costruzione di una corretta rete di conoscenze." Pages 161–93. In D. Parisi ed. *Per una educazione linguistica razionale*. Bologna, 1979.

Patte, "Exegesis"   Patte, D. "What Is Structural Exegesis?" In D. and A. Patte, *Structural Exegesis: From Theory to Practice*. Philadelphia, 1978.

Patte, *Exegesis*   Patte, D. *What Is Structural Exegesis?* Guides to Biblical Scholarship. Philadelphia: Fortress, 1976.

Patte, *Critics*   Patte, D. *Structural Exegesis for New Testament Critics*. Guides to Biblical Scholarship. Minneapolis: Fortress, 1989.

Patte, "Kingdom"   Patte, D. ed. "Kingdom and Children." *Semeia* 29 (1983).

Patte, *Matthew*   Patte, D. *The Gospel according to Matthew: A Structural Commentary on Matthew's Faith*. Philadelphia: Fortress Press, 1987.

Patte, *Paul's Faith*   Patte, D. *Paul's Faith and the Power of the Gospel: A Structural Introduction to the Pauline Letters*. Philadelphia: Fortress, 1983.

Patte, "Pronouncement"   Patte, D. "Jesus' Pronouncement about Entering the Kingdom Like a Child: A Structural Exegesis." *Semeia* 29 (1983) 3–42, esp. 4–11.

Perrin, *Redaction*   Perrin, N. *What Is Redaction Criticism?* Guides to Biblical Scholarship. Philadelphia: Fortress, 1969.

Pesch, *Entdeckung*   Pesch, R. *Die Entdeckung des ältesten Paulusbriefes. Die Briefe an die Gemeinde der Thessalonicher.* Freiburg, 1984.

Pesch, *Fischfang*   Pesch, R. *Der reiche Fischfang. Lk 5, 1–11/John 21, 1–14. Wundergeschichte, Berufungserzählung, Erscheinungsbericht*. Düsseldorf, 1969.

Pesch, *Markus*   Pesch, R. *Markusevangelium*. HTK. Freiburg, 1976.

Pesch, *Synoptisch*   Pesch, R., R. Kratz. *So liest man synoptisch: Anleitung und Kommentar zum Studium der synoptischen Evangelien*. Frankfurt am Main: Knecht, 1975.

Pesch, *Matthäus*   Pesch, W. *Matthäus der Seelsorger. Das neue Verständnis der Evangelien dargestellt am Beispiel von Mt 18*. SBS 2. Stuttgart, 1966.

Petersen, *Literary Criticism*   Petersen, N. R. *Literary Criticism for New Testament Critics*. Philadelphia, 1978.

Plett, *Textwissenschaft*   Plett, H. F. *Textwissenschaft und Textanalyse*. UTB 328. Heidelberg, 1979.

Polkow, "Method"   Polkow, D. "Method and Criteria for Historical Jesus Research." Pages 336–56. In *SBLSP 26*. Scholars, 1987.

Propp, *Morphologie*   Propp, V. J. *Die Morphologie des Märchens*. Munich, 1972.

Propp, *Morphology*   Propp, V. J. *Morphology of the Folktale*. 2d ed. Rev. and ed. L. A. Wagner. Austin: University of Texas Press, 1968.

QD   Quaestiones disputatae

Raible, "Gattungen"   Raible, W. "Gattungen als Textsorten." *Poetica* 12 (1980).

Raible, Lockmann, "Textsorten"   Raible, W., Lockmann. "Textsorten vs. Gattungen." *GermRomMonatsschrift* 55. New Series 24; n.d. 284–304.

Reder, "Prose"   Reder, L. M. "The Role of Elaboration in the Comprehension and Retention of Prose: A Critical Review." *Review of Educational Research* 50 (1980) 5–53.

Reedy, "Concerns"   Reedy, C. J. "Rhetorical Concerns and Argumentative Techniques in Matthean Pronouncement Stories." In *SBLSP 22*. Scholars, 1983.

Rehkopf, "Parallelismus"   Rehkopf, F. "Der 'Parallelismus' im Neuen Testament." *ZNW* 71 (1980) 46–57.

Reiser, "Alexanderroman"   Reiser, M. "Der Alexanderroman und das Markusevangelium." Pages 131–63. In Cancik, *Markus-Philologie*.

Reiser, *Syntax*   Reiser, M. *Syntax und Stil des Markusevangeliums im Licht der hellenistischen Volksliteratur*. WUNT 2, 11. Tübingen, 1985.

Reiß, *Texttyp*   Reiß, K. *Texttyp und Übersetzungsmethode. Der operative Text*. Kronberg, 1976.

Reiß, "Übersetzen"   Reiß, K. "Was heißt 'Übersetzen.' " Pages 33–47. In Gnilka, Rüger, *Bibel*.

Reitzenstein, *Mysterien-Religionen*   Reitzenstein, R. *Hellenistische Mysterien-Religionen*. Stuttgart: B.G. Teubner, 1910. Reprint. Darmstadt: Wissenschaftliche Buchgesellschaft, 1956. ET: *Hellenistic Mystery-Religions*. Trans. J. E. Steely. Pittsburgh: Pickwick Press, 1978.

Richter, *Exegese*   Richter, *Exegese als Literaturwissenschaft. Entwurf einer alttestamentlichen Literaturtheorie und Methodologie*. Göttingen, 1971.

Ricoeur, *Conflict*   Ricoeur, P. *The Conflict of Interpretations: Essays in Hermeneutics*. Edited by D. Ihde. Evanston: Northwestern University Press, 1974.

Ricoeur, "Méthodes"   Ricoeur, P. "Du conflit à la convergence des méthodes bibliques." Pages 35–53. In Barthes, *Exégèse*.

Rienecker, *Linguistic Key*   Rienecker, F. *A Linguistic Key to the Greek New Testament*. Ed. C. L. Rogers. Grand Rapids: Zondervan, 1980.

Riesner, *Jesus*   Riesner, R. *Jesus als Lehrer. Eine Untersuchung zum Ursprung der Evangelien-Überlieferung*. WUNT 2, 7. 2d ed. Tübingen, 1984.

Ritt, *Reden*   Ritt, H. *Das Reden Gottes im Sohn. Zur textlinguistischen Methode der neutestamentlichen Exegese.*

Ritt, "Übersetzungskritik"   Ritt, H. "Biblische 'Übersetzungskritik.' " *BZ* 20 (1970) 161–79.

Robinson, Cobb, *Hermeneutic*   Robinson, J. M., J. B. Cobb eds. *The New Hermeneutic. New Frontiers in Theology: Discussions among Continental and American Theologians,* vol. 2. New York: Harper & Row, 1964.

Roget, *Thesaurus*   Roget, P. M. *Roget's International Thesaurus.* 4th ed. Revised by R. L. Chapman. New York: Crowell, 1974.

Rohde, *Rediscovering*   Rohde, J. *Rediscovering the Teaching of the Evangelists.* Philadelphia: Westminster Press, 1968.

Rothkegel, Sandig, *Linguistische Modelle*   Rothkegel, A., B. Sandig. *Text, Textsorten, Semantik: Linguistische Modelle und maschinelle Verfahren.* Hamburg, 1984.

Sanders, "Autobiographical"   Sanders, J. T. "Paul's 'Autobiographical' Statements in Galatians 1–2." *JBL* 85 (1966) 335–43.

Sanders, *Stilistik*   Sanders, W. *Linguistische Stilistik, Grundzüge einer Stilanalyse sprachlicher Kommunikation.* Göttingen, 1977.

Sanders, *Stiltheorie*   Sanders, W. *Linguistische Stiltheorie.* Göttingen, 1973.

SANT   Studien zum Alten und Neuen Testament

SBB   Stuttgarter biblische Beiträge

SBL   Society of Biblical Literature

SBLDS   Society of Biblical Literature Dissertation Series

SBLMS   Society of Biblical Literature Monograph Series

SBLSP   *Society of Biblical Literature Seminar Papers*

SBS   Stuttgarter Bibelstudien

Scharbet, "Hermeneutische"   Scharbet, J. "Entstehungsgeschichte und hermeneutische Prinzipien der 'Einheitsübersetzung der Heiligen Schrift.' " Pages 149–68. In Gnilka, Rüger, *Bibel.*

Schelbert, *Formgeschichte*   Schelbert, G. *Wo steht die Formgeschichte: Methoden der Evangelien-Exegese.* ThBerichte 13. Zurich, 1985.

Schenk, *Philipperbriefe*   Schenk, W. *Die Philipperbriefe des Paulus. Kommentar.* Stuttgart, 1984.

Schenke, *Brotvermehrung*   Schenke, L. *Die wunderbare Brotvermehrung. Die neutestamentlichen Erzählungen und ihre Bedeutung.* Würzburg, 1983.

Schlieben-Lange, *Pragmatik*   Schlieben-Lange, B. *Linguistische Pragmatik.* Stuttgart: Kohlhammer, 1975.

Schlier, *Epheser*   Schlier, H. *Brief an die Epheser.* 6th ed. Düsseldorf, 1968.

Schlier, *Römerbrief*   Schlier, H. *Der Römerbrief: Kommentar.* Freiburg im Breisgau: Herder, 1977.

Schlingmann, *Methoden*   Schlingmann, C. *Methoden der Interpretation.* Stuttgart, 1985.

Schmidt, *Rahmen*   Schmidt, K. L. *Der Rahmen der Geschichte Jesu: Literarkritische Untersuchungen zur ältesten Jesusüberlieferung.* Darmstadt: Wissenschaftliche Buchgesellschaft, 1964.

Schmidt, *Texttheorie*   Schmidt, K. L. *Texttheorie, Probleme einer Linguistik der sprachlichen Kommunikation.* UTB 202. Munich, 1976.

Schnackenburg, *Ephesians*   Schnackenburg, R. *Ephesians: A Commentary.* Trans. H. Heron. Edinburgh: T. & T. Clark, 1991.

Schnackenburg, "Geschichtliche"   Schnackenburg, R. "Der geschichtliche Jesus in seiner ständigen Bedeutung für Theologie und Kirche."
Pages 194–220. In Kertelge, *Rückfrage.*

Schnackenburg, *John*   Schnackenburg, R. *The Gospel according to St. John.*
Trans. K. Smyth. New York: Herder & Herder, 1968–82.

Schneemelcher, *Apocrypha*   Schneemelcher, W. ed. *New Testament Apocrypha.* Trans. A. J. B. Higgins. Louisville: Westminster/John Knox Press,
1991–92.

Schneider, *Rhetorische*   Schneider, N. *Die rhetorische Eigenart der paulinischen Antithese.* Hermeneutische Untersuchungen zur Theologie II.
Tübingen, 1970.

Schnider, "Jesuserzählung"   Schnider, F. "Christusverkündigung und Jesuserzählung. Exegetische Überlegungen zu Mk 14, 3–9." *Kairos* 24 (1982)
171–80.

Schnider, *Söhne*   Schnider, F. *Die verlorene Söhne. Strukturanalytische und
historisch-kritische Untersuchungen zu Lk 15.* OBO 17. Göttingen, 1977.

Schober, *Funktionen*   Schober, O. ed. *Funktionen der Sprache.* Stuttgart,
1974.

Schober, *Text und Leser*   Schober, O. ed. *Text und Leser. Zur Rezeption von
Literatur für die Sekundarstute.* Stuttgart: P. Reclam, 1979.

Schreiner, *Einführung*   Schreiner, J. ed. *Einführung in die Methoden der
biblischen Exegese.* Tyrolia: Echter, 1971.

Schreiner, Dautzenberg, *Gestalt*   Schreiner, J., G. Dautzenberg. *Gestalt
und Anspruch des Neuen Testaments.* 2d ed. Würzburg, 1969.

Schroedel, "Bibel"   Schroedel, J. H. "Remythologisierung der Bibel?
Bemerkungen zu einer Situationsanalyse Eugen Drewermanns." *HerderKorr* 39 (1985) 275–79.

Schürmann, "Christus"   Schürmann, H. "Die Sprache des Christus.
Sprachliche Beobachtungen an den synoptischen Herrenworten." *BZ* 2
(1958) 54–84, 105.

Schürmann, "Voröster"   Schürmann, H. "Die vorösterliche Anfänge der
Logientradition. Versuch eines formgeschichtliches Zugang zum Leben
Jesu." Pages 39–65. In *Traditionsgeschichtliche Untersuchungen zu den syn-
optischen Evangelien. Beiträge.* Düsseldorf: Patmos, 1968.

Schweizer, *Grammatik*   Schweizer, H. *Metaphorische Grammatik. Wege zur
Integration von Grammatik und Textinterpretation in der Exegese.* St. Ottilien,
1981.

Schweizer, *Mark*   Schweizer, E. *The Good News according to Mark.* Trans.
D. H. Madvig. Richmond: John Knox Press, 1970.

Sebeok, *Style*   Sebeok, T. A. ed. *Style and Language.* Cambridge, Mass.:
Technology Press of MIT, 1960.

Second Vatican Council, "Dei Verbum"   Second Vatican Council. "Dogmatic Constitution: 'Dei Verbum.' " 21.

Second Vatican Council, "Liturgy"   Second Vatican Council. "Constitution on the Liturgy." 7.

Second Vatican Council, "Schriftgebrauch"   Second Vatican Council.
"Schriftgebrauch und -sinn in gottesdienstlichen Feiern." *Concilium* 11
(1975) n. 2.

Segovia, "Structure" Segovia, F. F. "The Structure, Tendenz, and Sitz im Leben of John 13:31–14:31." *JBL* 104 (1985) 491–93.

SémBib Sémiotique et Bible

Sowinski, *Textlinguistik* Sowinski, B. *Textlinguistik. Eine Einführung.* Stuttgart, 1983.

Stammerjohann, *Handbuch* Stammerjohann, H. *Handbuch der Linguistik.* Munich, 1975.

Steck, *World* Steck, O. H. *World and Environment.* Nashville: Abingdon Press, 1980.

Steiner, *Bibelübersetzungen* Steiner, R. *Neue Bibelübersetzungen vorgestellt, verglichen und gewertet.* Neukirchen, 1975.

Stine, *Translation* Stine, P. C. ed. *Bible Translation and the Spread of the Church: The Last 200 Years.* Studies in Christian Mission 2. Leiden/New York: E. J. Brill, 1990.

Stock, *Umgang* Stock, A. *Umgang mit theologischen Texten: Methoden, Analysen, Vorschlag.* Zurich: Benziger, 1974.

Stowers, *Diatribe* Stowers, S. K. *The Diatribe and Paul's Letter to the Romans.* SLBDS 57. Chico, 1981.

Strecker, *Problem* Strecker, G. ed. *Das Problem der Theologie des Neuen Testaments.* Wege der Forschung 367. Darmstadt, 1975.

Strecker, Schnelle, *Einführung* Strecker, G., U. Schnelle. *Einführung in die neutestamentliche Exegese.* Göttingen: Vandenhoeck & Ruprecht, 1983.

Stuhlmacher, *Gospel* Stuhlmacher, P. ed. *The Gospel and the Gospels.* Grand Rapids: Eerdmans, 1991.

Stuhlmacher, *Methoden* Stuhlmacher, P. *Methoden- und Sach-problematik einer interkonfessionellen Auslegung des Neuen Testaments: Vorarbeiten.* EKK 4. Zurich, 1972.

Stuhlmacher, *Philemon* Stuhlmacher, P. *Der Brief an Philemon.* Zurich: Benziger, 1975.

Stuhlmacher, *Verstehen* Stuhlmacher, P. *Vom Verstehen des Neuen Testaments: Eine Hermeneutik.* 2d ed. Göttingen: Vandenhoeck & Ruprecht, 1986.

Suleiman, Crosman, *Reader* Suleiman, S. R., J. Crosman. *The Reader in the Text: Essays on Audience and Interpretation.* Princeton, 1980.

SUNT Studien zur Umwelt des Neuen Testaments

Talbert, *Gospel* Talbert, C. H. *What Is a Gospel? The Genre of the Canonical Gospels.* Philadelphia: Fortress, 1977.

TDNT Theological Dictionary of the New Testament. G. Kittel, ed. 10 vols. Trans. G. Bromiley. Grand Rapids: Eerdmans, 1964–76.

ThBerichte Theologische Berichte

Theissen, *Followers* Theissen, G. *The First Followers of Jesus: A Sociological Analysis of the Earliest Christianity.* Trans. J. Bowden. London: SCM Press, 1978.

Theissen, *Miracle* Theissen, G. *The Miracle Stories of the Early Christian Tradition.* Trans. F. McDonagh. Edinburgh: T. & T. Clark, 1983.

Theissen, *Sociology* Theissen, G. *Sociology of Early Palestinian Christianity.* Trans. J. Bowden. Philadelphia: Fortress Press, 1978.

Theobald, *Anfang* Theobald, M. *Im Anfang war das Wort. Textlinguistische Studie zum Johannesprolog.* SBS 106. Stuttgart, 1982.

Theobald, "Primat"   Theobald, M. "Der Primat der Synchronie vor der Diachronie als Grundaxiom der Literarkritik: Methodische Erwägungen an Hand von Mk. 2:1–17/Mt. 9:9–13." *BZ* 22 (1978) 161–86.

THKNT   Theologischer Handkommentar zum Neuen Testament

Thompson, *Advice*   Thompson, W. G. *Matthew's Advice to a Divided Community: Mt. 17:22–18:35.* AnBib 44. Rome, 1970.

ThPh   Theologie und Philosophie

ThR   Theologische Rundschau

ThRev   Theologische Revue

Thraede, *Grundzüge*   Thraede, K. *Grundzüge griechisch-römischer Brieftopik.* Munich, 1970.

Titzmann, *Textanalyse*   Titzmann, M. *Strukturale Textanalyse.* UTB 582. Munich, 1977.

TLZ   Theologische Literaturzeitung

Tompkins, *Reader-Response*   Tompkins, J. P. ed. *Reader-Response Criticism: From Formalism to Post-Structuralism.* Baltimore, 1980.

Trilling, *Israel*   Trilling, W. *Das wahre Israel. Studien zur Theologie des Matthäusevangeliums.* SANT. 3d ed. Munich, 1964.

Trilling, *Untersuchungen*   Trilling, W. *Untersuchungen zum zweiten Thessalonicherbrief.* Leipzig, 1972.

TTZ   Trierer theologische Zeitschrift

Türk, *Wirkungsästhetik*   Türk, H. *Wirkungsästhetik.* Munich, 1976.

Ulrich, *Wörterbuch*   Ulrich, W. *Wörterbuch linguistische Grundbegriffe.* Kiel, 1981.

UTB   Uni-Taschenbücher

van Dijk. *Aspects*   van Dijk, T. *Some Aspects of Text Grammars: A Study in Theoretical Linguistics and Poetics.* Janua Linguarum, Series Maior 63. The Hague/Paris: Mouton, 1972.

van Dijk, *Textwissenschaft*   van Dijk, T. A. *Textwissenschaft. Eine interdisziplinäre Einführung.* Wissenschaft 4364. Munich, 1980.

van Iersel, "Exeget"   van Iersel, H. "Der Exeget und die Linguistik." *Concilium* 14 (1978) 313–18.

VD   Verbum domini

Venetz, "Beitrag"   Venetz, H.-J. "Der Beitrag der Soziologie zur Lektüre des Neuen Testaments. Ein Bericht." ThBerichte 13. Zurich, 1983, 87–121.

Voelz, "Language"   Voelz, J. W. "The Language of the New Testament." Pages 894–977. In W. Haase, ed., *Prinzipat II*, 25.2. Berlin, 1984.

von Brandt, *Werkzeug*   von Brandt, A. *Werkzeug des Historikers. Eine Einführung in die historischen Hilfswissenschaften.* Stuttgart, 1958.

Warning, *Rezeptionsästhetik*   Warning, R. ed. *Rezeptionsästhetik: Theorie und Praxis.* Munich: W. Fink, 1975.

Wegner, *Symposion*   Wegner, R. ed. *Symposion: Die Datierung der Evangelien.* Paderborn, 1982.

Weimar, *Enzyklopädie*   Weimar, K. *Enzyklopädie der Literaturwissenschaft.* UTB 1034. Munich, 1980.

Weinrich, *Kommunikation*   Weinrich, H. *Kommunikation, Instruktion, Text: Sprache in Texten.* Stuttgart, 1976.

Weinrich, *Literatur*   Weinrich, H. *Literatur für Leser.* Stuttgart, 1971.

Weinrich, *Textgrammatik*   Weinrich, H. *Textgrammatik der französischen Sprache*. Stuttgart, 1982.

Weinrich, "Theologie"   Weinrich, H. "Narrative Theologie." *Concilium* 9 (1973) 329–34.

Wengst, *Bedrängte*   Wengst, K. *Bedrängte Gemeinde und verherrlichter Christus. Der historische Ort des Johannesevangeliums als Schlüssel zu seiner Interpretation*. Neukirchen, 1981.

White, "Literature"   White, J. L. "New Testament Epistolary Literature in the Light of Ancient Epistolography." Pages 1730–56. In W. Haase, ed. *Prinzipat II* 25.2. Berlin, 1984.

White, "Philemon"   White, J. L. "The Structural Analysis of Philemon: A Point of Departure in the Formal Analysis of the Pauline Letter." Pages 1–47. In *SBLSP*. Ed. J. L. White et al. 2 vols. Scholars, 1971.

White, *Speech Act*   White, H. C. ed. *Speech Act Theory and Biblical Criticism*. Semeia 41. Atlanta: Scholars Press, 1988.

Wilckens, *Römer*   Wilckens, U. *Der Brief an die Römer*. Zurich: Benziger, 1978–82.

Wilcox, "Semitisms"   Wilcox, M. "Semitisms in the New Testament." Pages 978–1029. In W. Haase, ed. *Prinzipat II* 25.2. Berlin, 1984.

Wilß, *Übersetzungswissenschaft*   Wilß, W. *Übersetzungswissenschaft. Probleme und Methoden*. Stuttgart, 1977.

Wink, *Bibelauslegung*   Wink, W. *Bibelauslegung als Interaktion. Über die Grenzen historisch-kritischer Methode*. UTB 622. Stuttgart, 1976.

Wink, *Bible Study*   Wink, W. *Transforming Bible Study: A Leader's Guide*. Nashville, Tenn: Abingdon, 1980.

Wink, *Transformation*   Wink, W. *The Bible in Human Transformation: Toward a New Paradigm for Biblical Study*. Philadelphia: Fortress Press, 1973.

WMANT   Wissenschaftliche Monographien zum Alten und Neuen Testament

Wrede, "Task"   Wrede, W. "The Task and Methods of New Testament Theology." Pages 68–116. In Morgan, *Nature*.

Wrege, *Wirkungsgeschichte*   Wrege. H.-T. *Wirkungsgeschichte des Evangeliums*. Göttingen, 1981.

Wuellner, "Jakobusbrief"   Wuellner, W. H. "Der Jakobusbrief im Licht der Rhetorik und Textpragmatik." *LingBibl* 43 (1978) 5–66.

Wuellner, "Rhetoric."   Wuellner, W. H. "Paul's Rhetoric of Argumentation in Romans: An Alternative to the Donfried-Karris Debate over Romans." Pages 152–74. In Donfried, *Romans*.

WUNT   Wissenschaftliche Untersuchungen zum Neuen Testament

Zani, "Influsso"   Zani, L. "Influsso del genere letterario midrashico su Mt 2, 1–12." *StPat* 19 (1972) 257–320.

Zeller, "Heilung"   Zeller, D. "Die Heilung des Aussätzigen (Mk 1,40–45). Ein Beispiel bekennender und werbender Erzählung." *TTZ* 93 (1984) 138–46.

Zeller, "Pragmatik"   Zeller, D. "Zur Pragmatik der paulinischen Rechtfertigungslehre." *ThPh* 56 (1981) 204–17.

Zeller, "Wunder"   Zeller, D. "Wunder und Bekenntnis. Zum Sitz im Leben urchristlicher Wundergeschichten." *BZ* 25 (1981) 202–22.

Zerwick, Grosvenor, *Grammatical Analysis*   Zerwick, M., M. Grosvenor. *A Grammatical Analysis of the Greek New Testament.* Rev. ed. in 1 vol. Rome: Biblical Institute Press, 1981.

Zimijewski, *Rhetorik*   Zimijewski, J. *Elemente der literarischen Rhetorik. Eine Einführung für Studierende.* 7th ed. Munich, 1982.

Zimijewski, *Stil*   Zimijewski, J. *Der Stil der paulinischen 'Narrenrede.' Analyse der Sprachgestaltung in 2 Kor. 11:1–12, 10 als Beitrag zur Methodik von Stiluntersuchungen neutestamentlicher Texte.* BBB 52. Cologne, 1978.

Zimijewski, "Struktur"   Zimijewski, J. "Beobachtungen zur Struktur des Philemonbriefes." *BibLeb* 15 (1974) 273–96.

Zimmerman, "Formen"   Zimmerman, H. "Formen und Gattungen im NT." Pages 232–60. In Schreiner, *Einführung.*

Zimmermann, *Methodenlehre*   Zimmermann, H. *Neutestamentliche Methodenlehre. Darstellung der historisch-kritischen Methode.* Ed. K. Kliesch. 7th ed. Stuttgart: Katholisches Bibelwerk, 1982.

ZNW   *Zeitschrift für die neutestamentliche Wissenschaft*

Introduction ❖

Hendrikus Boers

> Our claim, then, will be that an adequate
> study of literature is inconceivable without
> an explicit insight into the general proper-
> ties of text structure . . .
>
> Teun van Dijk[1]

In the 1970 Society of Biblical Literature seminar on "The
Form and Function of the Pauline Letters," chaired by Nils A. Dahl,[2]
I was able to see for the first time that one could distinguish between
the meaning of Paul's statements taken by themselves and the way
they functioned in his letters. The contributions to this seminar
were wide-ranging, including the crucial formal studies by John L.
White;[3] Dahl's famous, unpublished but much quoted paper on
Galatians;[4] the identification of the genre of the Pauline letters as
paraenetic by Abraham J. Malherbe, illustrated with a study of
1 Thessalonians;[5] the discussion of the structure of that letter by
John C. Hurd;[6] and finally Wilhelm Wuellner's rhetorical study of
Romans.[7] Very important also are the preparatory articles[8] and

---

[1]Van Dijk, *Aspects*, 1.

[2]The principles on which the seminar was based were formulated in a working
paper by N. A. Dahl, "The Pauline Letters: Proposal for a Study Project of an SBL
Seminar on Paul," and a response by R. W. Funk, which formulated the title of the
seminar, "The Form and Function of the Pauline Letter: A Response to the Seminar
Proposal by Nils A. Dahl."

[3]For example, White, "Philemon," 1–47. See also W. G. Doty's unpublished
"Response to 'The Structural Analysis of Philemon,' by John L. White."

[4]"Paul's Letter to the Galatians: Epistolary Genre, Content, and Structure."

[5]"I Thessalonians as a Paraenetic Letter" (unpublished). See also the earlier
article, Malherbe, "Gentle."

[6]"Concerning the Structure of 1 Thessalonians" (unpublished). See also
Boers, "Thessalonians," which contains references to earlier work on various structural
features of the Pauline letters.

[7]Published as Wuellner, "Rhetoric."

[8]I mention only the two that are the most significant for us here: Betz,
"Composition" and "Defense."

subsequent commentary on Galatians[9] by Hans Dieter Betz. Significant about these studies in the present context is their recognition that Paul's letters could not be read without attention to the way in which the Apostle uses his language. This applies in general to the question concerning the genre of a letter; namely, whether it is (or all the letters are) paraenetic, as Malherbe maintains in the works mentioned above, or whether a letter is rhetorically apologetic, as Betz argued with regard to Galatians in his above-mentioned works.

If 1 Thessalonians is a paraenetic letter, then we have to read what Paul wrote in the letter in that light. To use a simple example: the discussion in the two apocalyptic sections, 4:13–18 and 5:1–11, should be taken not as if the sections are intended to provide apocalyptic information, but as if using such information were itself a basis for paraenesis. The interpretation of these passages involves the question of their function in the letter. That Paul may provide information that is partly different in another context, for example, in 1 Corinthians 15, is due to the information's altered function in the new context. A more extreme example is the different function of Paul's discussion of Jews, the Law, and faith in Galatians and in Romans. Even though he focuses sharply on this complex issue in large parts of both letters, no systematic Pauline conception of the Jews, the Law, and faith can be derived from them, because in each case the discussion is subject to its function in his paraenetic purpose.

Even more differentiated is Betz's work on Galatians. One may disagree with him, either in general or in detail, but he has shown that in the interpretation of a Pauline letter one cannot avoid asking what the rhetorical function is, not only of the letter as a whole, but also of each individual part.

What these studies have done is only a beginning. By focusing on the way in which language functions in Paul's texts, they have opened a window on the function of language not only in Paul's writings but in the New Testament as well. I refer to the studies above only to point to one of the ways in which a central concern in Wilhelm Egger's *How to Read the New Testament* has already been recognized in American New Testament scholarship. What is limited is the range of the view through this window. The study of language has remained the domain of a few special-interest groups: particularly the structuralist group in the SBL under the leadership of Daniel Patte;[10] those who are involved in biblical translation, an area in which significant work has been done on the use of language in the New Testament, particularly in the United Bible Societies under

---

[9]Betz, *Galatians.*
[10]For Patte's own work, see Patte, *Exegesis; Theory; Paul's Faith;* and *Matthew.*

the leadership of Eugene A. Nida,[11] but also in the work of Wycliffe Bible translators like John Beekman and John Callow;[12] and those working on discourse analysis in South Africa under the leadership of Johannes P. Louw.[13] Significantly the interest of both Nida and Louw moves beyond syntax to semantics, from the structure of a discourse to the meaning expressed in it, as the title of Louw's book shows.[14] Louw's method is fundamentally discourse analysis. The relationship between discourse analysis and semantics in Louw's and Nida's work is based on the insight that meaning comes to expression not in single sentences, let alone words, but in longer stretches of discourse. In the meantime, Louw and Nida have collaborated in the publication of a New Testament Greek lexicon based on some of the most recent principles of linguistics.[15] I will return to their lexicon below.

In order to indicate what new horizons might still come into view through the window opened on language and New Testament research by the above-mentioned studies, I will give an example from Robert-Alain de Beaugrande and Wolfgang Ulrich Dressler's *Introduction to Text Linguistics*,[16] in which they present their functional approach to language. It concerns the Saturday on which Tom Sawyer had been ordered to whitewash a fence, when he would rather have engaged in leisure activities.[17] He sees Ben, a neighborhood boy, come by, eating an apple which he himself would very much like to have. Tom uses language to *manage* the situation in such a way that in the end Ben whitewashes the fence and rewards Tom with the apple for the privilege. Through his behavior, pretending not to notice Ben except when it suits him, and interpreting the resented activity as something desirable, Tom achieves his purpose. When Ben remarks sarcastically, "Say—I'm going in a-swimming, *I* am. Don't you wish you could? But of course you'd druther *work*—wouldn't you?" Tom responds with a rhetorical question, "What do you call work?" When Ben replies that what Tom is doing certainly is work, Tom resumes whitewashing and answers carelessly, "Well, maybe it is, and maybe it ain't. All I know is, it suits Tom Sawyer," and then, "I don't see why I oughtn't to like it. Does a boy get a chance to whitewash a fence every day?" The end result of this remarkable managing of the situation through language and gestures is that Tom gives the brush to Ben

---

[11]Notably in the guidebook for translators: Nida, Taber, *Theory.* In United Bible Society translations circles it is fondly referred to as TAPOT.

[12]Beekman, Callow, *Translating.*

[13]See especially, Louw, *Semantics.*

[14]Louw, *Semantics.* With regard to Nida, see especially *Semantic.*

[15]Louw, Nida, *Lexicon.*

[16]de Beaugrande, Dressler, *Linguistics.*

[17]See ibid., 171–75.

"with reluctance in his face, but alacrity in his heart." The meaning of each of Tom's statements has to be taken in the context in which he uses them. For example, "Does a boy get a chance to whitewash a fence every day?" expresses an obvious truth in rhetorical form, but that is not its meaning for Tom. Its meaning does not reside in the words themselves, but in the meaning effect to which it contributes in the total context of the situation.

I cannot say that this use of language to manage a situation has remained completely unrecognized in New Testament scholarship. Jack T. Sanders's study of "Paul's 'Autobiographical' Statements in Galatians 1–2"[18] is not a linguistic study, but his conclusion reveals many of the marks of de Beaugrande and Dressler's linguistic interpretation of the Tom Sawyer incident. Sanders writes: ". . . the proper way to understand such seemingly 'autobiographical' statements made by Paul . . . is not to inquire into the historicity of the events alluded to in such statements, but to ascertain what point is being scored by Paul in his argumentation, and then to see how he makes 'autobiographical' events underscore that point."[19] Sanders's comment invites a study of the function of language in Paul, not only with regard to his autobiographical statements but also in general, and not only in Paul, but in the New Testament as a whole. This is the area of investigation to which Egger invites his readers in *How to Read the New Testament*, especially in Part 3, "Synchronic Reading."

How to Read the New Testament is not an introduction to linguistics and New Testament interpretation. As the subtitle indicates, it is more broadly conceived: an introduction to linguistic and historical-critical methodologies. Only one part (Part 3, "Synchronic Reading") can be considered primarily linguistic. The length of this section, however, more than a third of the book, indicates a heavy emphasis on linguistic matters. It is the one part of the book with which the traditional interpreter of the New Testament would be the least familiar. Traditional historical-critical methodologies are discussed in two shorter sections, in which Egger distinguishes between "Diachronic Reading" (Part 4), which concerns the literary history of the New Testament texts, and "Reading Historically" (Part 5), concerning the historical facts behind the texts and how information about those facts can be established. In these sections, as in the one which is primarily linguistic, Egger is less concerned to present the methods themselves than to show how they can inform a reading of the New Testament. There is a third methodological section, "Reading Hermeneutically" (Part 6), which concerns the ways in which the New Testament texts can be made

[18]Sanders, "Autobiographical."
[19]Ibid., 343.

relevant to the contemporary situation. These four approaches to reading the New Testament are not alternatives, but complementary. The demands of each text will determine which of these approaches, individually or in combination, would be the most fruitful. As the author states in the foreword, his methodology is an attempt to integrate a "sampling" of recent linguistic methods with traditional historical-critical exegesis. These four parts concerning the reading of New Testament texts are preceded by a clarification of the textual theory on which they are based (Part 1), and preparatory steps to the reading (Part 2).

Methodologically important for an understanding of this *Introduction to Linguistic and Historical-Critical Methodology* is the distinction between synchronic and diachronic, represented, respectively, by Parts 3 and 4. It is a distinction which goes back to the question of how meaning is conveyed in words. A diachronic understanding of the meaning of words is that they develop over time. Kittel's *Theological Dictionary of the New Testament* is based on such an understanding. In it the meanings of New Testament words are traced back to antecedents in the Hebrew Scriptures and in Second Temple Judaism, in Greek thought, the LXX, and finally in the New Testament itself.

An alternative to this understanding is the synchronic view, which was proposed by the Swiss linguist Ferdinand de Saussure, the father of structuralism.[20] According to this view the meaning of words is determined by their relationship to all other words in a given language. A simple way to explain this is by reference to colors. The meaning of the word "green" in a given language is determined by the other words used in that language to express the color spectrum: so the range of colors referred to by the word "green" may differ from language to language. It is even possible that in a single language the same word in different linguistic-cultural settings may not have the same meaning, depending on the existence of other words which bring the color spectrum to expression in each case. So, for example, as the color spectrum becomes more differentiated linguistically in a particular language, the color range to which "green" refers may become more restricted. In such a case it would be possible to trace the growing differentiation of the color spectrum diachronically, but the only way to determine the current meaning of "green" in that language would be to determine which other colors are differentiated in the color spectrum, and how they relate to "green." Similarly the meanings of words for "dwelling" in different languages differ according to the range of words that

---

[20]See de Saussure, *Course.*

are used to distinguish various types of dwellings. As a final example, the word for father in Zulu, "baba," is also used to refer to uncles on the father's side, distinguishing between a brother who is older than the father, "baba umkulu" (big father), and one who is younger, "baba umncane" (little father). The mother's brothers, on the other hand, are referred to as "malume," and the mother's sisters again as "mama," the word for mother, once more with distinctions between the older and younger aunts on the mother's side.

The following is an example that is closer at hand, from the New Testament. The English words "belief" and "faith" express discrete meanings that have to be conveyed by a single word in other languages, for example, Greek, πίστις, and German, "Glaube." To put it a little more technically, the semantic domain or the range of meaning that is brought to expression by πίστις in Greek and by "Glaube" in German is expressed in a more differentiated way by "faith" and "belief" in English. The range of meaning of πίστις and "Glaube" is wider, covering both the meanings of "faith" and "belief" in English, and accordingly less differentiated. But there is no verb for "faith" in the English language, which makes it necessary to revert to the single term "believe" to express the act of faith.

In Rom 3:3 Paul exploits the range of meaning expressed by the Greek term πίστις to play on yet another possible meaning, expressed by "trustworthy" in English and "vertrauenswürdig" in German. Τί γὰρ εἰ ἠπίστησάν τινες; μὴ ἡ ἀπιστία αὐτῶν τὴν πίστιν τοῦ θεοῦ καταργήσει. Paul's play on the range of meanings of πίστις and its derivatives in this verse leaves his meaning ambiguous, making it difficult to determine how one should translate: "What if some of them became distrustful (fell into disbelief), would their distrust (their disbelief, their lack of faith) not destroy the trustworthiness of God?" It may seem as if the meaning of πίστις τοῦ θεοῦ is relatively unambiguous, but the very next verse reveals that Paul is playing on another component of the meaning of πίστις when he relates the πίστις τοῦ θεοῦ to the truthfulness of God and human deceit: γινέσθω δὲ ὁ θεὸς ἀληθής, πᾶς δὲ ἄνθρωπος ψεύστης, "Let God be true, and every human being false" (Rom 3:4).[21]

An even more interesting case may be the term δικαιοσύνη, which can be translated only by a single term into German, "Gerechtigkeit," but by two terms into English, "righteousness" and "justice." The advantage of the two terms in English, compared with the single term in Greek and German, is that English can in this case again express more differentiated meanings. What is at issue is not

---

[21]For a thorough, understandable discussion of these matters, see Nida, *Analysis;* also "Referential Meaning" in Nida, Taber, *Theory,* 56–90. For an excellent but more technical discussion, see Baldinger, *Semantic Theory.*

so much the common meaning of the terms, but the distinct meanings that can be expressed by them. A certain moral quality is expressed in "righteousness" which is absent from "justice." When the owner of the vineyard in Matthew's parable of the Workers in the Vineyard (Matt 20:1–16) says to the persons standing around in the marketplace at the third hour of the day, ὑπάγετε καὶ ὑμεῖς εἰς τὸν ἀμπελῶνα, καὶ ὃ ἐὰν ᾖ δίκαιον δώσω ὑμῖν, "You too go into my vineyard, and whatever is just, I will give you" (v. 4), one can translate the Greek δίκαιον with "just," referring to a principle of action, distinguishing it from "righteous," referring to a quality of the actor. The same applies when the owner responds to the complaint of workers who worked the whole day, ἑταῖρε, οὐκ ἀδικῶ σε (v. 13). The owner means, stated in English, "I have not done you an injustice." The emphasis is on the principle that is operative in the relationship between him and the workers, not on his being right and they wrong. What is at issue is not the *righteousness* of the owner of the vineyard, but *justice* which governs the relationship between him and the workers. The owner is claiming to be not a righteous person but one whose actions are based on the principle of justice.

The advantage of the distinction of meaning that can be expressed by means of justice and righteousness in English becomes especially clear in Romans 10:3 where Paul writes about Israel, ἀγνοοῦντες γὰρ τὴν τοῦ θεοῦ δικαιοσύνην, καὶ τὴν ἰδίαν [δικαιοσύνην] ζητοῦντες στῆσαι, τῇ δικαιοσύνῃ τοῦ θεοῦ οὐχ ὑπετάγησαν. Neither the Greek nor the German can convey Paul's distinct meaning as well as it can be expressed in English: "Ignoring the justice of God, and seeking to establish their own righteousness, they did not submit to the justice of God."[22] God does not seek to be found righteous, but takes responsibility for justice in all of his creation. According to Paul, Israel sought to be found righteous, based on the fulfillment of the Law, and so did not integrate itself into the framework of God's justice.

This understanding of meaning in language was anticipated by William Wrede in his famous essay "The Task and Methods of New Testament Theology."[23] In this essay Wrede protests against the "wrong-headed" approach of squeezing "as much conceptual capital from every single phrase and every casually chosen expression used by an author." According to him, the sense of a term "has rather to be oriented on a few decisive conceptions of the author, so that the

---

[22]The fact that the second δικαιοσύνη may not be original in the text is of no significance. Its very absence indicates the degree to which the word could be presupposed. Not so in the English, because Paul could have used a distinctive "righteousness" for what Israel was seeking, in contrast with the "justice" of God.

[23]Wrede, "Task."

main lines of its meaning can be given. In the case of the concept πίστις, this will involve the characteristically Pauline view of its object, and in the case of σάρξ, what he says about ἁμαρτία, δι-καιοσύνη, νόμος, θάνατος, αἰών οὗτος, πνεῦμα, etc."[24] This is certainly not a sophisticated linguistic view, but Wrede understood clearly that in ordinary language the meaning of words is not inherent in the words themselves but is determined by their relationships to other words.

With the appearance of Louw and Nida's *Greek-English Lexicon of the New Testament Based on Semantic Domains* to which I referred above, New Testament scholarship has been placed in the fortunate situation of having at its disposal a lexicon which takes into account the most recent advances in linguistics concerning the ways in which meaning is expressed in language. An example from that lexicon will illustrate how the understanding of meaning through semantic domains opens up new insights into a language, in this case specifically New Testament Greek. In a traditional lexicon, like Walter Bauer's justly famous Greek-English lexicon,[25] all the meanings of a word are listed in a single entry by means of a series of definitions. So, for example, under σάρξ, σαρκός, ἡ, . . . *flesh,"* Bauer gives eight definitions coming from a variety of areas of meaning (semantic domains): "1. lit., of the material that covers the bones of a human or animal body"; "2. *the body* itself, viewed as substance"; "3. *a man of flesh and blood* ὁ λόγος σάρξ ἐγένετο"; "4. *human* or *mortal nature, earthly descent*"; "5. *corporeality, physical limitation(s), life here on earth*"; "6. *the external* or *outward side of life* as it appears in the eye of an unregenerate person, which is natural or earthly"; "7. In Paul's thought esp. *the flesh* is the willing instrument of sin to such a degree that wherever flesh is, all forms of sin are likew. present, and no good thing can live in the σάρξ"; and "8. The σάρξ is the source of the sexual urge without any suggestion of sinfulness connected w. it."

In Louw and Nida's two-volume lexicon all the words in the Greek New Testament are arranged in the first volume in semantic domains and subdomains of related meanings. The second volume has an index to a word's various locations in the first volume. In that regard it looks less like a traditional lexicon than like a thesaurus, with which it shares a fundamental understanding of meaning in a language. The arrangement in the two volumes is similar to the unabbreviated version of *Roget's International Thesaurus*[26] with its "Thesaurus of English Words and Phrases," listed in categories, such as "Abstract Relations," "Space," "Physics," "Matter," etc. in the first part, and the

---

[24]Ibid., 77.
[25]BAGD.
[26]See Roget, *Thesaurus.*

index in the second part by means of which one gains access to those words and phrases. The thesaurus then provides possible words for the meanings one has in mind. The principles of arrangement in Roget and in Louw and Nida's lexicon are different, as a comparison of *Roget's* "Synopsis of Categories" and Louw and Nida's "Table of Domains" immediately reveals. Nevertheless, Roget provides a good avenue to an understanding of Louw and Nida's lexicon. Examples of their semantic domains include: "1. Geographical Objects and Features," or "8. Body, Body Parts, and Body Products." The subdomains for domain 8 are: A. Body (entries 8.1–8.8); B. Parts of the Body (8.9–8.69); and C. Physiological Products of the Body (8.70–8.77). A word can appear in more than one domain or subdomain, depending on the range of its meanings. So, for example, σάρξ is listed eight times, twice each in domains 8 ("Body, Body Parts, and Body Products") and 9 ("People"), and once each in domains 10 ("Nation"), 23 ("Physiological Processes and States"), 26 ("Psychological Faculties"), and 58 ("Nature, Class, Example").

What makes it clear that Louw and Nida's work is indeed a lexicon and not a thesaurus is that the first volume lists not synonyms as in Roget, but single words with definitions. From here the closer relationship to Bauer's lexicon becomes clear. Even though Louw and Nida's domains do not agree precisely with those suggested by Bauer's eight definitions of σάρξ, Bauer's definitions also suggest different semantic domains for the various meanings of the word. So, for example, Bauer's first and second definitions clearly belong in Louw and Nida's domain 8; the third in domain 9; the fourth in domain 58; etc. But whereas Bauer is primarily concerned with the range of meanings of individual words, Nida and Louw's primary concern is the total range of meaning of Greek as it comes to expression in the vocabulary of the New Testament.

For the first meaning of σάρξ in Louw and Nida's lexicon, glossed as "flesh," the index volume refers to entry 8.63 in the main volume. Thus, in its first meaning σάρξ belongs in domain 8, "Body, Body Parts, and Body Products," subdomain B, "Parts of the Body." Its meaning is defined as "the flesh of both animals and human beings," followed by a single gloss, "flesh," and an illustrative example from the New Testament, Revelation 19:17d–18, δεῦτε . . . ἵνα φάγετε σάρκος βασιλέων . . . καὶ σάρκας ἵππων. This entry is preceded by 8.62 "μυελός, οῦ *m:* the soft material that fills the cavity in the bones—'marrow,' " and followed by 8.64 "αἷμα[a], τος *n*—'blood.' "[27] In

---

[27]The superscripted letter *a* after αἷμα indicates that this entry represents the word's first meaning. The absence of a superscripted letter after μυελός indicates that there is only one meaning for this term in the New Testament.

this way the lexicon shows where the first meaning of σάρξ belongs in the meaning structure of New Testament Greek, and to which other words it is closely related. Rather than define the meanings of individual Greek words, it opens to the reader both the range of meaning in New Testament Greek and the range of possibilities for expressing those meanings in words.

The sixth meaning of σάρξ, glossed as "human nature" and referred to as entry 26.7, belongs in domain 26, "Psychological Faculties." It is defined as "the psychological aspect of human nature which contrasts with the spiritual nature; in other words, that aspect of human nature which is characterized by or reflects typical human reasoning and desires in contrast with those aspects of human thought and behavior which relate to God and the spiritual life—'human nature, human aspects, natural, human.' " Entry 26.7 is flanked by the following entries: On one side by 26.5: "ἰσόψυχος, ον: pertaining to being of the same mind or attitude,—'having the same mind, . . .' " and 26.6: "σύμψυχος, ον: pertaining to similarity of attitude—'harmonious, united in spirit, being of one spirit' "; and on the other side by 26.8: "σαρκικός[a], ή, όν; σάρκινος[b], η, ον: pertaining to what is human or characteristic of human nature—'human, natural,' " and 26.9: "πνεῦμα[e], τος: the nonmaterial, psychological faculty which is potentially sensitive and responsive to God (πνεῦμα[e] contrasts with σάρξ, 26.7, as an expression of the divine in contrast with the purely human)—'spirit, spiritual, spiritual nature, inner being.' "

These illustrations reveal the complex structure of meaning in a language like Greek; the examples from Zulu reveal the differences in language structure between that language and English. Historical developments do affect the meanings of words in a language, but even then their current meanings are determined by the structure of the language in which they are used, not by the historical development that led to their current usage. There are cases in which the original meaning of a word was lost in the course of the historical development of its meaning. For some of the most significant progress in understanding how meaning comes to expression in language, I refer to the work of Kurt Baldinger, *Semantic Theory: Towards a Modern Semantics*,[28] and of Klaus Heger, *Monem, Word, Satz und Text*.[29]

In the discussion of meaning above I have remained largely within the limits set by individual words and their meaning within the structure of a language. There is another structural relationship among words that is equally important for the way meaning comes to expression in a language: the relationship between words in a

---

[28]See Baldinger, *Semantic Theory*.
[29]See Heger, *Monem*.

sentence and beyond a sentence in a discourse. The syntactic rules governing the relationships between words in sentences in the expression of meaning are well established and readily accessible for investigation in traditional grammar, and more recently in the advances made through transformational grammar, as developed by Noam Chomsky.[30] In traditional grammar it is readily understandable why the meaning of "house" is different in the following two sentences: "The house is large. One can house a number of families in it." The syntactic structure makes it clear that the first occurrence is a noun and the second a verb. Every speaker of the English language also knows that "house" is pronounced phonetically differently in the two instances.

The limits of traditional grammar can be shown by its inability to explain the ambiguity of the following sentence: "Flying airplanes can be dangerous." Transformational grammar makes it possible to clarify how two distinct underlying meanings, "To fly airplanes can be dangerous" and "Airplanes that fly can be dangerous," are transformed into a single sentence, based on the transformational rules of the English language. The following simplified—and not very precise—summary reveals the kind of transformational or re-writing rules involved. In the first sentence "to fly" is transformed into "flying" by the participle substitution rule, which results in our ambiguous sentence, "Flying airplanes can be dangerous." In the second sentence "airplanes that fly" becomes "airplanes flying," also by the participle substitution rule, which then in turn becomes "flying airplanes," by the adjectival shift rule, resulting in the identical ambiguous sentence, "Flying airplanes can be dangerous." A complete transformational clarification is far more complex and precise; this example merely shows the kind of process involved. The purpose of transformational grammar is not to give instruction on how ambiguous sentences can be constructed in English, but to clarify how acceptable sentences are constructed. The purpose of the illustration is to show how an ambiguous but grammatically acceptable sentence can result in English. The success or failure of a grammar depends on its ability to clarify how all possible acceptable sentences are constructed in a language. Transformational grammar can claim to do this better than traditional grammar, and it can show how similar meanings are expressed in syntactically different ways in different languages by using different sets of universally valid transformational rules.[31]

---

[30]Originally in Chomsky, *Structures*.

[31]For the latter, see especially, Fillmore, "Case." Fillmore shows in exceptionally clear reasoning how case is handled differently in different languages, but in such a way that the effect is sufficiently similar to be recognizable among languages.

In English, the subject and object of a sentence are determined by their placement, but in German by their case, i.e., nominative and accusative. Thus one could say with a certain emphasis "Den Mann hasse ich" in German, whereas a sentence formulated syntactically equivalent in English, "The man I hate," taken by itself, would appear incomplete. It will become clear that this does not have to be the case if the sentence occurs in a discourse. Indeed, an English speaker may, without a great deal of sophistication, immediately provide a context in which the sentence becomes understandable, by recognizing that it distinguishes between the man and another person, a woman or a child, for example. This reveals how it becomes necessary to move beyond the limits of a single sentence to clarify its syntax. It is not merely a question of semantics. An English-language speaker recognizes immediately that the sentence, taken completely by itself, is unacceptable syntactically. By expanding the sentence into a larger context, the sentence becomes syntactically acceptable, as the discussion below will show.

To begin with, the German sentence is ambiguous, depending on whether emphasis is placed on "den" or "Mann." In oral discourse this ambiguity would be avoided by means of emphasis, but even in a written account there would normally be no ambiguity. If the sentence is preceded by "A couple lives in the house across the street," even the English syntactic equivalent of the German "Den Mann hasse ich," "The man I hate," would be perfectly acceptable and clear. Thus, in English too, if the object of a sentence is made clear by the context, word placement can function to express emphasis. The meaning would not be the same if the sentence read "I hate the man," which says nothing about an attitude to the woman, whereas "The man I hate" unambiguously excludes the woman from the attitude to the man.

But the German "Den Mann hasse ich" can have a second meaning, which can be rendered in English only by inclusion of the demonstrative pronoun, "I hate that man." If mention of a certain man had come up in a conversation, and if a speaker wants to express emphatically her or his hate for him, the transformation rules of English require that the article be replaced by the demonstrative pronoun, and then a word order transformation can provide emphasis: "I hate that man" becomes emphatically "That man I hate." In German the same meaning can be expressed more effectively by retaining the article (in the accusative case, of course) by means of the word order transformation alone: "Ich hasse den Mann" becomes "Den Mann hasse Ich." A demonstrative pronoun transformation is possible, but redundant: "Jenen Mann hasse ich." And it could diminish the effect of the emphasis.

The discussion above reveals the advantages of noun-cases in languages like Greek, Latin, and German; but it also shows that languages without noun-cases, such as English and French, are not prevented from expressing the same meanings equally effectively. The discussion reveals at the same time the limitations of a grammar that remains within the confines of a sentence. There are sound reasons for maintaining that limitation in linguistics. The precision of the rules of sentence grammar does not apply when those limits are crossed. The attempt to maintain the same kind of precision is what characterized the early attempts at discourse analysis by Zellig Harris,[32] but as late as 1972 Teun van Dijk could still maintain that text-grammars do not yet exist.[33] Indeed, in subsequent studies by van Dijk and Kintsch it became clear that coherence in textual structures does not depend entirely on syntactic relationships. In an experiment they had one half of a group read texts with the sequence of the paragraphs intact and the other half with the sequence scrambled. Although it took much longer to read the stories with the scrambled paragraph sequences, the time it took those readers to produce summaries of the stories was not significantly longer than for the readers of the texts with the paragraphs intact. The summaries made by readers of the scrambled texts could not be distinguished (by other readers) from the summaries of the readers of the intact texts.[34] Indeed, in the reading of any text the reader organizes the material into what van Dijk calls a macro-structure, and as he points out, "everybody will construct the macro-structure for a text which is relevant to him, personally, and these macro-structures will be different for the same text."[35] One can even go so far as to say that a single reader will not read a text with exactly the same macro-structure every time,[36] but organizes the various parts of the text differently in each case. In no case does a reader take note of every detail in a text on an equivalent basis. In that regard the typical biblical commentary that scrutinizes every detail may represent the very opposite of the way texts are read.

The text itself does of course place certain restraints on the macro-structures we construct for our reading of them. Attention to those restraints can contribute in significant ways to our reading of a text. A useful text for illustrating this is Rom 6:1–14. The

---

[32] See, Harris, "Discourse."

[33] Van Dijk, *Aspects*, 1.

[34] Kintsch, van Dijk, "Histoires," and Kintsch, "Stories." For a summary, see Reder, "Prose," 25–27.

[35] Van Dijk, *Aspects*, 161.

[36] This is an example of Heraclitus' saying, "You cannot step twice into the same river; for fresh waters are ever flowing in upon you."

believer's participation in the death of Christ through baptism plays such an important role in this passage that a reader readily recognizes it as the main theme. The question is whether that is what Paul intended. Strong syntactic restraints in the text may help us answer that question. In a general way one can note that this section of the letter has an introduction, vv. 1 and 2, which formulates the theme in diatribe form, followed by two subsections, vv. 3–11, which clarify the point made in the first two verses, and vv. 12–14, which apply what is argued in vv. 3–11 as moral guidance for the readers. It is to the reasoning in vv. 3–11 that we give our attention first.

Verses 3–4 introduce the topic of baptism into the death of Christ as the basic argument. Paul cleverly introduces this topic in v. 3 as the fundamental premise about which there can be no dispute by presenting it as something that his readers are supposed to know: "Or do you not realize that we who were baptized into Christ Jesus were baptized into his death?" Note the parallel procedure in v. 16: "Do you not know that." In v. 4 Paul then immediately draws a conclusion from this premise. The connection between the premise and the conclusion is signified by οὖν.[37]

Γάρ, "for," in v. 5 signifies the introduction of further reasoning in support of this conclusion. This is then in turn supported with the participial construction of v. 6, which is again supported further by the very general principle of v. 7, introduced by γάρ. The same structure is present in vv. 8–10, except that the γάρ of v. 5 is now represented by δέ, signifying that the reasoning of vv. 8–10 is introduced as a parallel to that of vv. 5–7. The entire reasoning of vv. 5–10 supports the basic premise of vv. 3–4. With οὕτως, "so," in v. 11 Paul draws a conclusion from these supporting arguments, bringing the discussion back to the level of the premise of vv. 3–4.

This is then brought to a conclusion in vv. 12–13, the conclusion being signified once more by οὖν, "thus." This conclusion functions to demonstrate on the basis of the reasoning of vv. 3–11 the validity of Paul's reply to the rhetorical question of v. 1 in v. 2. The section is concluded with a general supporting statement, introduced by γάρ, "for." The syntactic structure of the section can be displayed graphically as follows:

---

[37]The importance of syntactic signals, such as οὖν, γάρ, εἰ, δέ, etc. becomes clear when one tries to analyze the text-syntactic structure of this passage from translations. Such an attempt also reveals how little attention translators give to such features. As with typical biblical translations, the focus of attention is on the individual details which comes at the cost of the overall structure.

Statement of the theme in diatribe form:

6:1–2 What then shall we say? Shall we sin in order that favor may abound? By no means! How can we who died to sin still live in it?

Introduction of the fundamental premise of the reasoning:

6:3–4 Or do you not realize that we who were baptized into Christ Jesus were baptized into his death? Thus we have been co-buried with him through the baptism into his death, in order that as Christ was raised from the dead through the glory of the Father, so we too might walk in the newness of life.

Two parallel sets of arguments in support of the fundamental premise:

6:5 For if we became co-physical in the similarity of his death, we will also be of his resurrection.

6:6 Knowing this: Our old self is co-crucified in order that the body of sin may be destroyed, no longer to be enslaved to sin.

6:7 For the one who died is freed from sin.

6:8 If we died with Christ, we believe that we will also co-live with him.

6:9 Knowing that Christ, being raised from the dead, will never die; death no longer reigns over him.

6:10 For the one who died, died once and for all to sin: The one who lives, lives for God.

Conclusion from the support arguments, returning to the level of vv. 3–4:

6:11 So we consider ourselves dead to sin and living for God in Christ Jesus.

Paraenesis concretizing the reply to the rhetorical question of v. 1 in v. 2:

6:12–13 Thus, do not let sin reign in your mortal bodies to be obedient to its lusts, nor put your members at the disposal of sin as weapons of evil, but place yourselves at the disposal of God as living from death, and your members as weapons of justice for God.

Universalizing support of the paraenesis:

6:14 For sin will not rule over you; for you are not subject to the Law, but depend on favor.

From this analysis it becomes clear that in this section Paul did not specifically intend to provide information on baptism as an incorporation into the death of Christ in anticipation of participation in his resurrection; rather, he used the conception of baptism as a metaphor to support the paraenesis of vv. 12–13. In those verses he concretizes his reply of v. 2 to the rhetorical question of v. 1. It would thus be a mistake to try to derive Paul's conception of baptism from his reasoning in this passage, in the same way that it is a mistake to reconstruct in a historically reliable way the actual events Paul refers to in Gal 1:13–2:14. This has been argued effectively by Jack Sanders in his study of "Paul's 'Autobiographical' Statements in Galatians 1–2" to which I referred above.

The following considerations reinforce this conclusion. The concluding, universalizing statement in Rom 6:14 prompts Paul to another rhetorical question in v. 15, parallel to the one in v. 1. The section following in vv. 15–23 has a syntactic structure parallel in many respects to vv. 1–14, but not in all. The key difference, however, is semantic: Instead of using baptism Paul now uses the social institution of slavery as a metaphor to argue the same point. This parallelism in itself amply shows that baptism and the institution of slavery are not the foci of Paul's reasoning but are interchangeable metaphors to underscore his paraenesis.

If we now consider Rom 5:12–21 and 7:1–5 we discover a feature that transcends all four sections: The transition from one state of existence to another which breaks all continuity between the two. In 5:12–21 Paul uses an Adam-Christ typology for that purpose, and in 7:1–5 a woman's binding to the laws of marriage only as long as her husband is alive. A certain carelessness in his choice of metaphors is evident in 7:1–5 when he parallels the death of the husband in v. 3 with the believer's death to the Law in v. 4. Here it is clear that Paul's concern is not the metaphor of marriage, but the completeness of the transition from one condition to another. The same should apply in principle to the other three metaphors. In the case of the Adam-Christ typology Paul also expects the metaphor to carry more weight than it can bear. In this case he is aware of it when he states in 5:15, ἀλλ᾽ οὐχ ὡς τὸ παράπτωμα, οὕτως καὶ τὸ χάρισμα.

These considerations reveal that the chapter divisions in the text of Romans are incorrect at this stage of the letter. The entire section 5:12–7:6 is a single unit. The existing chapter division is nevertheless correct in recognizing the special character of 6:1–23, with its stronger paraenetic emphasis. Within the larger framework of the transition from one form of existence to another in 5:12–7:6 it raises the concrete question of how one should behave when one has left behind the former form of existence for the new existence in Christ. That is the semantic macro-structure of this part of the letter. Further investigations of this kind will reveal the complete syntactic and semantic unity of the first 15 chapters of Romans, especially 1:18–11:36. Such an understanding of the letter reveals the impossibility of interpreting its meaning in a verse-by-verse commentary. A book like Romans, or any writing, biblical or otherwise, can be interpreted not by an additive process of interpreting its individual verses, but by recognizing the individual statements as the means of expressing its overall meaning. An interpretation has to begin by analyzing the book's syntactic and semantic macro-structure. The interpretation of the details should then be governed by the macro-structure, which is at the same time a testing of it. The problem with traditional biblical commentaries is not that they operate without macro-structures; they do have macro-structures. The problem is that the macro-structures operate without acknowledging their existence. What may be the most crucial aspect in the interpretation of a writing is left uncritically to the intuition of the interpreter. There is no methodological procedure for addressing it as a separate issue in the interpretation of texts.

The purpose of these illustrations is to shed further light on Egger's distinction between a synchronic and a diachronic reading. It is well-known that New Testament quotations from the LXX or from tradition frequently have meanings that differ from the originals. What I have in mind is not when an author explicitly interprets a quoted expression metaphorically, for example, when Paul applies Deut 25:4, οὐ κημήσεις βοῦν ἀλοῶντα, to his own situation in 1 Cor 9:9, but when an author quotes a passage, or a series of passages, to make a point, without careful attention to the meaning of what is quoted. For example, Paul quotes a series of passages from the LXX in Rom 2:10–18 and in 15:9–12. A diachronic reading of those verses can show how each of them changed in the course of the history of its transmission from the Hebrew through a variety of Greek versions to Paul's quotation. It is also possible to trace a history of the meaning of a passage diachronically further back, behind the Hebrew version. Such readings have validity in their own right, by shedding light on the history of the meaning of the passage in the course of its tradition, but they may not clarify the meaning of the passage in its New Testament context. That meaning is determined by the synchronic relationship of the quotation to the New Testament text in which it is embedded.

An interesting case of such a structural change in meaning is Matthew's integration of a cycle of Joseph stories (Matt 1:18–25; 2:13–15, 19–21) and a story of the Magi and Herod (2:1–12, 16–18) in his story of the birth of Jesus, which begins with: Τοῦ δὲ Ἰησοῦ Χριστοῦ ἡ γένεσις οὕτως ἦν (1:18). Matthew interpreted the meaning of his quoted material further by introducing the so-called formula quotations (1:23; 2:6, 15, and 18) and by concluding the composite account with a formulation of his own (2:22–23).[38] He does not appear to have changed the formulation of the original stories much, but by integrating them into a single story of the birth of Jesus, he moved the foci of the original stories from being on,

---

[38]See Boers, "Usage."

HOW TO READ THE NEW TESTAMENT

respectively, Joseph, the pious father of Jesus, on the one hand, and the contrasting figures of the Magi and Herod, on the other, to a single focus on Jesus as the only figure who plays a role in both stories. A shifting secondary focus concerns Joseph and the contrasting figures of the Magi and Herod. A diachronic reading makes it possible to recover the two originally discrete stories and to appreciate their distinctive meanings. But that is not Matthew's meaning, which is recognizable only by means of a synchronic reading of the passage as a single story. And so, a reading that takes note both diachronically how Matthew integrated the original stories to form his story of the birth of Jesus and synchronically how Matthew's story is unified structurally—like a bouquet of well-arranged flowers—reveals the remarkable literary achievement of Matthew.

Such a diachronic/synchronic reading can uncover the richness of meaning in the New Testament in other ways as well. So, for example, there is advantage to reading the parable of the Great Feast in Matt 22:1–10 and Luke 14:16–24 diachronically as well as synchronically, including Matthew's expansion by means of an originally separate parable in vv. 11–14. A first, diachronic, reading can uncover a simpler version of the parable behind the two versions of Matthew and Luke, and in the version in saying 64 of the Gospel of Thomas. A second, synchronic, reading can then note what each evangelist made of the parable as a structurally integral part of the meaning of his gospel.[39]

This brings me to what I consider one of the most significant advances in the understanding of meaning in texts, the semiotics of Algirdas Julien Greimas. Apart from Ferdinand de Saussure's structural understanding of meaning in language, the two most important antecedents to Greimas' semiotics of which I am aware are the work of the Russian formalist Vladímir Propp[40] and Claude Lévi-Strauss,[41] the father of structural anthropology.

The basic insight of Propp's work was that similar segments in fairy tales could be represented by different characters performing different actions, as the following examples clearly show:

1. A tsar gives an eagle to a hero. The eagle carries the hero to another kingdom.
2. An old man gives Súchenko a horse. The horse carries Súchenko away to another kingdom.

---

[39] It is a great loss to scholarship when Joachim Jeremias, in what is still one of the finest books on parable interpretation (see Jeremias, *Parables*), limits his interpretation to a diachronic reading that is interested only in what Jeremias considers the original meanings of the parables in the teaching of Jesus.

[40] Propp, *Morphology*.

[41] Especially important for our purposes is Lévi-Strauss, "Myth."

3. A sorcerer gives Iván a little boat. The boat takes Iván to another kingdom.
4. A princess gives Iván a ring. Young men appearing from out of the ring carry Iván away into another kingdom.[42]

Or

1. A dragon kidnaps a tsar's daughter or a peasant's daughter.
2. A witch kidnaps a boy.
3. Older brothers abduct the bride of a younger brother.[43]

On that basis Propp analyzed enough Russian fairy tales to enable him to conclude that the fundamental elements of Russian folktales were thirty-one functions and that they always occurred in the same sequence, although not all of them were present in a single tale. The following are examples, with Propp's numbering:

VIII. A villain causes harm or injury to a member of a family, or

VIIIa. A member of a family either lacks something or desires to have something;

IX. The hero is approached with a request or command: he is allowed to go or dispatched;

XIV. The hero acquires the use of a magical agent;

XVI. The hero and the villain join in direct combat;

XXVI. The task is resolved;

XXX. The villain is punished;

XXXI. The hero is married and ascends the throne.[44]

As the previous examples show, the actors who perform these functions and the way in which the performances take place could vary considerably without violating the genre of the (Russian) folk tale. Propp concluded that the storyteller was constrained in some features of the stories and free to create in others; for example, the storyteller was bound by the overall sequence of functions, but not by which functions he or she used. Significantly, the storyteller was also free to choose the means through which the functions were realized and the attributes of the characters, as the two sets of examples above reveal. Theoretically, according to Propp, the freedom in this case was absolute. "A tree may show the way, a crane may give a steed as a gift, a chisel may spy, etc."[45]

[42]Propp, *Morphology*, 19–20.
[43]Ibid., 31.
[44]Ibid., 27–65.
[45]See ibid., 112–13.

The relationship between Propp and Lévi-Strauss became clear in a review published by the anthropologist after the appearance of Propp's *Morphology* in English in 1958.[46] The critical edge of Lévi-Strauss' review was to point out the difference between Propp's morphology and a structural approach. His critique was that the morphologist separated the form from the content, whereas the structuralist understood these as inseparable. Propp interpreted the structure of the fairy tale as a chronological succession of story elements or functions that were qualitatively distinct, each constituting an independent "genre." Through the structural study of myth it had become possible to establish that the functions, the elements of myths, or "mythemes" as Lévi-Strauss calls them, were not linked in a mere succession, but that many of them were transformations of one and the same function. So, for example, what Propp identified as two distinct functions, the combat between the hero and the villain (XVI) and the difficult task he performs (XXVI), became recognizable as transformations of one and the same function. What made it possible to recognize such actions as transformations of the same function was the realization that they were not discrete, but functioned in relationship to others.

The significance of Lévi-Strauss' proposed transformations for New Testament interpretation is easily recognizable in the above-mentioned four metaphors Paul uses to express the completeness of the transition from a previous form of existence to the being in Christ in Rom 5:12–7:6, the Adam-Christ typology, baptism into the death of Christ, the institution of slavery, and a woman's freedom from a legal binding to her deceased husband.

The most important feature of Lévi-Strauss' structural approach for the interpretation of the New Testament may be his understanding of myth. In contrast with Rudolf Bultmann, who understood mythological language as an objectifying form of presenting otherworldly matters in this-worldly terms,[47] Lévi-Strauss understood myth as the attempt to cope with irresolvable contradictions without resolving them.[48] Whereas Bultmann interpreted New Testament myths by demythologizing them, reformulating their

---

[46]Lévi-Strauss, "Structure." Although Lévi–Strauss was not directly influenced by Propp's 1928 work—his first encounter with the work was in the original 1958 English translation—he recognized with genuine appreciation its indirect influence through his association with Roman Jakobson.

[47]Bultmann, "Mythologie."

[48]". . . since the purpose of myth is to provide a logical model capable of overcoming a contradiction (an impossible achievement if, as it happens, the contradiction is real), a theoretically infinite number of slates will be generated, each one slightly different from the others. Thus, myth grows spiral-wise until the intellectual impulse which has produced it is exhausted" (Lévi-Strauss, "Myth," 226).

meanings in the non-objective categories of Martin Heidegger's existentialist thought, Lévi-Strauss insisted that myths had to be interpreted in terms of their own logic, the logic of myth, not positive, that is, philosophical logic. The logic of myth, though not philosophical, according to Lévi-Strauss, was as rigorous as philosophical logic. Myths were not primitive ways of expressing philosophical truths as Bultmann presupposed; therefore, the task of interpreting them could not be to reformulate them in philosophical language. Whereas philosophical logic was non-contradictory, the logic of myth accepted contradiction; myth was a way of coping with fundamental contradictions by transforming them into more ordinary, recognizable forms.

The need to accept contradiction can be illustrated very well in philosophy, of all places. In Plato's latest period he had become aware of the irreconcilable contradiction facing any philosopher attempting to understand "being," τὸ ὄν. Most intriguing in the presentation of this issue is that he has Parmenides, by name or as the Eliatic stranger, instruct Socrates in these problems, even though Parmenides' understanding that being was one and unchanging represents only the one pole of the unresolvable contradiction. The other was Heraclitus' understanding that being was subject to constant change. After clarifying the impossibility of accepting either of these contradictory views as the only correct understanding of being, Parmenides does not suggest rejecting either or both of them, but as children do when asked to choose one of two hands held forward or behind the back, we should take both, and so accept the contradiction: ὅσα ἀκίνητα καὶ κεκινημένα, τὸ ὄν καὶ τὸ πᾶν συναμφότερα λέγειν (Sophist 249D). The typical behavior of children functions here as a myth that makes the irresolvable contradiction tolerable.[49]

Lévi-Strauss' method of uncovering the meaning expressed in mythical texts is to read them not only syntagmatically, i.e., with the flow of the stories, but also paradigmatically, by tabulating the recurrence of similar story elements or mythemes in a myth or a series of myths. The examination of a sufficient number enables him to discern structural patterns of oppositions between groups of mythemes. He compares it with the reading of a musical score, which must be read not only horizontally with regard to its melody, but also vertically with regard to the harmony of the various voices and of the instruments or singers.[50] He then illustrates this method, first with an analysis of the Oedipus myth,[51] and then the

---

[49]See Boers, "Theologie," 69–74.
[50]Lévi-Strauss, "Myth," 208.
[51]Ibid., 209–14.

North American Zuni myth of origin and emergence.[52] I will illustrate it by a partial analysis of the mythical structure of justification in Paul's letter to the Romans. Paul is not telling myths—he actually intends his reasoning to be positive; the following sets of mythemes nevertheless reveal the mythical structure on which his thinking is based.

JUSTIFICATION BY WORKS	JUSTIFICATION BY FAITH	DISBELIEF OF ISRAEL	INCLUSION OF ISRAEL
	1:16a–b For I am not ashamed of the gospel, for it is the power of God to salvation for all who believe,		
			1:16c–d to the Jews first, and to the Hellenes.
	1:17 For God's justice has been revealed in it from faith to faith, as it is written, "The just will live by faith."		
2:13 Not the hearers of the Law are just before God, but the doers of the Law will be justified.			
			2:25a Circumcision is useful if you practice the Law;
	2:25b if you are a transgressor of the Law, your circumcision has become no circumcision. **2:28** For not who is it in the open is a Jew, nor is circumcision in the open in the flesh,		
			2:29a–b but who is it in secret is a Jew, and circumcision is of the heart, in the spirit, not the letter. **3:1–2** What then is the prerogative of the Jew, and what the use of circumcision? Much in many ways, in the first place, that they were

---

[52]Ibid., 215–26.

JUSTIFICATION BY WORKS	JUSTIFICATION BY FAITH	DISBELIEF OF ISRAEL	INCLUSION OF ISRAEL
			entrusted with God's revelation.
		3:3 What then? If some of them became distrustful, will their distrust not destroy God's trust?	
	3:20 Through works of the Law no one will be justified before him, for through the Law is the recognition of sin. **3:21a** But now the justice of God has been revealed without the Law		
			3:22 the justice of God through the faith of Christ to all who believe. There is no distinction
		3:28 For we consider that a person is justified by faith without works of the Law.	
			3:30 God is one who justifies the circumcised from faith, and the uncircumcised through faith.
4:2a–b If Abraham was justified from works, he would have reason to be proud,			
	4:2c but not before God.		
4:4 For the person who works, the reward is not considered a favor, but in accordance with what is due,			
	4:5 but for the person who does not work, but trusts in him who justifies the ungodly, his [or her] act of trusting is reckoned as justice. **4:9c** For we say, faith was reckoned to Abraham as justification.		

JUSTIFICATION BY WORKS	JUSTIFICATION BY FAITH	DISBELIEF OF ISRAEL	INCLUSION OF ISRAEL
			4:10–12 How was it reckoned? When he was circumcised or uncircumcised? Not circumcised, but uncircumcised. And he received the sign of circumcision, a seal of the justification of faith while uncircumcised, so that he would be the father of all who believe while uncircumcised, that [justification] would be reckoned to them, and the father of the circumcised for those who are not only circumcised, but who also trace the foot steps of the faith while uncircumcised of our father Abraham.
	4:13 For it was not through the Law that the promise was made to Abraham and to his seed that he would be the inheritor of the world, but through the obedience of faith.		
4:14–15a For if those who are from the Law are inheritors, faith has become empty, and the promise destroyed. For the Law engenders wrath;			
	4:15b–16b where there is no Law, there is also no transgression. For that reason it is through faith		
			4:16c–e in order that it would be as a favor, so that the promises would be secure for every seed, not only for the one who is from

JUSTIFICATION BY WORKS	JUSTIFICATION BY FAITH	DISBELIEF OF ISRAEL	INCLUSION OF ISRAEL
			the Law, but also for the one who is from the faith of Abraham, who is the father of all of us.
	9:2 I have a great sadness and an unceasing heartache.		
			9:3–5b For I pray that I myself would be a curse away from Christ for the sake of my brothers, my kinsmen in the flesh, who are Israelites, to whom it belongs to be a child and the glory and the covenants and the giving of the Law and the worship and the promises, of whom are the Fathers and from whom is Christ in the flesh.
		10:2–3 I witness concerning them that they have a zeal for God, but without understanding. Ignorant of the justice of God, and seeking to establish their own, they did not submit to the justice of God.	
			10:15–16 For if their rejection is the reconciliation of the world, what is their reintegration except life from death; and if the firstfruits is holy, so also the dough. And if the roots are holy, so also the branches.

In this double set of oppositions we have a suggestion that just as the rejection of Israel stands opposed to its inclusion, so justification through works stands opposed to justification by faith. It would be a mistake to claim that Paul understood the opposition in this way, but these parallel sets of oppositions open a window to what, at a deeper level, Paul was struggling with in his letter. The answer, as we know very well, is not a simple equation of the rejection of Israel with justification through works and Israel's inclusion with justification by faith. In Rom 2:25–29 Paul interprets doing what the Law requires positively. The relationship between these mythemes resides in the relationships of opposition, not in the components taken by themselves. One may formulate the structure of the oppositions as follows: the opposition between the disbelief of Israel and its inclusion with the gentiles as inheritors of the promise to Abraham[53] finds confirmation in the opposition between justification through works and justification by faith. Romans is mythical to the extent that it attempts, not only to live with, but to affirm both sets of oppositions without resolving them. Paul affirms the Law as well as faith in this letter without trying to reconcile them,[54] but he tries consciously to resolve the opposition between Israel's disbelief and its inclusion with the gentiles as inheritors of the promise to Abraham, for example, by claiming, "if the first-fruits is holy, so also the dough" (11:16a);[55] the degree to which he did so he abandoned mythical thought; the degree to which he failed, making repeated attempts throughout chapter 11,[56] but in effect conceding that he was unable to do so in his appeal to the mysterious depths of the wisdom and knowledge of God,[57] he submitted to the mythical power of his thinking.

At the root of Lévi-Strauss' structural method are the insights of Ferdinand de Saussure, to whom I referred above, that meanings do not reside in words, but in the structural relationships between words. Lévi-Strauss extended de Saussure's insight to formulations larger than single words, i.e., to what, in the context of the interpretation of myths, he calls mythemes. With regard to our own material this means that we could now move beyond the individual formulations in terms of which New Testament Christians expressed the experience of salvation in Christ, as if they were discrete entities, to the recognition of them as transformations of functions which had meaning only in relationship to other functions, similarly transformed into concrete formulations. In this way the structure of the conceptual world in terms of which New Testa-

---

[53]See especially 3:10–11 where the promise to Abraham concerns, not the circumcised, but the uncircumcised; the only way in which Israel was able to participate in the promise was through an uncircumcised faith (3:12).

[54]Romans 3:31, νόμον οὖν καταργοῦμεν διὰ τῆς πίστεως; μὴ γένοιτο, ἀλλὰ νόμον ἱστάνομεν; similarly in Gal 3:21.

[55]Here one notices Paul's desperation about the salvation of all of Israel; he grasps at a straw with the argument that the remnant of Israel who accepted Christ are the firstfruits, which guarantees the sanctification of the entire nation.

[56]11:1, 4, 11–12, 13c–16, 23–24, 28.

[57]11:22, 25–26, 30–36.

ment Christians experienced salvation in Christ becomes exposed, giving an even better understanding of their language and thinking than had been possible for the history-of-religion school, which had still taken the formulations very much as individual expressions, even though anyone who has read Richard Reitzenstein's *Hellenistische Mysterien-Religionen*[58] knows that the thrust of that work, like many others from the history-of-religion school, was toward the entire conceptual world in which Christianity was born. The investigation of the individual formulations was no mere "parallelomania" for that school, but an attempt to understand the language and thinking of Hellenistic times as a means of interpreting the New Testament. For our purposes we can consider the work of Lévi-Strauss as a further step in what was started by the history-of-religion school.

Some of the most important of these features, insofar as they are relevant for the investigation of meaning in texts, including New Testament texts, are brought together in the semiotics of Greimas, recently with the collaboration of Joseph Courtés, in *Sémiotique: Dictionnaire raisonné de la théorie du langage*.[59] It is formulated in its most comprehensive form in the generative trajectory.

GENERATIVE TRAJECTORY			
		syntactic component	*semantic component*
Semio-narrative structures	**deep level**	FUNDAMENTAL SYNTAX	FUNDAMENTAL SEMANTICS
	surface level	SURFACE NARRATIVE SYNTAX	NARRATIVE SEMANTICS
Discourse structures		DISCOURSE SYNTAX	DISCOURSE SEMANTICS
		Discoursivization actorialization temporalization spatialization	Thematization Figurativization

The trajectory has two components, the one syntactic and the other semantic, clarifying how words and larger units are linked

---

[58] Reitzenstein, *Mysterien-Religionen*.

[59] Greimas, Courtés, *Sémiotique*. English *Semiotics*. The following are some of Greimas' most important works, leading up to this dictionary: *Sémantique* (English *Semantics*), *Sens* (English *Meaning*), *Maupassant*, and more recently, following the dictionary, *Sens II*.

(syntax), and how meaning is brought to expression by such linkage in a text (semantics). It is not intended to reveal how a text is produced (what is called pragmatics in linguistic theory), as if an author goes through its various levels as she or he produces a text, but an abstract presentation of what is involved grammatically in a text. As one moves through the various levels of the trajectory, it is not as if one moves from earlier to later stages in the text's production. All the features are present at the same time. There is also no pretension that these features are concretely present but hidden in the text. They are abstractions, products of linguistic theory, by means of which it becomes possible to understand the grammar of a text, syntactically and semantically.

The generative trajectory is the central feature of a syntactic-semantic grammar which provides the means of analyzing a text at its various levels, beginning with the concrete level of its syntactic and semantic discourse structures and moving down to the deepest, most abstract levels of the fundamental syntax and semantics. It is not necessary to reach for this grammar all the time in the interpretation of a text, even though it can be very useful. Where something like it becomes crucial is when difficulties arise, similar to the reaching for the grammar (syntax) of a foreign language with which one is reasonably familiar only when one stumbles on a problem in reading.[60]

(1) *Taking note of the semantic component first:* At the concrete level of the discourse structure, "figurativization" refers to the concrete expression of the text's meaning in figures. They are equivalent to Lévi-Strauss' mythemes, such as I presented above in connection with the mythical structure of Romans. At a deeper level, which is achieved by reading the text vertically in the columns as I presented them above, the thematic linkage of the figures becomes revealed. At the still deeper level of the narrative semantics, the analysis of a text reveals the system of values which is brought to expression in the themes, and finally at the deepest level of the fundamental semantics, the micro-universe out of which the text is generated semantically. It is represented, according to Greimas, by either the existential opposition between life and death, or the cultural opposition between culture and nature.[61]

(2) *Turning then to the syntactic component:* At the concrete level of the discourse structures we find the text's formulation in

---

[60] For a comprehensive discussion of the generative trajectory as a means of clarifying the structure and meaning of a New Testament text, see Boers, *"Mountain."*

[61] For my somewhat different understanding of the micro-universe as a single opposition at an even deeper level between the polarities life/death and good/bad, see Boers, *"Mountain,"* 97–104.

terms of concrete characters, in space and time. At the deeper level of the surface narrative syntax, the characters are mere subjects, either in circumstances of conjunction or disjunction with objects, or performing actions to change undesirable circumstances. As the means of analyzing this level of the text, Greimas has provided the following narrative schema.

NARRATIVE SCHEMA			
A NEED	B PREPAREDNESS	C PERFORMANCE	D SANCTION
A subject of a circumstance, disjointed from a desirable object, or conjoined with an undesirable object	An active subject, willing or obliged, and able (having the power), to overcome the need, specified in A, by a performance	The active subject performing the action transforming the circumstance specified in A into its opposite	Recognition of the success or failure of the performance, or of the achievement of a desired value

In the four phases of the narrative schema, Greimas succeeded in incorporating all thirty-one functions of Propp.

The designation "narrative schema" does not limit its use to "story" texts. As an example, the statement "For freedom Christ has set us free" in Gal 5:1a can be analyzed as follows: The statement itself is a sanction (phase D) that a performance, "set free," (phase C) has been performed successfully by an active subject, Christ who was obviously prepared, that is, was willing or obliged and able, to perform the action (phase B), which had the objective of overcoming the need of transferring "us" to the condition of freedom (phase A). Not all phases of the schema have to come to expression in a text; they are nevertheless presupposed.

What happens at the level of the narrative schema can be formalized further at a deeper level of abstraction in terms of narrative programs in which the actual subjects become purely formal, either active subjects or subjects of circumstance in the following function.

$$F_1 [S_1 \Rightarrow (S_2 \geq O_1) \rightarrow (S_2 \leq O_1)]$$

In this narrative schema F_1 represents a *function* in which an active *subject*, S_1, takes an *action*, represented by $\Rightarrow$, *to transform*, $\rightarrow$, the undesirable circumstance of a *second subject*, represented by S_2, who is *disjoined*, represented by $\geq$, from an *object*, O_1, into a *circumstance of conjunction*, $(S_2 \leq O_1)$. The brackets delimit the function, and the parentheses the circumstances.

In an analysis of Gal 5:1a, Christ would be S_1, we (us) would be S_2, and freedom O_1. That Christ carried out the performance presupposes that he was qualified to do so, which can be written formally as the following function, assuming that Christ himself was the active subject responsible for the action through which he became qualified, for example, by his act of obedience unto death (Phil. 2:6–8).

$$F_2 [S_1 \Rightarrow (S_1 \geq O_2) \to (S_1 \leq O_2)]$$

Through his act of obedience, formalized here as F_2, S_1 transformed his circumstance of a lack of preparedness, disjunction from O_2, into preparedness, $(S_1 \leq O_2)$.

The next step in such an analysis is to establish the formal relationships between these functions. This is done by means of the semiotic square, a formal means of analyzing the relationships between circumstances and actions in a text.

The two functions analyzed above would appear as follows on a logical square:

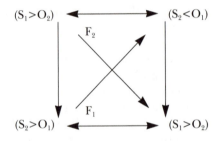

The semiotic square is based on the logical square according to which the top horizontal double arrow represents contraries, and the bottom double arrow subcontraries. Contraries cannot both be true at the same time, but subcontraries can. The vertical arrows represent implication: If what is at either of the two top corners of the square is true, what is at the bottom corner below it is also true. The diagonal lines represent contradiction: If what is on one side of the diagonal line is the case, what is on the other side cannot be the case. On the logical square the diagonal lines are double arrows, indicating purely logical relationships without a concern for which of the two is case. This is the only difference between the logical and the semiotic square as I interpret it.[62] In the case of the semiotic

---

[62]Greimas and other semioticians who follow him use the logical square slightly differently. See Greimas, Courtés, *Semiotics*, under "Square, semiotic." The differences can be reconciled.

square the arrow indicates that an existing circumstance was transformed into its opposite.

What our analysis by means of the semiotic square reveals about Gal 5:1a is that the performance of F_1 presupposes F_2, because circumstance $(S_2 \geq O_1)$ implies $(S_1 \geq O_2)$: Christ had to be qualified before he could make us free.

These are the kind of riches Egger gives his readers in Part 3, "Synchronic Reading." The distinction between Part 3 and Part 4, "Diachronic Reading," is important for understanding this work. Both are "literary" readings. A diachronic reading is historical in a particular sense; it concerns the literary history of a text. Thus Egger distinguishes a diachronic reading from a historical reading which concerns the events behind the texts which gave rise to them (Part 5). Both diachronic reading and historical reading are historical, but in different ways. Part 4, "Diachronic Reading," is a traditional discussion of the actual production of the texts. In this part, Egger's concern is with the distinction of source material and the way in which sources are incorporated into the New Testament writings in their present form. He is also concerned with how a text may change in meaning as it becomes incorporated into a new text-syntactic setting in the New Testament. Part 5, "Reading Historically," is distinguished from the previous diachronic reading by its concern, not with the history of the texts themselves, but with the history behind them; in particular, what can be discerned about Jesus behind the synoptics.

A diachronic reading thus shares its literary nature, its focus on the texts, with a synchronic reading, and it shares its historical nature with what Egger refers to distinctively in Part 5 as a historical reading. Similarly, he takes "reading hermeneutically" (Part 6) in a historical sense. It concerns the way in which the text was interpreted in the past and guides into how it can have meaning in the present. His concern is not with contemporary hermeneutic theory as practiced in New Testament studies by Rudolf Bultmann, Ernst Fuchs and Gerhard Ebeling under the influence of Martin Heidegger and Hans-Georg Gadamer,[63] but with the history of interpretation, and factors that need to be considered in making the New Testament relevant in the present.

What Egger discusses in this part should also be distinguished from the pragmatics of a text, a text-linguistic feature which concerns the way in which meaning is communicated in texts. Egger correctly discusses pragmatics under synchronic reading in Part 3, §10, "Pragmatic Analysis." Pragmatics is a feature of the text itself, not the actual reading of the text by a real reader. An example of

---

[63]For a comprehensive discussion, see Robinson, Cobb, *Hermeneutic*.

text pragmatics is the way in which the author of the Fourth Gospel engages and disengages in the story of the woman at the well (John 4:4–42). By telling a story the author avoids directly addressing his reader(s), but in v. 9 the author (or an editor) reengages by addressing them directly when the author clarifies the woman's rhetorical remark, "How is it that you, a Jew, ask me, a Samaritan woman for a drink [of water]?" with the explanation, "Jews and gentiles do not share utensils." After the explanation the author becomes once more disengaged by continuing the telling of the story. An even more interesting case occurs in vv. 31–38 when the author has the disciples return from the village so that Jesus, one of the participants in the story, assumes the role of clarifying what was happening. Instead of once more reengaging to give this explanation, the author has Jesus, one of the participants in the story, do so. The sole function of the disciples in the story is to enable Jesus to give this clarification, for which the author prepared readers with the remark earlier that they had left for the village to buy food (v. 8). The ultimate effect of the two clarifications is the same, the readers are aided in their understanding of the story, but in each case the author used a different pragmatic approach to achieve this.[64]

Thus the relationship between the main parts of Egger's *Introduction to Linguistic and Historical-Critical Methodology* becomes clear. Part 3 is linguistic; Parts 4–6 are historical-critical. On the other hand, Parts 3 and 4 are both literary, concerning the texts themselves, whereas Parts 5 and 6 concern historical events, not the history of the texts themselves, but the history behind the texts and the history of the effects which the texts have had and continue to have on their readers and interpreters.

Egger does not promote a particular linguistic or semiotic theory, but tries to clarify the way in which texts function by taking note of the various theories in terms of which a text can be understood linguistically. I remember a statement of the philosopher-metaphysician Gottfried Martin to the following effect: If one considers the variety of metaphysical systems from the point of view of the answers, they represent the confusion of philosophy, but if one considers them from the point of view of the questions to which they are possible answers, they represent the wealth of philosophy. Egger's book manifests the wealth of linguistics as it relates to New Testament interpretation. By not promoting a specific theory Egger highlights language itself. That is a strength of the book; its focus is on the text of the New Testament from the perspective of a variety of linguistic and other theories. A person who is looking for an in-depth presentation of a

---

[64]For a fuller discussion, see Boers, *"Mountain."*

specific text-linguistic or semantic theory will be disappointed, but this book should make readers aware that textuality should not be taken for granted. It shows that there are a number of aspects of textuality, covered in the various sections, that need to be taken into consideration in the interpretation of a text. It is an introduction to the various aspects of the text of the New Testament, not an advanced book on linguistics, but it could prepare readers to take the next step of investigating some of the theories in more detail.

§1
Introduction: Methodology as a Guide to Reading

EVERY METHODOLOGY IS A GUIDE TO THE RIGHT UNDERSTANDING OF texts. Since there is only one way to understand texts, namely, reading, any New Testament methodology is first and foremost a guide to correct reading of the texts of the New Testament.

The first pointers for correct reading arise out of reflection on how the meaning of texts is disclosed through reading. Thus to study method is to study understanding. Such a study of understanding, which gets under way with reading, does start out with something that is very personal and subjective, but we are dealing with an area in which the reader, thanks to personal experience, is competent to proceed.

INTRODUCTORY LITERATURE ABOUT REFLECTION ON READING: ISER, *Reading*, provides an extensive discussion on the reading of texts. See also WEIMAR, *Enzyklopädie*, 163–227. Weimar offers a thorough hermeneutics of the specific problems raised by the reading of literary texts. GLINZ, *Textanalyse*. Glinz provides a detailed treatment of the situation, intentions, and interests of author and reader. SCHOBER, *Text und Leser*. This anthology of texts offers a good overview. Representatives of current reading theories are cited in their own words, while introductions by the editor establish the context of the excerpts.[1]

1. READING AS ACCESS TO THE MEANING OF THE TEXT

1.1 EXPERIENCES WITH READING AND UNDERSTANDING

When we read a text, understanding sets in automatically. Anyone who reads a text in a familiar language instinctively connects the material read with a meaning. This simply cannot be avoided. "The

---

[1]Further literature: Assmann, Hardmeier, *Schrift; Funk-Kolleg Literatur;* Detweiler, "Reader"; Eco, *Lector;* Fowler, "Reader"; Grimm, *Literatur;* Iser, *Reading;* Schlingmann, *Methoden;* Link, *Rezeptionsforschung;* Magaß, "Thesen"; Tompkins, *Reader-Response;* Suleiman, Crosman, *Reader;* Türk, *Wirkungsästhetik;* Warning, *Rezeptions-ästhetik;* Weinrich, *Literatur.*

activity of understanding is a spontaneous response to reading."[2] The reader gives the words the sense she is familiar with; she draws connecting lines between what is read and her own subjective experience. She connects the statements in the text with other statements whose meaning is familiar. Through reading the new text becomes a personal possession.

> The understanding acquired in the first reading still has a highly subjective and personal coloring.

Among the factors that shape the first understanding are intensity of the reading, knowledge of the language, breadth of reading, the condition of the reader, etc.

Thus understanding gets started through reading. But a first reading does not guarantee the correctness of the understanding, for at the first reading we often find incomprehension and misunderstanding. In many passages the reader notices an incapacity to understand the text, for example, when she meets with unknown terms or an unfamiliar "world." It can also happen that the reader thinks she understands the text but in reality misunderstands it. Unawares, she mistakes her misunderstanding for the meaning of the text. Such incomprehension and misunderstanding occur because the reader may, perhaps, understand words in the sense familiar to her or because she relates the text to the kinds of texts used in her everyday environment, etc.[3]

Since reading is thus always exposed to the danger of incomprehension and misunderstanding, the reader must employ certain strategies to press forward to the sense of the text and in a way that does not succumb to the "dangers" of the text.

If in the course of a conversation any statement made by our interlocutor is not clear to us, we can ask for a clarification. Sometimes as the conversation proceeds it turns out that a misunderstanding exists. Asking questions and considering the context of the discussion are ways to ascertain the correctness of our understanding. Another form of grasping the sense of a conversation consists in the listener's distancing herself from the situation. From that distance many things "sound" different from the way they first seemed. As in conversation, so too in reading, there are forms for ascertaining that the text has been rightly understood. Attentive and

---

[2]Weimar, *Enzyklopädie*, 287. For spontaneous understanding see Coreth, *Hermeneutik*, 119–23.

[3]Weimar, *Enzyklopädie*, 300 and 297. On the limits to understanding cf. Coreth, *Hermeneutik*, 123.

repeated reading of a text leads more easily to the sense of the text than does a quick and superficial reading. A letter read a second time has a different effect on the reader.

> Certain forms of ascertaining the correctness of our understanding are familiar to us from daily life.

With ancient texts understanding is further made difficult by temporal, linguistic, and cultural distance. Such texts resist understanding. Hence as a rule the reader of ancient texts exercises in advance a certain caution. Of course it can also be the case, as with the Bible, that the texts are familiar and thus have already been read in a certain way.

1.2 SCHOLARLY READING AS ASCERTAINMENT

1.2.1 The Peculiar Nature of Scholarly Reading

The scholarly approach to texts is a special form of reading.[4] Like other forms of reading, scholarly concern with texts also begins with reading the text and with a first understanding of the text conditioned by various subjective factors. Scholarly reading differs from other kinds of reading through its systematic effort to ascertain the correctness of one's understanding. As early as the first reading, scrutiny of the understanding acquired and reflection upon it come into play.[5] Ascertainment is achieved by the reader's carefully recording the phenomena of the text and trying to make connections, striving for a certain completeness in considering the many aspects of the text, presenting the arguments for her own understanding of it, and thus making it possible for another person to duplicate the process of understanding.

> Scholarly reading ascertains the sense of the text through the most complete, systematic recording possible of the phenomena of the text and through grappling with the reasons that speak for or against a specific understanding of it.

In this way scholarly reading avoids the danger of "pigeonholing" the text and furnishing it with the sense that upon first

---

[4]On the connection between reading and literary scholarship see Weimar, *Enzyklopädie*, 46–70.

[5]Weimar, *Enzyklopädie*, 305.

reading seems obvious. And so scholarly reading leads from a strongly subjective reading to a "distanced" reading, which acknowledges the strangeness of the text. Such reading always takes a critical stance toward both the subjective and the group-conditioned forms of understanding texts.[6]

1.2.2 The Competent Reader

By the reader's "competence" I mean in this context her ability to grasp the meaning of a text. True, every reader reads subjectively at first, but she is also competent to do correct reading. For despite the influence of subjective factors on the understanding of the text, reading is not purely subjective and arbitrary. Reading is like a conversation: The reader lets the text take her as an interlocutor into the world of the text. She observes the peculiar nature of the text. She gains insights that are evident to her. In addition the reader can turn to certain authorities to check the correctness of her reading.

Such competence means, on the one hand, the ability to let oneself be led to the meaning of the text by the text itself, and, on the other hand, the ability to recognize the "dangers" of the text, that is, those circumstances that could be the occasion of incomprehension and misunderstanding. Thus competence implies the possibilities and limitations of the individual reading.

Every reader is competent to make observations about the text, to reach conclusions and have feelings about it.

The reader's competence can be seen in various ways. The reader of a text is competent, first of all, to make full observations about the text and to establish connections.[7] Just as the viewer of a building is able, even without a guide, to make certain observations (number of windows, distinctive features, etc.), the reader too can make various observations about the text and establish a connection between these observations.

Beyond that the reader is competent to draw conclusions from observations and comparisons. Someone who views a house from a given side and observes no doors can nonetheless infer that the house does have a door (at least under normal circumstances).

---

[6]To this extent it is an ongoing responsibility of exegesis to be not just historical, but also critical.

[7]This capability is the source of both simple and scholarly reading of the Bible. In the light of that fact there is no essential difference between both forms of reading.

The reader is capable of reaching this conclusion on the basis of cultural knowledge. In the same way the reader can make inferences from observations on the text concerning, say, the author, the audience, the time and place of composition, etc. The reader can extend her competence to make observations and draw conclusions by acquiring supplementary information.

Beyond that the reader is in every instance competent to have feelings about the text. She can say whether a text is pleasing or irritating, etc.[8] One could at most ask whether such reactions are appropriate. The reader should also develop a certain awareness of the limits to her own ability (regarding languages, cultural knowledge, etc.). Such an admission of one's own limits and the caution that grows out of it will guard one from many misinterpretations.

The individual steps in a methodology lead to observations about the text and show how conclusions can be drawn. This book on methodology aims to help develop the competence whose foundations are already given to the reader. The reader is to apply her competence in making observations, establishing connections between them, and drawing conclusions from them in order to attain a better understanding of the biblical text. Scholarly reading of the Scriptures builds on this competence.

1.2.3 Ways to Check the Correctness of Reading

The problem of incomprehension and misunderstanding arises daily in many conversations. In those instances it can be overcome by posing questions and asking for clarification. In reading, the text does not react when it is misunderstood. That is why the reader must always take care to see whether her understanding is correct. She is referred to certain authoritative ways of checking and confirming the correctness of her reading.

The reader has at her disposal authoritative sources for checking the correctness of reading, that is, aids for scrutinizing the correctness of her understanding.

A first way of checking is repeated reading, continual questioning, comparison, and giving attention to the context. Only someone who questions the text again and again will arrive at its meaning.[9]

---

[8]On this point cf. books on practical Bible work that make use of psychological methods, such as Wink, *Bible Study;* Barth, Schramm, *Bibel.*

[9]Observations about the text can also be collected with the help of a question grid, with items such as: Who is doing what, where, when. The question grids of this

A second check on the correctness of the reading is to consider different people's experience of the text. This can occur by means of reading in a group. "One should not interpret by oneself."[10] When several people read a text, they observe more things in it than a single individual could, just as they can draw more conclusions from their observations. Then if the individual participants in the understanding of the text achieved through observations and conclusions do not agree, it becomes necessary to examine the proposed understanding of the text, namely, by looking into the arguments put forth. In this way reading becomes intersubjective and articulated. In exegesis considering other people's experience takes place most frequently by consulting secondary sources. When the reader compares her insights with those of other readers, as found in commentaries, etc., a confrontation emerges with other viewpoints (which are naturally based on observations and conclusions of their own).[11] The recourse to these "authorities" is meaningful, however, only when a reader has already made her own observations about the text. Otherwise the danger exists that the reader will just uncritically accept the observations of other readers.

While the two "authorities" mentioned for checking on our interpretations are no doubt valid for all readers, the Catholic reader of the Bible, for example, is directed by the church's documents to a special kind of "authority."[12] Biblical texts are not to be read in isolation but in a larger context—the context of the whole of sacred Scripture and the believing life of the church, its tradition,

---

methodology also aim to help the reader to make observations. Weimar, *Enzyklopädie,* 178: "There is only one way to follow up the feeling or the awareness of the inadequacy of the first understanding, and to avoid the domination of self-deception and misunderstanding: question, question, and question again. In this way even an amateur, who otherwise admires and condemns without asking questions, can train himself to be a literary scholar. For the scholar's 'talent' is the ability to question." Cf. also Grimminger, "Kommunikation," in *Funk-Kolleg Literatur,* 110–16, especially p. 109: "Every reflection on texts, every interpretation presupposes that the interpretations that have been sketched out by the reader and that have a psychic existence can be compared again with the text and thus be checked."

[10]This sentence could have been taken from a practical handbook for the Bible (cf. Egger, *Gemeinsam,* 10); but it comes in fact from Weimar, *Enzyklopädie,* 309. Glinz puts it still more clearly in *Textanalyse* I, 47–48: " . . . If scholarly intersubjective understanding is to be achieved, and if spontaneous acts of understanding are to be made conscious and explained in scholarly analysis, then for every text several individual ways of understanding, and wherever possible different ones, have to be brought face to face."

[11]Often the reader pays attention to the character of texts only when her attention is called to it. Likewise the effort to verify the correctness of conclusions often presupposes a confrontation with other views. Thus pragmatics and research history are an indispensable help in exegesis, enabling us to come closer to the meaning of the texts.

[12]Second Vatican Council, "Dei Verbum," n. 12.

and that of its magisterium. This "authority" is an essential feature of Catholic Bible reading.[13]

1.3 A SCHOLARLY MODEL OF READING

> The reading of texts becomes a scholarly engagement with texts when it is bound up with systematic reflection on the correctness of understanding.

The model of scholarly reading takes its point of departure from the fact that scholarly reception of texts, like other kinds of reading, is influenced by all sorts of subjective factors. Among these factors must be included both precedents set by other scholars and personal circumstances. The process of scholarly reading itself begins, like all knowledge of the text, with the act of reading. The task at hand is either to scrutinize the first understanding of the text, in which incomprehension and misunderstanding are often mixed together with correct insights, or else to examine on the basis of the text itself the prior understanding that, with familiar texts, has already been steered in specific directions. This scrutiny occurs through the use of observations and conclusions. Its findings must be presented in a way that is rational and intersubjectively verifiable. Part of this process is confronting the so-called secondary literature, in other words, the "reading experiences" of other scholars.[14]

2. EXEGETICAL METHODS AS AIDS TO SCHOLARLY READING AND UNDERSTANDING

Biblical exegesis sees itself as scholarly engagement with Holy Scripture. As a scholarly form of reading the Scriptures it displays characteristics that are valid for the scholarly reading of texts in general. It seeks, with the help of tested procedures, to ascertain the meaning of the text and to give the results an intersubjective verifiability. It tries to do justice to the peculiar difficulties of understanding the biblical text as a historical document. Thus exegesis must always be both historical and critical (as opposed to simplistic "pigeonholing").

---

[13]Of course in every reading of Holy Scripture (and not just in "Catholic" reading) there is a series of factors that have already influenced the first reading: in each case a certain pre-understanding makes itself felt. This in turn is based on the reader's life story, education, confessional affiliation, etc.

[14]Cf. Glinz, *Textanalyse* (see n. 10).

Such scholarly ascertainment is not equally necessary for every reader. There are also other legitimate and necessary forms of ascertaining what is in a text: personal, uninhibited reading of Scripture, listening to the word of God in the liturgy and the church's preaching, discussions about Scripture, and practical Bible study. The individual forms differ according to the person's intention, the intensity of the work, the degree of reflection, the relatedness to real life, the communications situation, etc.[15]

2.1 THE VARIETY OF SCHOLARLY METHODS AND THEIR INTEGRATION

> To do justice to the varied aspects of New Testament texts, a varied set of methodological instruments is used in scholarly dealings with the New Testament.

Scholarly researchers generally acknowledge the complex of methods summed up in the phrase "historical-critical method." Its components include textual criticism (reconstruction of the original Greek text of the New Testament), literary criticism (determining the written sources of the New Testament), traditions criticism and the history of traditions (the oral prehistory of the texts), redaction criticism and redaction history (the collection and editing of the material).[16] These methods read the text primarily under its diachronic aspect, that is, with a view to the genesis of the text, and see the way to the meaning of the text above all in reconstruing its historical origin. These already classic methods have been supplemented in recent days by impulses from many departments of modern linguistics (textual linguistics, structuralism, semantics, pragmatics). These new methods strive primarily to grasp the text synchronically. They complete the historical-critical approach by making the observation of textual phenomena an explicit step in analyzing the text, and they continue the process of classifying (Formalisierung) texts that began in form criticism.

This division into synchronic and diachronic aspects has made itself at home in the discussion of methodology. "Synchronic" (Greek for "simultaneous") methods explore a system in the form

---

[15]On reflection about non-scholarly dealings with Scripture cf. Egger, "Bibellesens"; Kremer, "Bibel"; idem, *Buch*. Among the aids to practical work on the Bible may be mentioned: Erl, Gaiser, *Methoden;* and Egger, *Gemeinsam.*

[16]The four-part division proposed by Zimmermann in *Methodenlehre* (1st to 6th edition) gives an overview of the practical steps in the historical-critical method. Most methodologies offer a sharper division between methods.

that it has at a definite point in time, for example, the English language of today or of the nineteenth century. In synchronic analysis of New Testament texts the text is explored in the form that it has at a specific point in its history. In every case attention is also paid to the communications system in which the text is embedded.[17] Synchronic analysis can be undertaken on the level of final editing as well as in the different versions of the text on all the levels of tradition.

The origin of, and changes in, a system (with texts this would be the use and revision of sources), on the other hand, is explored with so-called diachronic methods. The more recent methods of exegesis often place a very strong emphasis on the need for procedures of synchronic analysis. The historical-critical method is especially concerned with the genesis of texts, but it should not be simply equated with diachronic methods, for it also takes note of many synchronic features, just as not all recent methods view the text in a purely synchronic fashion.

The newer approaches have to be integrated into the already classic methods.

Through the questions it poses every method calls our attention to certain aspects of the text. Matching the variety of these aspects is a variety of methods. Lest we overlook the unity of the text while observing its many aspects, we must clarify the connection between the methods. This is accomplished primarily by means of the theoretical model of "communication through the texts"[18] and hermeneutic reflections on the act of "reading and understanding."[19]

2.2 APPLICATION OF VARIOUS METHODS

The function of the various methods can best be described by a comparison: There are a number of ways to grasp a landscape, with its peculiar character and beauties. Each way reveals something of these; and someone who uses only one way is overlooking a great deal. Of course, there can be ways that are especially rewarding, so that other ways can only offer a supplement or a weak substitute for them.

---

[17]Synchronic analysis does not necessarily mean a purely text-immanent interpretation.

[18]See §§2–4.

[19]See §1 and the introduction to Part 6.

> For every text we must seek out the approach and method best suited to it.

Methods are not means to be applied mechanically to grasp the sense of the text. Methods should be understood as indicating the direction we should take in collecting observations about the text and as showing how we can most appropriately draw conclusions as to the meaning of the text.

Upon beginning scholarly work on the text, however, it is advisable to carry out the individual methodological steps in a specific order, which can vary according to the genre of the text. In this way nothing important will escape the beginner. In the course of work on a concrete text, it will then be seen what methodological step is especially suited to the text and is, for that reason, a fruitful approach.

3. PECULIAR FEATURES OF THIS METHODOLOGY

3.1 KEY POINTS

The methodology presented here is meant as a guide to scholarly work on New Testament texts. An especially characteristic mark of this methodology is the attempt to use a theoretical model of the text and to use a hermeneutic reflection on the act of reading in order to create an organic connection between the methods of historical-critical exegesis and a selection from some more recent methods derived from linguistics.[20]

The individual practical steps to be followed as well as the presuppositions underlying them are reflected on, insofar as this is feasible, since reflection on the possibilities and limits of a scholarly discipline is also a function of that discipline.[21] The primary element in this reflection is reflection on the link between methodology, textual theory, and hermeneutics.

---

[20]Fundamental material on the necessity of integrating the methods can be found in: Richter, *Exegese*, 9–48; Ricoeur, "Méthodes," 35–53; Hardmeier, *Texttheorie*, 28–44; Marguerat, *Strukturale*, 31–84. Schweitzer, *Grammatik*. A brief sketch of an integrated methodology is provided by: Kremer, "Alte," 3–12; Frankemölle, "Kommunikatives," 30. Books on methodology that carry out this integration include Berger, *Exegese;* and for the Old Testament, Fohrer, *Exegese AT.* New editions of methodologies of the historical-critical method expand the method by treating the linguistic aspect: Zimmermann, *Methodenlehre* (starting with the 7th edition); Schreiner, Dautzenberg, *Gestalt,* 2d ed.

[21]What matters is recognizing the possibilities and illusions inherent in every method; cf. Ricoeur, "Méthodes" (see n. 20), 36.

For a number of reasons there have to be restrictions in presenting the material. First of all, a choice must be made from the available methods (this is especially true for the newer methods). The criteria for selection were: The methods should allow many observations and yet not be too difficult to apply.[22] In the process at least one method should be offered for each individual aspect of a textual exploration (linguistics, semantics, etc.). For selecting among newer methods I also employed the criterion that the methods have, on the one hand, won a certain acceptance among experts in the field of linguistics[23] and, on the other hand, can be connected to the traditional historical-critical method.[24] The idea behind this is that without the connection to historical-critical research, a large part of the literature on this subject will remain a closed book to the student.

One further restriction had to be made concerning the extent of reflection on the methods. It is true that controversial methods must be reflected on, but in this context, given the intended purpose of this methodology, and given the inevitably complicated discussion of methods with their (often bemoaned) difficult terminology, I can present only the most important reasons in each case for the choice made and for the order of methodological steps to be followed. In keeping with the book's intended audience, the bibliographical citations have been kept brief. [Whenever possible bibliographies of English-language works have been included. Ed.]

3.2 READERSHIP

This introduction to the methods of New Testament exegesis aims above all at helping students of the New Testament to become theoretically and practically familiar with the ways that biblical scholarship works. To reach that goal, in presenting the individual methods the theoretical underpinnings of the method will also be set forth in each case. The appropriateness of the method will be demonstrated by means of concrete texts, and practical hints will be supplied for individual exercise.

The book, then, is directed to that rather broad group of readers who need a precise, verifiable understanding of texts[25] and who would like to gain insight into the workings of New Testament

---

[22]For this reason the semantic theories of Greimas, among others, will be presented only in a rudimentary form, although there are a series of studies that make use of this method.

[23]This is the case with regard to the practical steps of linguistic-syntactic, semantic, and pragmatic analysis (though not always in that sequence). Cf. the introduction to Part 3.

[24]See n. 20.

[25]On the wording of this see Glinz, *Textanalyse* I, 3.

exegesis, insofar as it has been influenced by the results of recent studies in linguistics.

3.3 STRUCTURE OF THE PRESENT METHODOLOGY

The considerations that have led to the ordering of the practical steps and hence to the structuring of the method may be briefly spelled out here. The text is first conceived under its synchronic aspect as a structure (an ordered aggregate of elements and relations between the elements) and as part of a comprehensive situation involving communication, action, and life. Thereafter the text is viewed under its diachronic aspect as the product of a long evolutionary history. On the basis of such a theory of the text we can justify the necessity of integrating procedures of both synchronic and diachronic analysis, since the text is both a structure and an element of communication as well as the result of a long genesis.

In the second part I shall present the preparatory steps for work on the text: establishing the form of the text through textual criticism, through clarifying the preliminary understanding with which readers approach the text and which strongly influences them in their first reading of the text, and through the drawing up or use of translations.

In the third part I shall present the procedures for the actual reading of the text from the synchronic standpoint.[26] First to be addressed are the problems that arise from the demarcation of the texts from one another. Then, along with the methods of linguistics (partly, however, with an eye to the practical steps of the historical-critical method) the following topics will be discussed in detail: linguistic-syntactic analysis (language, style, structure, articulation of the text), semantic analysis (meaning contained in the text),[27] pragmatic analysis (effect intended by the text), and analysis of genres (common features of similar texts). Observations about the elements of the text and their interconnection, something that the synchronic methods are especially conducive to, also form an important precondition for diachronic analysis.

In Part 4, in close connection with the practical steps of the historical-critical method, I shall present the diachronic methods: literary criticism, tradition criticism, historical analysis of tradition,

---

[26]Separate presentation of the synchronic and diachronic methods makes sense not only because of the theoretical difference between "synchronic" and "diachronic," but also on didactic grounds: Since the historical-critical method operates in a predominately diachronic fashion, only a separate presentation of the diachronic methods provides the possibility of understanding the secondary literature, which often works with this method. In addition the synchronic method is easier to put into practice.

[27]Narrative analysis will be handled along with semantic analysis.

and editorial history. Of course, some findings that emerge in this part will differ from other outlines of methodology, since here I shall take up only those practical steps that closely correspond to the diachronic point of view (history of textual origins). Elements of historical-critical exegesis that are better suited to a synchronic viewpoint have already been built into the presentation of the synchronic methods.

In Part 5 I shall present the reading of the text in its historical aspect. Here the question is, how can the reader go from the text to the reconstruction of historical data.

In Part 6 I shall deal with the hermeneutical problem of reading. Here the issue is, how can the text speak to today's reader through exposition of the originally intended meaning and through an updating that will promote a personal appropriation of the text?

The individual chapters each have a similar structure. After a short definition of the aspect being analyzed, I shall explain the theoretical features of the method and the practical approach of the analytic procedure in question. Then in the summary practical suggestions will be provided for personal work on the New Testament texts. Finally, sample texts will bring to light the possibilities of, and limits to, the individual methodological steps.

Part 1 🏵

Textual Theory

GUIDES FOR ANALYSIS AND INTERPRETATION MUST BE SUITED TO THE peculiar nature and historical origins of the texts being explored. Thus any methodology is always based on a specific notion of the text under investigation and the elements and factors influencing the origins, the peculiar features, and the expressive power of the text. Such a comprehensive concept of the text can be characterized in a quite general sense as textual theory.[1]

The texts of the New Testament, both in their original situation and in their reception by the reader (through whom, after all, they first awaken to life), are part of a larger communications process. From this perspective "New Testament textual theory" deals with the different factors through whose interplay communication by means of the New Testament texts becomes possible.

> New Testament textual theory analyzes the elements and factors involved in the origins of the New Testament and tries to determine how communication through New Testament texts actually works.

The textual theory presented in the following section builds on the findings of historical critical exegesis, which is also undergirded by a "textual theory," that is, a notion about the nature and origin of the texts. With regard to the biblical texts, the advocates of the historical critical method have, for all their disagreements, reached a broad consensus on the nature, intended effect, and origins of the texts, although formal theories on these matters have scarcely been developed.[2]

---

[1]Questions on this subject are treated in linguisitcs under the headings of "(semiotic) textual theory," "textual scholarship," or "textual linguisitcs." The following items may be cited from the literature: Akmajian, Demers, Harnish, *Linguistics;* van Dijk, *Textwissenschaft;* Eco, *Semiotics;* idem, *Trattato;* Güttgemanns, *Linguistik;* idem, "Texttheorie," 85–111; Große, "Semiotik"; Hardmeier, *Texttheorie;* Hennig, Huth, *Kommunikation;* Kallmeyer, *Lektürekolleg*; Kalverkämper, *Orientierung;* Sowinski, *Textlinguistik.* Further literature will be cited for the individual chapters.

[2]Cf. the methodologies of the historical critical method (insofar as they address "textual theory") and the exegetical studies that make use of the historical

In the next section this textual theory of the historical critical method will be expanded with the help of the findings of modern linguistics. The New Testament texts will be considered within the framework of textual theory and in greater detail than usual. My intention is to explain, in the wake of the efforts by modern textual theory, the connection between the factors involved, which differ in their nature, function, and origin.

Scholarly approaches to communication through texts and reflection on reading are often concerned, of course, with texts in contemporary language, with utility texts, or with fictional texts. Since the biblical texts were composed, for the most part, under circumstances quite different from those of the present-day texts, and since these ancient texts also present today's readers with problems altogether different from those raised by contemporary texts, the models of text-linguistic theories have to be differentiated and clearly circumscribed in order to apply the perspective of textual theory to biblical texts.

Textual theory has consequences for the methodical handling of texts, for the reconstruction of the process of communication in which the texts are embedded, as well as for a scholarly model of reading biblical texts.

---

critical method. In the Catholic world this sort of consensus on the peculiar nature and origin of Holy Scripture is presented in the Constitution on Revelation of the Second Vatican Council (1965), and, as far as the Gospels are concerned, in the "Instruction on the Historical Truth of the Gospels" (1964).

§2
Text as a Structured Quantity

ANYONE WHO HEARS OR READS SEVERAL WORDS OR SENTENCES strung together usually notices without much reflection whether she has before her a complete text, an excerpt, or an incoherent sequence of words. Both "textual linguistics" and structuralism address questions of the internal coherence of the elements in a text.

INTRODUCTORY LITERATURE: DE BEAUGRAND, DRESSLER, *Linguistics* provides an introduction to the problems of textual linguistics. For another approach to the same topic, see HALLIDAY, *Explorations*. *Funk-Kolleg Sprache* I, 115–206, familiarizes the reader with the key concepts of structuralism.[1]

Because of all the revisions undergone by the biblical texts by tradition and editing, we find all more urgency in the questions, what actually makes a text a text, and of what does its textuality consist?

1. THE TEXT AS A STRUCTURED, COHERENT LINGUISTIC STATEMENT

The very word "text" (Latin *textus* = web, structure) expresses the idea that the text reveals a correlation of elements. When someone utters a series of words or sentences, we can decide whether one or more texts are present by checking the unity and coherence of the statement. If the words and sentences of the statement are related to one another, the statement is to be qualified as a (unified) text. If the connection between elements is lacking, then we are dealing with two or more texts, perhaps with fragments of texts or with meaningless sequences of words.

---

[1]Further literature: Barthes, "Introduction"; Fages, *Structuralisme;* Fossion, *Leggere;* Marguerat, *Strukturale;* Groupe d'Entrevernes, *Analyse;* idem, *Signes;* Panier, "Introduction"; Patte, "Exegesis"; Parisi, Castelfranchi, "Comprensione."

> A linguistic statement establishes itself as a text by the fact that its parts
> refer to one another and can be explained only from the context.

1.1 STRUCTURE

A text should be viewed as a system whose elements (words, sentences, sections, but also semantic contents, etc.) are interrelated.
Relations between the elements are ordered in keeping with definite
rules (from the rules of grammar through the rules of logical correctness, and so forth) and can be more or less close. Every element
need not be connected to every other one.

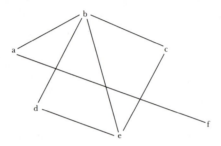

DIAGRAM 1: THE TEXT AS A STRUCTURE

As Diagram 1 shows,[2] there is a variety of orderly relations
between the elements of a text. The sum of the relations between the
elements of a text (a,b,c . . .) is characterized as the "structure" of the
text, in keeping with the definition of structure as an "aggregate of
the relations that connect the elements of a system with one another."[3]

> The structure of a text means the network or sum of the relations
> between the elements of the text.

For this reason the approach that sees structures as primary in the text
is called "structuralist."[4]

---

[2] In connection with Fossion, *Leggere*, 24.
[3] *Funk-Kolleg Sprache* I, 118.
[4] Structuralism, it is true, belongs to the synchronic methods, but this does not
mean that texts exist only in a synchronic system of relations. One extreme branch of
structuralism proposes a theory of the text (not supported in this methodology) according
to which the text before us has absolute priority. This sort of method becomes antihistorical. Granted, the text has to be viewed as a coherent whole, but it is never a
completely closed system. Texts exist in manifold relations to extratextual factors (e.g.,

1.2 Factors Governing the Coherence of Texts

A text is more than a mere sequence of words and sentences. Various factors constitute the text as a structure that transcends the sentences in it. The relations between the individual elements are not consistently firm. There are texts in which the elements are rather loosely interconnected. An example of such a loose assemblage would be some of the series of moral directives in the Pauline epistles, Phil 4:4–7 among others. But then some texts display a high degree of coherence. In the brief section Gal 3:23–29 we find only one sentence that lacks a connecting particle. The combination of the elements is subject to certain rules of connection.[5]

The factors that link the elements of a text with one another and thus contribute to its coherence are of various kinds and function on various levels of the text.

1.2.1 Levels of Coherence

The connectedness of the elements can be established on different levels. On the level of syntax and style the following coherence factors play a particularly important role: pronominal reference (referring to prior or subsequent material in the text with the help of pronouns and substantives), conjunctions, certain repetitions (refrains, among other types). An example of high syntactic coherence can be found in Rom 8:1–17, with its numerous particles and conjunctions, which assure the continuity of the sentences in the text. On the level of semantics (the study of meaning) the text becomes coherent through its subject, through repetition of key words, etc. Thus the text of Rom 8:1–17 is marked by the recurrence (repetition) of the expressions πνεῦμα (spirit) and σάρξ (flesh). On the level of pragmatics (intended effect) the text and its various elements are given unity and coherence through the intent to produce a unified effect on the reader. The account in Gal 1–2 of Paul's life and work first becomes an integral unit by means of linguistic-syntactic and semantic coherence factors, but then it reaches that

---

within a process of communication). In its extreme form structuralism is antihistorical (only the system), antipsychological (only the work and the connections present in it), antisociological (no "Sitz im Leben"). In our methodology structuralism will be used as one method among others. Cf. on this point Ricoeur, "Méthodes" (see §1, note 20), 37–39.

[5] Plett, *Textwissenschaft*, 61. On the coherence factors see de Beaugrande, Dressler, *Linguistics*, 48–83; Kallmeyer, *Lektürekolleg* I, 177–252; Plett, *Textwissenschaft*, 60–70; Egger, "Bergpredigt." These factors will be mentioned in detail in the sections on the individual methods.

end primarily through the pragmatics of the text. The whole text is shaped by Paul's intention of moving the Galatians to trust him as a person and the gospel he preaches.[6]

1.2.2 Degree of Coherence

The degree of coherence on the individual levels can be more or less strong. Some texts have a very tight syntactic interconnectedness; others have an especially dense "fit" through semantic recurrence (in a weather report, for example, we hear nothing but meteorological expressions). In any case it takes the interplay of all the coherence factors to create the coherence of the text.

1.2.3 Lack of Coherence

In some New Testament texts, of course, we note a lack of coherence. We find breaks in the linguistic-stylistic form, discontinuities, disrupting repetitions, and so forth. In short there are "tensions" in the text.[7] In accordance with the notion that a text becomes a coherent whole on the levels of syntax, semantics, pragmatics, and genre, if we have a breakdown of coherence, in other words, a complete lack of coherence in a linguistic statement, then we must assume that we are dealing with two or more texts. We have to keep in mind, however, that coherence need not be equally strong on all levels; nor does a lack of coherence on one level necessarily mean a lack of coherence in the text as a whole. Furthermore, with ancient texts, on the level of semantic and pragmatic coherence, the coherence factors that we apply to modern texts are not unconditionally valid. The kind of argumentation used by the author can differ from what modern logic expects, just as the intended effect of a text can be achieved through different strategies from those of modern texts. Under certain circumstances stylistic breaks and rapid semantic transitions can correspond to an author's or an editor's specific intention.[8]

---

[6]Egger, *Galaterbrief* (consult under this passage).

[7]In literary criticism observations about such "tensions" in the text are used as an indication of its genesis: If tensions can be identified in the text, then we must assume that sources have been worked up. In the case of a text with such tensions we are apparently dealing not with a single text, but with several. Such literary operations have been carried out on the Gospels (especially concerning the Synoptic question) and the Pauline letters (problem of the unity of 1 and 2 Cor, Phil, 1 Thess). According to Richter, *Exegese*, 49–72; Fohrer, *Exegese AT,* 44–56; Strecke, Schnelle, *Einführung,* 40–41, literary criticism, as the determination of unity/disunity, constitutes the starting point of analysis. Merklein rightly stresses in "Einheitlichkeit" that the classic criteria of literary criticism are consistently criteria of incoherence, which help to track down a lack of textual coherence. Before the search for tensions, breaks, etc. scholarly textual analysis must determine the degree of coherence in the text.

[8]"Tensions and breaks in the text are relevant not primarily for signaling the presence of different layers and sources; rather they point to the pragmatic intention

With regard to the so-called tensions in the text, the rule is that at least as much attention must be paid to the coherence factors as to the tensions. Neither the unity nor the disunity of the text is certain a priori. If the analysis is done in an orderly fashion, one can pass judgment about unity/disunity on the basis of the ascertained coherence factors and breaks in coherence.

2. THE STRUCTURALIST MODEL OF READING

Structuralism makes use of a method appropriate to it. Since the text is conceived as a network of relations in which the elements are interrelated, the text can also be employed as a system of reference. One element refers (because all the elements are related) to the other. Thus, as a means of decoding, a method is used that systematically inquires about the relations between the elements of the text.

Structuralism gives directions on how to determine the relations between the elements of a text.

This method provides help in discovering elements and relations between the elements. We are not, to be sure, dealing with a more or less mechanical procedure of discovery, since in semantic analyses the cultural knowledge of the reader plays a particularly significant role. With ancient texts, such as the Bible, this cultural competence of the reader is even more crucial.

From the standpoint of hermeneutics the structuralist approach presents us with the task of seeking the meaning of the text above all in the text itself, that is, in the relations among the elements of the text. The text, then, is to be understood from this perspective as the sum of elements and relations. The text in the reader's hands, with its structures, is the privileged locus of the search for the meaning of the text.[9] Accordingly, anyone who wishes to understand a text must look to its structures. Needless to say, in decoding a text we must also take into consideration, among other things, its historical contexts.[10]

---

of the author who wishes to catch the listener/reader's attention with the breaks," Frankemölle, *Handlungsanweisungen*, 26.

[9]Barthes, "L'analyse," 188.

[10]As opposed to a narrowly conceived structuralism (see above, n. 4).

§3
Texts as Part of a Process of Communication

TEXTS ARE NOT ISOLATED QUANTITIES, BUT ARE EMBEDDED IN A larger context. They are one of the elements in a linguistic process of communication.

LITERATURE: HALLIDAY, *Explorations* investigates how language functions in communication. GÜLICH, RAIBLE, *Textmodelle*, 14–58; and BREUR, *Texttheorie*, 44–71, offer a good beginner's introduction to the theory of "communication through texts." For a textual theory appropriate to biblical texts the reader is referred to HARDMEIER, *Texttheorie*, 52–153; and FRANKEMÖLLE, "Kommunikatives." Under the entry "Pragmatics" (understood in the broad sense), Frankemölle presents a comprehensive theory of the text, into which the historical-critical method is supposed to be integrated through a reorientation.[1]

1. COMMUNICATION THROUGH
(WRITTEN) TEXTS

First let me present a model that holds true for linguistic communication in general and that is often characterized simply as the "model of the text."

In the model shown[2] in Diagram 2 only the most important factors are cited. The speaker/sender shares a certain subject matter with the listener/receiver. Speaker and listener are at the same place

---

[1]The article by Frankemölle, "Kommunikatives," 61–90, is cited emphatically in Frankemölle, *Handlungsanweisungen*, 19–49. Comments on the "text in communication" can also be found in Hennig, Huth, *Kommunikation;* Kahrmann, *Erzählertextanalyse,* 15–50.

[2]The presentation has been taken, with modifications, from *Funk-Kolleg Sprache* I, 141. Cf. Kallmeyer, *Lektürekolleg* I, 26–60; Plett, *Textwissenschaft,* 45; Schmidt, *Texttheorie,* 107–11. For use of such a model in exegetical work: Hardmeier, *Texttheorie,* 106, 108; Frankemölle, "Kommunikatives," 28; Altpeter, *Exegese,* 24–28.

and speak/listen at the same time. Understanding and exerting influence are possible between speaker and listener only when they have at their disposal a common code, a common aggregate of signs, a common "language." Otherwise they speak different "languages." Of course, the listener can immediately expand the aggregate of signs at her disposal by asking questions of the speaker in conversation. The listener/receiver can make use of the information. Speaker and listener are in some cases linked together through the extralinguistic communication situation, so that, for example, sensory perception or common knowledge about certain matters of fact will make understanding easier.

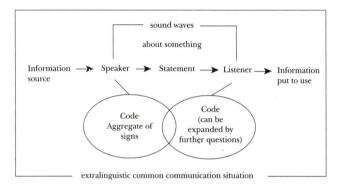

DIAGRAM 2: MODEL OF LINGUISTIC COMMUNICATION IN GENERAL

For communication through written texts, such as the New Testament, such a model is insufficient. Not only do written texts exist in a definite, special way,[3] but there are quite specific problems concerning author-text-reader bound up with written statements[4] that are not present in oral interchanges. In a conversation, for instance, expressions such as "I," "today," and "here" are clear without further ado. In written texts such terms are comprehensible only when (in the case of a letter) there is an address, a date, and a signature. Also important is the fact that instead of a direct connection between speaker and listener a temporal distance now comes

---

[3]For texts as written linguistic statements Weimar's conclusions in his *Enzyklopädie* are correct: The duration of texts is independent of their situation (§80). Texts belong to two temporally separate situations (§81). Texts always exist in the present (§82). And despite "historicity," texts do not change (§83). Texts are timeless and complete (§84). A text is a real presence of part of the past (§85). Texts are the sound of language transformed into lines (§86).
[4]Ehlich, "Textbegriff"; Rothkegel, Sandig, *Linguistische Modelle*, 9–25; and Frankemölle, *Handlungsanweisungen*, 19–49, deal with the de facto separate existence of texts (those that have been detached from the original communication situation) created by the material autonomy of the medium.

between author and reader. The result is a "severely extended speaking situation."[5] "Writing and reading can thus turn into processes as far-removed from one another as one wishes; they are in any case non-simultaneous processes."[6] With biblical texts the length of the temporal interval between the time of composition and that of reading again complicates things. The text as a written aggregate of signs remains the same, but the problem which arises for new readers is whether they possess the necessary aggregate of signs (code) for understanding the text.

In the model of communication through written texts, which is more precisely formulated from the standpoint of written communication in Diagram 3, the factors of time and space have been inserted.[7]

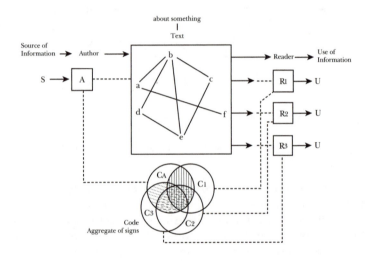

DIAGRAM 3: MODEL OF COMMUNICATION THROUGH
WRITING-CONSTITUTED TEXTS

This sketch is to be read as follows: Information comes from the source to the author, who at a certain point in time, at a certain place, and under certain conditions composes a text. The text is transmitted through a channel (e.g., papyrus) that is subject to

---

[5]Ehlich, "Textbegriff," 18.

[6]Grimminger, "Kommunikation."

[7]In connection with the models of Ehlich, "Textbegriff," 18; and Frankemölle, *Handlungsanweisungen*, 28.

disturbance. The reader (reader 1 to reader *x*) lives at a different place. The aggregate of signs that the author and the reader have at their disposal (from familiarity with the Greek language to cultural knowledge) can vary greatly.

In the model of Diagram 3 today's reader has a precisely defined place as a reader. Even if she is not identical with the original intended audience of the text (in the case of the Pauline letters, for example; the situation is different with the Gospels, which as the transmitters of the Jesus tradition are aimed at a broader public), and even if the conditions of reception today are different from those obtaining for the first readers, the present-day reader receives the text directly, without having to wait for mediation of earlier readers.[8]

2. COMMUNICATION THROUGH WORKS
FROM THE DISTANT PAST

When communication takes place through texts from the distant past, consequences emerge for the process of understanding.[9]

Knowledge about the temporal gap between author and reader influences the writing and reading of texts.

The following explanations have been organized around the two poles of communication: the conveyance of information by the author and the reception of it by the reader. The statements that follow are partly self-evident, but they play a major role (from a hermeneutical point of view) in understanding texts.

2.1 THE ROLE OF THE AUTHOR

In shaping the text the author is influenced by the factors mentioned above, that is, by the aggregate of signs (concepts, language)

---

[8]Of course the history of the text's effects and the tradition in which the text is transmitted are influential in guiding the reader.

[9]The comments by Grimminger in "Kommunikation," 104–16 on the reading and writing of literary texts are also valid, with some modifications, for forms of communication with other written texts. Cf. too on the subject of the situation, intention, and interests of senders and receivers, Glinz, *Textanalyse* I, 67–105; II, 42–48 (with a list of the influencing factors).

at her disposal, by the sources available, by the image she has of the reader, and by the intended result. In particular this means:

- The author composes the text as a "child of her time." Her movements are framed against the horizon of the thought and life of that day. She avails herself of a specific and limited aggregate of signs in the form of concepts, linguistic tools, etc.

- The author "processes" her ideas and, where this is applicable, the material borrowed from oral or written sources into a new integral unit.

- The reader intended by the author (not to be equated with the actual reader) can be a specific person or a community, people of a certain time, or even future readers. The picture that the author has of the reader exerts an essential influence on the shaping of the text. This is especially relevant to the choice of the code and the "completeness" of the text. If the author can presume that the intended reader knows a good deal about the past, she need not mention these prerequisites for understanding the text. The less the author knows about the intended reader, the more complete and more thoroughly organized the text will have to be.

- The author aims to bring the intended reader to a certain way of thinking, feeling, and acting, to confirm or change ideas and behavior. She aims to direct the reader. As a means to this end the author has at her disposal the tools of language. Tools from the world beyond the text, which play such a commanding role in oral conversation, are as a rule not available.

- As soon as the text is composed and out of the author's hands, it becomes autonomous and goes its own way. Apart from a few exceptions, the author can no longer guard her text against incomprehension and misunderstanding. Since after a certain time one can no longer ask questions of the author, a "one-way street" kind of communication sets in.

2.2 RECEPTION OF THE TEXT BY THE READER

Written statements have become autonomous. Texts may be accompanied by extratextual aids to understanding, for example, clarifications by the person who presents the text. With New Testament texts, only the text itself provides access to understanding. For that reason this "communication without a partner" takes place in a "narrowing of the focus of perception to the text."[10] This fact has the following consequences for the reader trying to understand the text:

- The reader of the text, who need not live at the same time as the author, is, like the author, a child of her time. She has at her disposal a certain aggregate of signs in the form of cultural knowledge, ideas, linguistic tools, etc. Since author and reader are both children of their own time, the modern reader does not automatically possess the code necessary for understanding ancient texts. The problem is, how can the reader acquire this code?

- Not every reader of a text is the reader actually intended by the author. But under certain conditions even the unintended reader can understand a text that is not aimed at her.

- The reception of the text by the reader can be disturbed, for example, by a fragmentary transmission of the text, faulty transmission as a result of copying errors, and so forth. The reception can also be hindered by defective knowledge of the language and ideas of the author. The text can be misunderstood. A text can also have effects not originally intended by being read and applied in new situations.

- The text has endured. In this case the reader can continually question the text and check her interpretations against the text.

3. READING AS A WAY OF RECONSTRUCTING THE PROCESS OF COMMUNICATION

The text is part of a process of communication and depends on the many factors involved in such a process. In order to understand the text, it is also necessary to reconstruct the process of communication in which the text is embedded, for only when the interpreter has a complete picture of the various factors involved in the evolution of the text is an appropriate interpretation possible.

With biblical texts, as a rule, we can enter into the process of communication only via the text itself. By carefully applying our proposed model of communication, however, we can draw

---

[10]Grimminger, "Kommunikation," 105.

some conclusions from the text as to the other factors in communication, that is, the author and her time, the intended reasons, etc.

> The application of the model of communication to ancient texts allows us to a certain extent to reach conclusions about the process of communication in which the text is embedded.

The extent of the findings that can be derived from such inferences varies from text to text. It is greater in the case of the Pauline letters than of the Gospels because Paul often discusses the ideas and attitudes of his addressees, while this occurs only indirectly in the Gospels.

The methodical steps taken to reach conclusions are sketched out in Diagram 4. They will be described more precisely in the presentation of the individual methods.

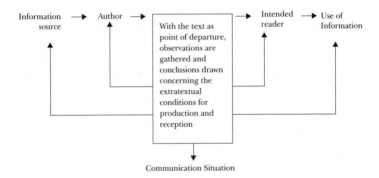

DIAGRAM 4: STEPS REQUIRED FOR RECONSTRUCTING
THE PROCESS OF COMMUNICATION

The reconstruction of the process of communication in which the text is embedded comes to a close when we get an answer to the following questions:[11]

Author: Who is communicating?

Reader: To whom?

---

[11]See also Lewandowski, *Linguistisches,* under the entry for "Textanalyse." Systematic textual analysis will have to orient itself to Lasswell's formula, "Who says what in which channel to whom with what effect?" (in Bryson, *Ideas,* 37).

Subject:	About what? What?
Time:	When?
Place:	Where?
Code:	Common aggregate of signs shared by author and reader?
Desired Effect:	Why?

§4
Texts as the Result of Reception and Editing

THE NEW TESTAMENT TEXTS ARE NOT ONLY EMBEDDED IN A SYN-chronic network; they are also involved in a diachronic develop-ment, insofar as they are the result of a long process of oral and written transmission.

INTRODUCTORY LITERATURE: HALLIDAY, *Expectations,* provides basic mate-rial. KOESTER, *Literature,* gives a comprehensive history of New Testament and other early Christian literature. DEWEY, *Orality,* is a discussion of the move from oral discourse to written text by a number of scholars. KELBER, *Oral,* is a basic work on the topic. In books on the methodology of the New Testament, when the individual steps of the method are presented, a brief exposition is also given to notions about the origins of the texts. HARD-MEIER, *Texttheorie* (on the Old Testament), and MUßNER, "Methodologie,"[1] are noteworthy as approaches to a systematic theory on the origin of the texts.

1. THE ORIGIN OF THE
NEW TESTAMENT SCRIPTURES

> The New Testament texts are products of a long process of oral and written editing and transmission.

The handing down of the words and deeds of Jesus and of the message of death and resurrection amounts to a reception and editing of texts. The sensory experience of the life, death, and resurrection of Jesus of Nazareth was handed down in a reflective, up-to-date fashion. At the various stages of tradition new emphases were put in, and some aspects receded into the background.

---

[1]Hardmeier, *Texttheorie,* 109–53; Mußner, "Methodologie," 118–47. The fol-lowing reflections are closely linked with the comments of these two authors.

1.1 STAGES IN THE EMERGENCE OF THE TEXTS

The emergence of the New Testament scriptures can be divided into three stages: pre–Easter period,[2] post–Easter oral tradition, and writing down of the texts.[3] Diagram 5 sketches out the stages in the development of the most important groups of texts in the New Testament.

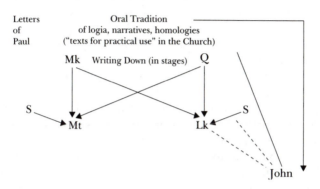

Logia of Jesus
Narratives about Jesus
Creeds and Professions of Faith

Letters   Oral Tradition
of   of logia, narratives, homologies
Paul   ("texts for practical use" in the Church)

Mk   Writing Down (in stages)   Q

S   S

Mt   Lk

John

DIAGRAM 5: THE STAGES OF THE EMERGENCE OF THE NEW TESTAMENT TEXTS

What triggered the emergence of the text was the word and work of Jesus of Nazareth or, more exactly stated, the words uttered by Jesus himself (logia) and the texts about Jesus (narratives) shaped by witnesses. Even at this stage, to be sure, a certain process of reception was under way, insofar as Old Testament texts were being critically received. As early as the time before Easter the apostles were disciples in the genuine sense of the word. They were gathered around Jesus, taking part in his travels and his way of life. They felt that they were committed to his person.[4] The (pre–Easter) logia tradition begins with them. A series of observations about the words of Jesus confirms this concept of text production and reception already operating in the pre–Easter period:[5] (a) As messianic material

---

[2]In classical form criticism the significance of the pre–Easter period for the formation of tradition was passed over in silence. A new perspective on the subject was opened by Schürmann, "Voröster," 39–65.

[3]This division was chosen by the Constitution on Revelation, "Dei Verbum," of the Second Vatican Council, ch. 5.

[4]Cf. Riesner, *Jesus*, 408–19.

[5]The following list of peculiar features is taken almost word for word from Riesner, *Jesus*, 433 (which has references for each item). Fundamental for this conception is Schürmann, "Voröster."

the sayings of Jesus demanded to be memorized; (b) Jesus was used to giving terse summaries of his teaching; (c) some expressions of Jesus can be understood as inviting the listener to learn them by heart; (d) the mysterious and prophetic character of many of Jesus' words suggested that they be preserved for meditation; (e) the deliberately mnemonic formulation of most of the synoptic tradition of Jesus' words was conducive to, indeed it called for, inculcation. And the method chosen for inculcation, we may assume, was learning by heart, memorizing.[6] Thus as far back as the pre–Easter period, the production of narrative texts and the reception of Jesus' logia by the disciples[7] were subject to the conditions which form criticism has brought to light,[8] especially with regard to post–Easter tradition. These conditions include, for example, selection, reshaping, and reinterpretation.[9]

The Easter experience leads to the production of new texts. This experience is formulated in the Easter confessions[10] as a homology that "God has raised him from the dead." These new texts then become part of the tradition. They are received and passed on (cf. 1 Cor 15:30). Along with them the Jesus logia and the Jesus narratives are also handed down, though now, of course, they are seen in a new light. At this time the letters of Paul emerge as new texts. They witness to the production of new texts, but also to the reception of old texts, in that they contain formulas of faith, a missionary vocabulary, and Old Testament quotations. The reception of traditions is subject to certain conditions.[11]

With the writing down of the proclamation in the Gospels (or their prototypes) as well as in the other New Testament scriptures (Acts, Epistles, Revelation) the reception and reshaping of texts reaches a new level.[12] The texts are now given a fixed, definitive linguistic form. The originally isolated brief texts become part of a larger whole, and hence they must be read in this new context. The texts become in a certain sense autonomous; they break away from the group that handed them down as well as from their addressees. The formation of the canon is the seal on the reception of the normative scriptures, as carried out in the church.

---

[6]Riesner, *Jesus*, 440–43.
[7]Ibid., 423–24.
[8]Lampe, Luz, "Overview," 431.
[9]Cf. Hahn, "Jesus," 11–77, esp. 14–26 (of course, here primarily on the subject of the transition from the pre– to the post–Easter period).
[10]The Easter narratives belong to a different genre.
[11]See below.
[12]Cf. above on the peculiar nature of (written) texts. In research on the Gospels Güttgemanns, *Questions*, was notable for calling attention to this difference between "writtenness" and orality.

1.2 A MODEL OF TEXT-PROCESSING

The emergence of the texts of the New Testament scriptures is the result of a series of textual revisions. At every stage of the process texts are received and (re-)produced. In each case the reworking of the text must also be thought of as part of the process of communication. The result of this reworking can serve as the point of departure for a new revision.[13] Diagram 6 shows the course of the editorial process.

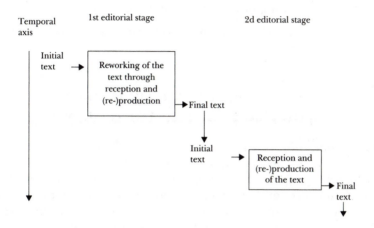

DIAGRAM 6: THE HANDING DOWN OF THE TEXT
AS A CONSEQUENCE OF EDITORIAL REVISIONS

Through revision the texts come to have a new effect on a different group of addressees; they become a response to changed situations. The most important factors that influence revision (selection, alteration and reshaping, reinterpretation) are the following:[14]

- The influence of an explicit Christology. The significance of the person of Jesus was recognized with increasing clarity and found expression also in the texts, above all through the introduction of confessional formulas into the texts of the Gospels; cf., for example, Mark 8:27–30.

- The influence of the Old Testament through both quotations and the available narrative models (e.g., of the Suffering Servant in the Passion narrative).

---

[13]The model is taken, with modifications, from Hardmeier, *Texttheorie*, 80.
[14]Presented in detail by Hahn, in "Jesus," 14–26.

- The more or less negligible textual changes and doublets; the miracle of the loaves and fishes, say, or the versions of the Lord's Prayer.

- The influence of popular narrative modes, for instance, the heightening of the miraculous element.

- Contamination by originally separated texts.

- The orientation of individual pericopes to the story of the Passion.

- The opening of Christian communities to the gentiles.

- The growing confrontation with Judaism, especially Pharisaic Judaism.

2. READING AS A SEARCH FOR THE TRACES OF TEXTUAL ORIGINS

The ongoing process of the production, reception, and revision of the text has left its traces in the New Testament. Some texts (or partial texts) reflect a one-time, non-repeatable situation, in which Jesus found himself before Easter vis-à-vis Israel. There are texts that contradict the post–Easter missionary situation. Some texts advance an open, vague (or "indirect") Christology and soteriology, etc. Other partial texts betray the influence of christological confessions and post–Easter soteriology, post–Easter experience of mission and persecution, the attempt to unravel obscure sayings of Jesus, etc.[15] Thus the text carries with it the vestiges of its origins. For the exegete such observations about the text indicate how to trace the origins of the text.

---

[15]Mußner, "Methodologie," 133–34, 136–37, cites these and other observations as criteria that show whether a logion is authentically Jesus' or a post–Easter formulation. Still, these observations can also be applied in a quite general way as clues to the genesis of the text.

Part 2 ▧

Preparatory Steps in Analysis

IN CARRYING OUT THE ACTUAL ANALYSIS OF TEXTS CERTAIN PREPARA-
tory steps are necessary: establishing the original form of the text
through textual criticism, making one's own (provisional) translation of the ancient text (or choosing from the translations already
available), and arriving at a first orientation toward the text.

§5
Establishing the Form of the Text (Textual Criticism)

ONE OF THE FIRST TASKS IN DEALING WITH THE NEW TESTAMENT texts consists in making sure that the text before us agrees with the one that came from the hands of the author. One special branch of New Testament scholarship, textual criticism, is concerned with just this.

> Taking its starting point from the available manuscripts, New Testament textual criticism attempts to reconstruct the original text of the New Testament (now no longer preserved).

Because of the highly specialized nature of research in textual criticism only a few of its basic concepts can be presented here. But these will at least enable the beginner to make appropriate use of the two most widely used handbook editions of the New Testament, the *Nestle-Aland Novum Testamentum*, 27th edition (NA[27]), and the United Bible Societies' *Greek New Testament*, 4th edition (UBS[4]). Subsequent reference will be made to these editions. Beyond that the student should be familiar with the most important manuscripts and manuscript families of the New Testament and should be able, bearing in mind the criteria of textual criticism, to duplicate its decisions as found in commentaries and scholarly works.[1]

LITERATURE: Almost all books on methodology also offer an introduction to the methods of textual criticism. K. & B. ALAND, *Text*,[2] may be considered

---

[1] Conzelmann, Lindemann, *Interpreting*, 14–15, also propose a similar learning objective. See as well Fee, *Exegesis*, 51–60.

[2] Metzger, *Text*, as well as the introductory works by Kümmel and Wilkenhauser-Schmid provide extensive introductions to, and practice in, textual criticism. Brief introductions may be found in Conzelmann, Lindemann, *Interpreting*, §4, 17–26; Strecker, Schnelle, *Einführung*, 23–39; Zimmermann, *Methodenlehre*, ch. 1; Metzger, *Commentary*, xiii–xxxi; Martini, *Il testo*, 502–52. See also Greenlee, *Text Criticism*.

the standard introduction and the basic reference work on these matters, thanks to its rich documentation.

1. THE THEORY UNDERLYING TEXTUAL CRITICISM ON THE ORIGIN OF VARIANTS AND TYPES OF TEXTS[3]

Until the discovery of the art of printing, the Greek text of the New Testament was disseminated in manuscripts. The originals of the New Testament scriptures have not been preserved, but transcripts of the texts in Greek and the texts of translations (i.e., versions, some of them very old) have survived. The manuscripts that we do have cover a span from A.D. 130 to the fifteenth century. The most important manuscripts are the papyri from the beginning of the third century and the great codices of the fourth century. Alongside the direct testimony of the Greek text in the manuscripts we have indirect evidence in the writings of the Fathers of the church.

1.1 THE ORIGIN OF VARIANTS

The manuscripts offer the text of the New Testament with many variants (alternate readings), whether trivial or more significant.

Variants come about from the fact that texts are incorrectly copied, or else corrections are deliberately entered.

No two manuscripts are completely alike.

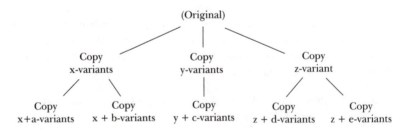

DIAGRAM 7: EMERGENCE OF VARIANTS

Unconscious sources of error include mixing up letters by the copyist (ΛΛ for M), mishearing (while copying from dictation, especially since ει and ι were pronounced the same), false separation of words (since

---

[3]On this point see esp. Aland, K. & B., *Text*, 48–71.

scriptio continua was the usual custom), doubling of letters or words, leaving something out (by skipping over material, such as when sentences have the same beginning or end), adding marginal notes, assimilating parallel passages familiar to the copyist (Mark 1:34 to Luke 4:41).

Deliberate correction can be based on the intention of correcting passages of the text that strike the copyist as erroneous (Mark 1:2, "in the prophets" instead of "in the prophet Isaiah"; Luke 2:43, "Joseph and Mary," instead of "his parents"; Luke 24:13, "a hundred and sixty" instead of "sixty" stadia; changes in spelling, grammar, and style (e.g., elimination of asyndeton), and so forth.

Changes can be either accidental or systematic. When we have a systematic change (and thus the formation of a text by means of specific criteria), we speak of revision or recension. Of course, just how far the types of texts (to be mentioned shortly) are the result of recension is disputed in the research.

1.2 THE ORIGIN OF MANUSCRIPT FAMILIES AND TYPES OF TEXTS

The list of the most important manuscripts with the necessary details can be found in NA[27] and UBS[4]. Here are some statistical data on the manuscripts:[4]

Quantity	Name	Designation	Material	Age
88	Papyri	$\mathfrak{P}$ + number	Papyrus	up until 8th century
274	Majuscules	A, B, C, etc. 01, 02, 03 . . .	Parchment	4–9th cent.
2800 (ca.)	Miniscules	1, 2, 3 . . .	Parchment	9–15th cent.
2110 (ca.)	Lectionaries	11, 12, 13 . . .	Parchment	

Some manuscripts are so important that in the *Nestle-Aland* edition they are cited for every passage.[5] The most important manuscripts are considered to be $\mathfrak{P}^{45}$, $\mathfrak{P}^{66}$, $\mathfrak{P}^{75}$ (especially valuable), B (Codex Vaticanus, especially valuable), ℵ (Codex Sinaiticus), D (with many problems), W, and Θ.

The first Christian centuries saw the development of so-called local texts.[6]

---

[4]Data from ibid., 83–160.
[5]List in ibid., 239–42.
[6]On the "local texts" see also Metzger, *Commentary*, xvii.

When new communities were founded in the vicinity of great cities such as Alexandria, Antioch, and Rome, copies of the sacred scriptures were passed on to them in the textual form customary in those cities. From the middle of the second century on, "the emergence of every new Christian community means the emergence of new New Testament manuscripts."[7] When copies were made, they displayed the same variants as the texts used in the mother communities (and new mistakes would perhaps be made in copying). Thus "text families" arise, i.e., groups of interdependent manuscripts whose stemmata can be reconstructed, for example, families 1 and 13, which have been attested to by manuscripts since the twelfth century.[8] In the individual geographic regions there were different attitudes toward exactness in transmission.[9] The text was still a "living text."[10] In some regions fidelity to the letter counted as the supreme duty, for example, in connection with the ideas of textual criticism, as found back in antiquity. This was probably the case in the region of Alexandria, more particularly the manuscripts $\mathfrak{P}^{66}$, $\mathfrak{P}^{75}$ and manuscript B (Codex Vaticanus). In other areas a freer attitude prevailed toward literal fidelity to the letter (in the region, say, of $\mathfrak{P}^{45}$). The local origin of manuscripts and the manner of copying were among the preconditions leading to the development of several types of texts in the New Testament. When after the epochal Constantinian shift in the fourth century many communities had to be supplied with manuscripts, those textual forms and manuscripts that served as patterns in the church scriptoria acquired a decisive influence.[11] Four types of text receive primary attention in the research.[12]

The Alexandrian type is attested to by papyri $\mathfrak{P}^{66,\ 75}$ and codices B, ℵ, A (Acts of the Apostles), as well as by the old Coptic versions. The archetype of this form can be traced back to the second

---

[7] Aland, K. & B., *Text*, 55.

[8] Martini, *Il testo*, 509.

[9] This can be proved on the basis of an analysis of the errors found in the individual manuscripts: cf. Martini, *Il testo*, 519: $\mathfrak{P}^{75}$ has primarily spelling mistakes, $\mathfrak{P}^{66}$ has missing syllables, $\mathfrak{P}^{45}$ transpositions of words.

[10] Aland, K. & B., *Text*, 69.

[11] Ibid., 70–71.

[12] By "textual type" Martini, *Il testo*, 509, means not so much a group of manuscripts as a totality of variants that are found in certain codices and seem to have a common origin. The division of manuscripts according to textual type has played a great role in New Testament research, cited by Zimmermann, *Methodenlehre;* Metzger, *Commentary;* and Martini, *Il testo;* along with Conzelmann, Lindemann, and Strecker, Schnelle. Aland, K. & B., *Text*, 48–71, groups the manuscripts less according to textual types, but distinguishes more sharply an "early" text (which existed as a normal text, as a freer text and as a solid text) and the later textual forms (Alexandrian-Egyptian, Antiochene-Byzantine) that were created through a certain "convergence of the various text streams" (Kanalisierung). Other textual forms, especially the "Western" variety, are uncertain, as Aland sees it. On the lists and manuscripts, organized by families, see Metzger, *Commentary*, xxix–xxxi; Martini, *Il testo*, 521–30.

or third century. It is characterized by brevity and strictness of expression. This text is in general shorter than the other types of text and reveals fewer grammatical and stylistic improvements.

The "Western text," whose prior and parallel forms can be traced back as far as the third or fourth century, is attested to by codices D, W (for Mark 1:1–5, 30), $\mathfrak{P}^{38}$ and $\mathfrak{P}^{48}$, the Old Latin versions, and Latin church writers. This textual form (especially in the D version) loves paraphrase, changes the position of words, and makes corrections. The text of the Acts of the Apostles is around ten percent longer than in the other manuscripts. The peculiar character and the value of this textual type are questioned in the research.[13]

The Byzantine type, which includes almost all manuscripts since the seventh or eighth century, is a fairly unified type, displaying linguistic polish (preference for syntactic links), elegance of expression, and stylistic changes (aorist instead of the historical present). This textual form is the result of an editorial process that most likely started in Antioch and then was continued in Byzantium. This text was used as a *koinē* (common) text in the Byzantine Empire. Important manuscripts of this type include A (Gospels), E, F, G, H, K.

The research often admits a fourth textual type, from Caesarea, represented by $\mathfrak{P}^{45}$ and the manuscripts Θ and W (Mark 5:31–16:20).

1.3 MODERN EDITIONS OF THE GREEK NEW TESTAMENT

With the help of textual criticism we can reconstruct the form of the text that was circulating in the churches around the middle of the second century. Research in textual criticism has led to the scholarly editions of the New Testament.[14] For a person beginning scholarly work on the New Testament the handbook editions already mentioned, *Nestle-Aland* and *The Greek New Testament* are sufficient. Both editions offer as their main text the text of the New Testament that has been reconstructed on the basis of the critical work by internationally and interdenominationally recognized experts. In the wording of the main text these two editions are identical.[15]

The Greek New Testament is a critical edition for translators in which the most important variants (around 1440) are noted and extensively documented. In addition the editors provide an evaluation of the individual variants, a list of parallel passages, and—an important item for translators—a punctuation apparatus, which

---

[13]In particular, Aland, K. & B., *Text*, 54–55, opposes the idea that the West developed its own textual form. According to *Text*, 240, Codex D therefore carries special weight when it agrees with the other major documents.

[14]For an overview of the research history of textual criticism, see Aland, K. & B., *Text*, 3–47. See also Epp, Fee, *Theory and Method*.

[15]On the genesis of this new "standard text" see Aland, K. & B., *Text*, 30–36.

shows how the text of the New Testament is divided into sentences in the most important modern translations. In a supplementary volume reasons for the textual decisions of the editors are presented.

Nestle-Aland[16] offers a much more extensive critical apparatus than *The Greek New Testament* and, in addition, a copious list of parallel passages.

2. THE METHOD OF TEXTUAL CRITICISM

The reconstruction of the Greek text takes place in the following steps. After the collection of the available variants for a biblical passage[17] and the grouping of variants, inferences are made about the probable original text from the material at hand.

> For the reconstruction of the original text external (to the text) and internal criteria are in force.[18]

With an eye to external criteria (i.e., on the basis of the particular character of the manuscripts) we can say that a variant reading was probably in the original text

- if the reading is attested in many manuscripts. This is characterized as multiple attestation.

- if the reading is found in old manuscripts otherwise known to be reliable (such as Codex Vaticanus), or when it is attested by a generally reliable textual type. The principle is, The greater age of a manuscript speaks for better quality, and quality before quantity.

- if the reading is attested to in manuscripts that are genealogically and geographically independent. A reading is thus original if it has support from different types of texts. This criterion is especially important for evaluating variants from Codex D.

---

[16]*Nestle-Aland*, 26th edition, is a completely new version, as compared with the 25th edition, with regard to variants cited, introductions, etc. The 27th edition follows the purpose of the 26th edition, and their texts are identical. Minor changes in punctuation or rare changes in paragraphing occur. The apparatus has been expanded.

[17]Today this is possible only at great institutes, such as the Institute for New Testament Textual Research in Münster/Westphalia.

[18]On this point cf. Aland, K. & B., *Text,* 281–82: "Zwölf Grundregeln" (Twelve basic rules) and the inroductions to textual criticism, especially Metzger, *Commentary,* xxv–xxviii.

With an eye to internal criteria (i.e., by comparing the variants and drawing on the understanding of how texts in general are handed down) we can say that a reading probably was in the original text

- if the reading is materially difficult and so provided the copyist with the occasion to make a change. The more difficult reading is more likely to be original (*lectio difficilior potior*).

- if the reading is the shorter one (*lectio brevior potior*).

- if the reading most readily corresponds to the style, the vocabulary, and the theological frame of reference of the author in question, as well as to the immediate context.

- if the reading betrays no influence from parallel passages. The alteration of texts by adaptation to parallel texts is explained by the fact that in copying, words slip in from a parallel passage familiar to the copyist.

Most likely to be original is the reading where the findings of external and internal criteria coincide. Yet it very often happens that the criteria do not point in the same direction. Thus, for example, a *lectio difficilior* attested to only by a single manuscript can hardly be the original one. By a kind of countercheck we must then explain why the original text was changed in a specific way in the copying process.

PRACTICAL POINTERS FOR TEXTUAL CRITICISM

- Using the more recent editions of the New Testament, determine what variants exist for a given passage.
- Can the variants be related to specific textual types?
- What differences in meaning result from the different variants? Do these variants change the sense of the text?
- Applying the external and internal criteria of textual criticism, consider which reading might be the original one.
- Draw up a stemma of the formation of variants for back-checking the preferred reading.
- With the use of commentaries, determine what criteria are used for decision-making in textual criticism.

3. EXAMPLES

One of the instructional goals of this section was to enable the student to replicate text-critical decisions in commentaries and scholarly works. In keeping with this goal, special attention will be given in the following examples to text-critical decisions that have been made in such works.

3.1 Eph 1:1: ἐν Ἐφέσῳ

The location, "in Ephesus," is missing in the important old manuscripts. Thus the problem arises, To whom is the letter addressed? This text-critical question is in turn bound up with the question of who the addressees of the letter were, since Ephesians contains no references to concrete addressees or to their situation.

The difficulty of the text-critical problem is evident already in the current editions of the New Testament: *The Greek New Testament* and *Nestle-Aland* have ἐν Ἐφέσῳ in the main text, but place brackets around the phrase.[19] In *The Greek New Testament* the insertion of ἐν Ἐφέσῳ is given a rating of *C*, signifying that the editor has serious doubts whether the better reading is in the main text or in the critical apparatus.

The facts are as follows: A number of important manuscripts testify to the shorter text without the address. These are 𝔓⁴⁶ B* ℵ* 424c 1739 as well as manuscripts mentioned by Basil and the text that was used by Origen. The longer text is found in most manuscripts. The variant reading was entered by correctors in ℵ and B as well.

For the briefer reading, which is both a *lectio brevior* and a *lectio difficilior*, and which in addition is attested to by old manuscripts of the best quality, we can say, "By all the rules of textual criticism this reading is the best one."[20] The translation of the short text runs,[21] "to the saints and believers (there) in Christ," in which case τοῖς οὖσιν would not be meaningless, given the absence of an address, but because of an idiom attested to by Greek papyri might also mean "there."

Given these circumstances Schnackenburg and Mußner[22] opt for the short text. Both explain the insertion of the address by arguing that the readers felt the absence of an address (of the sort

---

[19] The editors of *The Greek New Testament* (UBS³/⁴) justify this by citing the difficult textual situation. See Metzger, *Commentary*, 601.

[20] Schlier, *Epheser*, 30.

[21] According to Schnackenburg, *Ephesians*, see under this passage.

[22] Ibid.; Mußner, *Epheser*, 35–36 ("seems . . . not to be original").

found in all the Pauline letters) and that someone inserted this one, knowing that Paul had long worked in Ephesus. Although application of the external and internal criteria speak for the shorter text, Gnilka stands by the position that the address comes from the original text. He maintains that the lack of an address would be unprecedented, and that there are "no examples of a community usurping a letter."[23]

3.2 MARK 1:1: υἱοῦ θεοῦ

At the beginning of the Gospel according to Mark we find the reading, υἱοῦ (τοῦ) θεοῦ, an important christological title for Mark not attested to by some old manuscripts.

This problem in textual criticism does not find any permanent solution in *The Greek New Testament*, 4th ed., or in the *Nestle-Aland* 27th ed. In the main text of both editions υἱοῦ θεοῦ is in brackets. *The Greek New Testament* rates the originality of the longer text as *C* (subject to considerable doubt).

Applying the external criteria suggests that the longer version is more likely the original one, for the longer version has much stronger attestation, quantitatively speaking, than the short version (see the critical apparatus). It is also attested to by representatives of various types of text (Alexandrian and Western). The shorter version, however, is very old. The abbreviation of the short version might be explained by a copyist's error, since the scribal abbreviations usual with holy names θεός, Υἱός could mislead the copyist into an oversight ("homoioteleuton"). The internal criteria speak, in part, for the short version. We are dealing here with a *lectio brevior* attested to by sound and important textual evidence. An expansion of the short version could be explained by the endeavor to insert christological titles.[24] But this assumption is opposed by the fact that the designation "Son of God" at the very beginning of the work fits the theology of Mark. This Gospel is concerned with the gradual revelation of the Χριστός (Mark 8:29), and then of the Υἱός Θεοῦ (Mark 15:29).[25] By using this title at the beginning Mark creates a tension-filled arc embracing the entire work (cf. also 1:11; 8:29; 9:7; 14:61) and gives the reader useful assistance.

---

[23]Gnilka, *Epheserbrief,* 7; Lindemann makes the same point in "Bemerkungen," 235–51.

[24]Primarily for this reason Pesch, in *Markus,* I, 74, maintains that the brief version is the original one.

[25]Even if the title "Son of God," which is often used in Mark, does not go back to editorial formation, as Pesch assumes in *Markus,* I, 74, the Son-of-God Christology is typical of Mark.

§6
First Orientation to the Text

IN PREPARING THE ACTUAL ANALYSIS OF A TEXT, A FIRST ORIENTATION to the text being analyzed will be of help. At the very outset problems can arise over the scope of the text under investigation. We must also decide to what extent we will be working on the Greek original or/and how far, at least in the first stage, we will be referring to translations and putting them to specific use. In the latter case we must choose the translations we wish to work on.

To begin, it would be of some use to reflect on the reasons why a particular section is made the object of a scholarly exploration.

LITERATURE: LOUW, *Semantics,* provides a comprehensive linguistic introduction to the investigation of New Testament texts, including discourse analysis which is particularly relevant here. GLINZ, *Textanalyse,* and WEIMAR, *Enzyklopädie,* 163–81, discuss how to get a first orientation to the text.

1. DEMARCATION AND BREAKDOWN
OF THE TEXT (SEGMENTATION)

> "For success or at least convenience in doing analyses correct segmentation of the text into smaller reading units is often crucial."[1]

Since a text reveals its meaning only when it is viewed as a whole, it would by rights be necessary to analyze a text in its entirety, that is, to address an entire book of the New Testament. But except for the letter to Philemon this is scarcely possible in the detail called for by exegetical work. Still, it is true that "portions of texts are . . . meaningful units only when they manifest a link between their contents and the general sense of the text."[2] Thus the question arises, what part of a text[3] should be chosen from a longer text, and

---

[1]Glinz, *Textanalyse,* I, 52.
[2]Weinrich, *Textgrammatik,* 29.
[3]The terms are: part of a text, segment of a text, pericope (= "section").

how is the segmentation to be carried out and justified? Once a part
of a text is chosen, another segmentation must be undertaken.

1.1 DETERMINING THE BEGINNING AND END
OF THE TEXT UNDER INVESTIGATION

The beginning and end of a section are not to be defined by means
of the chapter and verse citations in editions of the Bible, since this
does not represent a division into meaning-segments. Determining
the beginning and end of a textual unit is crucial for the proper
understanding of the text. At the start of the investigation, however,
it can be undertaken only in a preliminary fashion. In the course of
the investigation it will then become clear how appropriate to the
text this demarcation was. One can embark on a preliminary demarcation of the text using conventional editions of the Bible, provided
one remembers that in the course of exploring the text notions of
beginning and end will, in some cases, have to be revised. Since the
text is a structured quantity in which the individual elements are interrelated, precise analysis will establish the boundaries of the text.

The exact demarcation of the text under investigation, that is, the
determination of the beginning and end of the textual unit can be justified
only in the course of analysis. In the first stages the demarcation can be
undertaken with the usual editions of the Bible.

For a first determination of the beginning and end of a text
it will be helpful, from a methodological standpoint, to compare the
various editions of the Bible. The comparison will show whether
there are problems with the boundaries of the text: If editions of the
Bible reveal considerable differences in this regard, such problems
are present. In that case we must inquire into the reasons for these
differences. The most important signals of the division are indications of time and place, along with changes of subject matter; hence
all of these are aids in segmentation.[4]

As an example of textual segmentation we may cite Matt
7:7–12. *The Greek New Testament* joins the verses in Matt 7:7–12
together under the heading, "Ask, Seek, Knock." *Nestle-Aland*, which
has no intermediate headings, breaks the text down into two sections, 7:7–11 and 7:12. The New American Bible (NAB) superscribes
Matt 7:7–11 with "The Power of Prayer," and 7:12 with "The Golden

---

[4]More precise explanations of the structure and organization of texts may be
found in §8.

Rule." For 7:7–12 the Comtemporary English Version (CEV) has as its heading, "Ask, Search, Knock," and for 7:13–14, "The Narrow Gate," thereby inserting a pause before 7:13. The New Revised Standard Version (NRSV) labels 7:7–11, "Ask, Search, Knock," and isolates 7:12 entirely, calling it "The Golden Rule." NRSV terms 7:13–14 "The Narrow Gate." Now we have to decide on the boundaries of the text under investigation. A caesura seems out of place between Matt 7:11 and 7:12, because Matt 7:12 is connected to the preceding verse by the particle οὖν. The demand that one behave in accordance with the Golden Rule ensues almost as a sort of consequence of God's behavior. Since there is no such linguistic-syntactic link between 7:12 and 7:13, and a new subject begins with 7:13, this seems a better place for a caesura.[5]

1.2 CONSIDERATION OF THE CONTEXT

The meaning of words, sentences, and parts of texts is substantially shaped by context. That is why we must always pay heed to the connection between a part of the text and the text as a whole. Otherwise the part of the text will be easily misunderstood. Right from the start, therefore, we must determine the remote and the immediate context, what place a part of the text has in the thematic progression of the text as a whole, and, where applicable, what position it occupies in the narrative development of the text. Thus, for example, the Lazarus story in John 11:1–46, which occurs toward the end of the Johannine account of Jesus' public life, forms a high point (as the last of the "signs") and is related in many ways to the Passion story that follows. And it is from that source that the narrative also acquires its peculiar coloring.[6] Consideration of the relation between the pericopes and the text as a whole is especially crucial for redaction criticism.

1.3 DIVISION OF THE TEXT INTO THE SMALLEST READING UNITS

At the very beginning of our work a division of the text into the smallest reading units makes it possible for us to get a better overview of it.[7] The usual breakdown into verses that one finds in editions of the Bible cannot do this. As a rule the best way to divide up the text for reading is to break it down into sentences, which includes even one-word sentences (e.g., "Woe"). A still more detailed approach is to divide up the text into lines of meaning, as we find

---

[5]Cf. Egger, "Bergpredigt," 182.
[6]Kremer, *Lazarus*.
[7]See Schweizer, *Grammatik*, 21–25.

in the new editions for liturgical use. In a breakdown into lines of meaning we can also see clearly the subordination of the sentences and clauses.[8]

First Thessalonians 1:1 can be divided up into the following lines of meaning:

> Paul, Silvanus, Timothy,
> to the church of the Thessalonians,
> in God our Father
> and the Lord Jesus Christ:
> Grace to you and peace.

1.4 DETERMINING THE UNITY OR DISUNITY OF THE TEXT

Determining whether a text is unified or composite is crucial for understanding it. At the beginning of an analysis only a few observations can be made about this. Only when the synchronic analysis has been done will we see whether certain observations about the text can be explained solely by recourse to the use of sources,[9] in other words, whether the text in question is really a unit or a composite.

POINTERS FOR SEGMENTING THE TEXT

- With the help of various editions and translations of the Bible determine where the text under investigation begins and where it ends.
- Divide the text up into lines of meaning.
- Determine the context of the text, especially with regard to the subject and the action narrated.

---

[8]Busseman, Van der Sluis, *Bibel,* 76. Schnackenburg, *Ephesians,* offers the translation divided into meaning lines.

[9]Richter, *Exegese,* 49–50, and Fohrer, *Exegese AT,* 25, place the literary investigation, that is, the determination of unity/disunity at the beginning of scholarly work. Thus for Fohrer the sequence of practical steps is textual criticism, literary criticism, linguistic analysis, etc. Since the decision of whether a text is unified or disunified presupposes an exact analysis of its linguistic-syntactic, semantic, and pragmatic character, it cannot be made until after this analysis. Of course, from the very beginning we have to reckon with the possibility of a disunified text.

2. OBJECTIFICATION OF THE FIRST
UNDERSTANDING OF THE TEXT

As already pointed out in the reflections on the reading, the
first reading of a text can be bound up with incomprehension
and misunderstanding. Since this first incomprehension and misunderstanding has many consequences for interpretation, interpreting begins with seeking objective grounds for the first
understanding.[10]

Objectifying the first understanding of the text means that the reader
frames her understanding of the text in words, and thus makes it into
something tangible that she can observe and scrutinize.

2.1 ROUGH TRANSLATION AND THE USE OF TRANSLATIONS

A first objectification of one's understanding of the text is achieved
by drawing up a rough translation of the New Testament text under
investigation. Scholarly work is done with the Greek original of the
New Testament. Many supporters of structuralism argue that it
makes no difference whether one works with the Greek text or with
translations, but this overlooks the significance that the linguistic-
syntactic form of the text has in and of itself for the understanding
of that text. We must work on the basis of the textual form that has
been reconstructed in textual criticism through the use of manuscript evidence.

  Although a translation that does full justice to the original
text is possible only as the culmination of scholarly engagement with
a text,[11] at the very beginning of analysis a preliminary translation
has to be prepared. This rough translation betrays immediately the
translator's initial understanding. The rough translation has to be
worked on during all phases of textual analysis. The tools for rough
translation are the usual grammars and reference works.[12]

  In addition a look at the translations available for a text will
prove helpful. This sort of comparison makes it immediately evident
in which passages there are problems with translation—and therefore
with understanding.

---

[10]Weimar, *Enzyklopädie*, §305.
[11]See §7 on the translation of the text.
[12]The usual grammars, especially BDF, and dictionaries, especially BAGD;
Rienecker, *Linguistic Key*, and Zerwick, Grosvenor, *Grammatical Analysis*, are particularly
intended for beginners. Also Louw, Nida, *Lexicon*.

2.2 REFLECTION ON THE FIRST UNDERSTANDING OF THE TEXT

A clarification of the preliminary understanding and an objectification of the understanding of the text acquired in the first reading are viewed as an essential first step, not only in practical work on the Bible but in literary studies as well.[13] In objectifying the first understanding of the text, which is often still blurry, one can also find help in methods that, while they derive from practical work on the Bible, must have their place in any scholarly methodology that recognizes the importance of subjectivity. Such methods are useful to scholarship insofar as they help to clarify the initial personal and subjective reading (by which all further reading is influenced).[14]

The punctuation method and experiential analysis are especially useful for objectifying one's first understanding of the text.

The punctuation or sign method[15] consists in the reader's jotting down symbols in the margin of the text. For passages that are unclear a question mark is placed in the margin. Passages that seem important get an exclamation point (or the passage can simply be underlined). Passages that seem existentially important are marked with an arrow. This procedure, which also corresponds to conventional reading techniques, helps the reader to get an overview of the problems posed by the text. Now the text is no longer incomprehensible in its totality. Its difficulties have been precisely circumscribed. Thus the reader can set about solving material difficulties with additional information and can take a stand on her emotional responses to the text. The punctuation method is especially well suited for group work because it spells out the practical steps to be followed. The discussion is begun by the participants who have put a question mark next to a given passage. They present their problem; then there is a response by the group members who have not marked the passage, in other words, the readers who find it comprehensible. Anyone who has insights to offer on the issue completes the conversation and continues it in new directions.

Experiential analysis[16] is designed to explore one's own attitude toward the message of the Bible. The reader asks herself how the text affects her. Depending on her general outlook, her life history, experiences, and anxieties, each reader will be moved in her own way. In approaching the Bible from the standpoint of one's own experience it will often be appropriate to ask what the reader liked

---

[13]This position is defended especially by Glinz and Weimar (see above).

[14]If these methods are used in groups, the group can function as the first authority to check the correctness of understanding.

[15]Erl, Gaiser, *Methoden*, 109–11; see also *Praktische Bibelarbeit heute* published by the Catholic Bible Society (Stuttgart, 1973), 71–73; Egger, *Gemeinsam*, 48–49.

[16]See Egger, *Bibelkunde*, 20.

in the text, what disturbed her, where she sees the central problem, and what might be the significance of individual sentences, as well as problems and things mentioned in the text.

POINTERS FOR OBJECTIFYING THE
FIRST UNDERSTANDING OF THE TEXT

Along with the punctuation methods and experiential analysis the following approaches will be of some service:

- Note the expectations you have as you set about reading a specific text.
- After reading, note your impressions and compare your results with those of a seminar group.

---

§7
Translation of the Text and Use of Translations

FOR MOST BIBLE READERS ONE BEGINS TO DEAL WITH BIBLICAL TEXTS by making one's own (preliminary) translation or consulting another's translation.

> Translation is the written reproduction of the Greek text of the New Testament in a specific target language.[1]

In scholarly work likewise one often begins dealing with biblical texts by using language translations of both the Bible and texts from the milieu of the biblical scriptures.

> At the very beginning of scholarly work one must get an overview of important problems of translation, such as the principles underlying theories of translation, the possibilities and limits of translations, and the function of the most important translations in the reader's native language.

A good translation presupposes exegetical knowledge, acquired through long work, of the text to be translated, as well as knowledge of the language and the audience. Thus translation marks the completion of scholarly work on the text. Translation is the objectification, in its most compressed form, of the understanding of the text acquired by the interpreter. The translation sets forth the understanding of the text arrived at by the interpreter. Translation is possible only after the groundwork is laid and as the result of the successful reception of the text by the interpreter.[2]

INTRODUCTORY LITERATURE: NIDA, TABER, *Theory*, provide an extensive introduction to the theory and practice of biblical translation based on contemporary linguistic principles. Similarly, BEEKMAN, CALLOW, *Translating*.

---

[1] This is how Koller, *Übersetzungswissenschaft*, 12, defines "translating."
[2] Translation as a conclusion intrinsically belongs to interpretation.

Louw, *Lexicography*, provides essays on lexicography as it relates to Bible translation. Koller, *Übersetzungswissenschaft*, acquaints the reader with the usual problems of scholarly translation.[3]

1. THEORIES OF TRANSLATION

1.1 Translation as a Process of Communication

Translation and translating are presented in Diagram 8 within the framework of a theory of communication.

Author ⟶ IL-Text ⟶ Reader
                             Translator
                             Reader becomes Transmitter ⟶ TL-Text ⟶ Reader

DIAGRAM 8: TRANSLATION AS A PROCESS OF COMMUNICATION

Translation is a process of communication. The original message (which is transmitted in a specific language, the so-called initial language [IL], and is embedded in a specific process of communication) is supposed to become a specific message for, in certain cases an appeal to, readers who are not familiar with the initial language and who live in a different culture. For them the translator is the mediator.

The business of translation begins with the translator's becoming a reader of the text. Thus the first phase of translation is the phase of understanding, in which the translator of the initial text analyzes it with respect to its meaning, intention, conditions of development, proposed guidance for the reader, etc. The second phase concerns the intellectual transfer of the meaning structures that have been discovered into the language of the audience. The third phase is the phase of reconstruction, in which the translator "reproduces" the original language text, whose linguistic, semantic, pragmatic, etc. aspects have now been analyzed, "under optimal consideration of communicatively equivalent standpoints."[4] In order

---

[3]Koller, *Übersetzungswissenschaft;* Gnilka, Rüger, *Bibel.* Further literature: On the general theory of translation: Reiß, *Texttyp;* Wilß, *Übersetzungswissenschaft;* Nida, "Signs." On the translation of biblical texts: Buzzetti, *Tradotta;* Meurer, *Bibel;* Nida, "Einige Grundsätze"; Kassühlke, "Übersetzung"; Ritt, "Übersetzungskritik." On English translations see Grant, *Translating the Bible.* Reflections on methodology in translation can also be found in the discussions of Müller, "Funktion"; Frankemölle, "Bibel."

[4]Nida, "Signs," 98, speaks of three phases, "analysis, transfer, restructuring"; in the same way, in connection with Nida, see Kassühlke, *Übersetzen*, 43. Wilß, *Übersetzungswissenschaft*, 72, mentions two phases: the phase of understanding and the phase of linguistic reconstruction.

for translation actually to become a process of communication a whole series of factors and elements has to be taken into account:[5] e.g., initial language, target language, linguistic shape of the text, content (sense, meaning), genre, intended audience.

For the translation itself, translators must ask themselves the following questions—and answer them through translation:[6]

- *Who* is saying *what* (surface of the text, wording, vocabulary, and syntax) *about which subject* (theme, content)?

or

- *What is not being said* (presumed knowledge, prior knowledge about the subject, socio-cultural background information)?

- *How* (tone, style, range) is something being said?

- *When* and *where* (situation in time and space) is something being said, and *through what media* (spoken or written language, genre, type of text)?

and

- *To whom* (audience) is something being said, and *for what purpose* (purpose and desired effect of communication)?

Depending on which question is seen as taking precedence over the others, the translation will turn out differently. For a communications theoretical approach it is vital to ask not just about the content and the linguistic form of the original, but also about which audience will use the translation. If we adhere to this sort of pragmatic or sociolinguistic theory of translation, no single translation will qualify as the best. Depending upon who the members of the audience are, there will have to be various kinds of translations.[7] In any case the translation must be such that the recipient can understand the text with her own aggregate of signs. The initial language text and the target language text should be as equivalent as possible, which means that the quality of the original text should be preserved. "Quality" is understood here as the peculiar nature of the text, created by the following factors: phonology (sound, rhythm), syntax, semantics (theme), pragmatics, type of text (and its communicative functions), and the history of the origins of the text.[8] Since these factors cannot be reduced to a 1:1 correspondence in

---

[5]In connection with Koller, *Übersetzungswissenschaft*, 114–34; Kassühlke, *Übersetzen*, 35; Ritt, "Übersetzungskritik," 167; K. Reiß, "Übersetzen," esp. 36–40.

[6] Reiß, "Übersetzen," 41.

[7]Nida, "Einige Grundsätze," 15–17; on Nida, see Koller, *Übersetzungswissenschaft*, 86.

[8]On the individual factors, cf. Koller, *Übersetzungswissenschaft*, 125–33.

different languages, and since, beyond that, they are located on different levels, translation means the search for the greatest degree of equivalency on the different levels.[9]

1.2 TYPES OF TRANSLATION

In modern translations of the Bible, there are two kinds of translations in primary use (these are standardized types that do not appear in their pure form). Depending on the sort of equivalency that is sought, the translation will be formally or dynamically equivalent.[10]

In formal translations the goal is word-for-word translation. As far as possible the translation should have a 1:1 relationship to the original text, beginning with word order. This is "a kind of translation that aims to make the audience familiar with the message through verbal and syntactic imitation of the original."[11] Deviations from the word order of the original occur only when the target language demands it. This sort of translation is supposed to preserve fidelity to the original. Since formal translation strives above all to attain an equivalent reproduction of a message's form and content, it is strongly author-oriented. Formal translations can go so far as concordance-translations, where any given Greek expression in the New Testament is always translated by the same word in the target language.[12]

The value of formal translations consists primarily in the fact that they serve as a vehicle for a biblically framed language. For religious communities that need a common language as well as religious and theological terminology,[13] formal translations are surely indispensable.

The value of formal translations of the biblical texts lies in the fact that they supply a mode of expression in order to formulate religious experience (which is based on scripture as God's word).

---

[9] On equivalency: ibid., 85–88 (on Nida) and 176–91.
[10] On the types of translations see Reiß, "Übersetzen," 34–36.
[11] Kassühlke, Übersetzen, 39–40; Reiß, "Übersetzen," 34–35, make a further distinction between interlinear (word-for-word translation) and literal translation ("grammar translation").
[12] In synopses, for example. [Or interlinears. Ed.]
[13] Just as certain disciplines, such as mathematics, medicine, etc., for reasons of linguistic economy and precision, cannot dispense with specific technical terms, neither can faith that aims to express its experience dispense with technical terms, such as "grace, kingdom of God." In this sense we are speaking of technical theological terminology. On the necessity of a specific linguistic form to preserve the common explicit memory of salvation, cf. Ritt, "Übersetzungskritik," 178.

Formal translations are especially appropriate for study because they bring the reader close to the original. A translation that is close to the original and even, under circumstances, rough is the only way to do meaningful work on the Synoptic Gospels.

Formal translations include most previous translations, such as the New American Standard Bible, the King James Version and the New King James Version, and the Modern Language Bible (MLB).

A second model of translation, the dynamically equivalent translation,[14] is based on the idea that a translation should exercise the same influence on today's reader as the original text did on its audience back then.

> The value of a dynamically equivalent translation lies in its approach, which is strongly oriented toward the reader and reception.

The process of translation in accordance with the dynamically equivalent method runs as follows: analysis of the text by breaking it down into its elements (in semantic analysis this is done especially with the help of componential analysis[15]), intellectual transferral, and construction of a new textual unit in the target language. Accordingly Rom 1:17 is translated:

NA[27]	MLB	CEV	NIV
δικαιοσύνη	For		For in the gospel a righteous-
γὰρ θεοῦ	God's righteousness	The Good News	ness from God
ἐν αὐτῷ	is disclosed	tells how	is revealed
ἀποκαλύπτεται	in it	God accepts	a righteousness that is
ἐκ πίστεως	through faith	everyone who has faith	by faith
εἰς πίστιν	and leading to faith	but only those who have faith	from first to last

The Contemporary English Version offers the text in a new rendition.[16] After decoding the text on the basis of certain categories (such as object, event, relationship), the text is newly encoded. The translation then makes it clear who is acting (God), that the point at issue here is God's action, and that through this action new relationships are established. In spite of the text's distance from us, the essential semantic contents of δικαιοσύνη τοῦ θεοῦ are preserved.

The significance of this theory of translation also lies in the fact that it has been used as the foundation of international

---

[14]Müller, "Funktion," 237, proposes "funktionale Übersetzung" as a translation of "dynamic equivalent translation."

[15]Componential analysis plays a large role in Nida's theory of translation: In "Signs," 64–67, he presents the semantic classes of object, event, abstractions, relations, and their meaning for translating.

[16]On Rom 1:17 cf. also the reflections of Buzzetti, *Tradotta*.

Bible projects.[17] This theory rightly ranks as the one that has been most intensely reflected on in the field of Bible translations.[18] The reception-oriented approach will merit particular attention in the future.[19] The disadvantages of this theory are, first, the relatively great distance from the text to which such translations lead, and, second, the many exegetical decisions preceding the actual translation whose form they essentially determine. Formal translations avoid this heavy input of exegetical decisions into translation.

The distinction, sharply emphasized before, between translation and a free rendering can scarcely be maintained any longer today. Given the newer theories of translation the difference between translating and freely rendering as an equivalent reproduction has become fluid.

Sometimes too the question of "revision" plays a part in translation. If, because of its importance, a Bible translation is so greatly treasured that people are reluctant to depart from it in any essential way, but it has nonetheless become necessary to adapt it to modern literary sensibilities, or new findings by biblical scholarship need to be worked into the translation (as in the Revised Standard Version), then the existing translation will be improved only where necessary. In the meantime the familiar language will otherwise be kept. This is how the Revised Standard Version was revised, with the final result, the New Revised Standard Version, published in 1989.

1.3 ASSESSING TRANSLATIONS

Keeping the theory of communication in mind when we review a translation, two aspects ought to be examined.

The quality of a translation is measured not only by its fidelity to the author and the text but also by its degree of orientation to the reader.

Fidelity to the original, together with expressiveness in the target language, has always been seen as a standard of a good translation. For recent theories of translation, paying attention to the reader, to the reader's cultural presuppositions and capacity for understanding, is part and parcel of the standards of judgment. Depending upon the sort of reader the translation is intended for, it will proceed differently. For readers not familiar with religious and ecclesiastical language

---

[17] Meurer, "Weltbundes," 173–89.
[18] Müller, "Funktion," 236.
[19] Frankemölle, "Bibel," 122.

many biblical expressions found in formal translations are no longer understandable. For such readers a translation that dispenses with foreign words and (so far as possible) with special terms from church tradition will be useful. It will have a propaedeutic and pastoral function. Such a translation, of course, will hardly be appropriate for Christians who have reflected on their faith and consciously profess it.[20]

The comparison of translations has both descriptive and critical goals.[21]

2. OVERVIEW OF ENGLISH-LANGUAGE TRANSLATIONS OF THE NEW TESTAMENT

Earliest developments of the English Bible have their roots in Jerome's translation of the Latin Bible, commonly known as the Vulgate. In fifth- and sixth-century England people learned the stories of Jerome's Latin Bible in their own language through pictures, poems, and songs. Such representations evolved into Old English translations of the Psalter (ca. A.D. 700) and bits and pieces of the Gospels as well as the Old Testament; these were invariably composed for the sake of the religious "professionals," and it is not until the advent of John Wycliffe (ca. 1330–84) and his followers that the idea of a Bible for ordinary people became a reality. Wycliffe set the course—an often violent and controversial course followed by such luminaries as William Tyndale and Miles Coverdale—for the plethora of today's Bible translations.[22]

The so-called King James Version, commissioned by James I in 1604 at the recommendation of the president of Corpus Christi College, Oxford, Dr. John Reynolds, appeared in 1611. Also known as the Authorized Version, perhaps no other version has influenced English-language culture as much. Despite its relatively poor manuscript base by today's standards, it continues to be cherished and used as the "authoritative" translation of many Protestant Christians.

If Wycliffe set the course for Protestant translations, the Douai-Rheims Bible, which emerged out of the so-called Douai Bible, itself the product of several revisions, set the course for Catholic translations. This translation relied upon Latin versions rather than the Greek manuscripts and was in part a direct response to Protestant translations. While the Douai-Rheims Bible never

---

[20]Ibid., 123–24.

[21]On the comparison of translations in linguistics cf. Bright, *International Encyclopedia;* Asher, *Encyclopedia of Linguistics;* Koller, *Übersetzungswissenschaft,* 192–216; see also Barnwell, *Semantics and Translation.*

[22]See, e.g., Bruce, *History.*

quite had the influence of the Authorized Version, it nevertheless is an important milestone in Bible translation.

Although numerous versions of the English Bible have appeared since the Authorized Version and the Douai-Rheims, translations remained relatively static until the 1881 publication of the Revised Version. The Revised Version (with its counterpart American Standard Version in America) incorporated the latest nineteenth-century Greek manuscript evidence and sought to bring the translation itself up to (then) contemporary standards.[23] Despite these strides, the Revised Version never supplanted the Authorized Version as the translation of choice among Protestant Christians. In 1946 the Revised Standard Version New Testament appeared, followed in six years by a revision of the New Testament and the issuance of the Old Testament.

In the last fifty years churches have witnessed a virtual flood of Bible translations; only the most popular and notable can be mentioned here. In response to Pius XII's famous encyclical *Divino afflante Spiritu* and the decrees of Vatican II, Catholic translation efforts have exploded, with the focus being on working with the original Greek manuscripts rather than basing a translation on the Latin Vulgate. Perhaps the most significant Catholic translation for study purposes is the New American Bible, produced by members of the Catholic Biblical Association and appearing in 1970. The New Testament was revised in 1986 and the Psalms in 1991. The translations are also self-consciously designed for use by the lay reader. The New Jerusalem Bible (1985; preceded by the Jerusalem Bible, 1966), for example, functions as the official English-language liturgical text used in Catholic churches throughout the world. Among Protestant churches numerous New Testament versions appeared in the twentieth century, including those of individual translators like E. J. Goodspeed, James Moffatt, and J. B. Phillips. Translations of the entire Bible include the rather literal Modern Language Bible and the New American Standard Bible. The more flowing New International Version (1973, 1978), a committee translation carried out under the direction of the International Bible Society, has been widely accepted and adopted because of its fluid and easy-to-read translation based on Eugene Nida's theory of "dynamic equivalence."[24] On another front the United Bible Societies produced the Contemporary English Version New Testament (designed to replace the Good News Bible) to further bridge the gap between the lan-

---

[23] The impetus for revision resulted from two major manuscript finds, Vaticanus (Codex B) and Sinaiticus (Codex ℵ), and from the vision of two Cambridge scholars, B. F. Westcott and F. J. A. Hort.

[24] Nida, *Science of Translating.*

guage of the Bible and the modern reader. Perhaps the most notable and sometimes controversial translation in the last decade is the New Revised Standard Version.[25] Published in a Catholic edition as well as an edition geared more for Protestant use, its sensitivity to gender issues,[26] sometimes at the expense of the original sense of the language, has earned it both friend and foe.

3. PREPARING THE TRANSLATION

To begin with, the translator must lay down the textual foundation of the translation.[27] Here the criteria for textual criticism are applicable; and should they arise, questions concerning the canon will have to be settled.[28] For the translation itself both the initial language and the target language have to be taken into consideration.

In analyzing the initial language text the translator is first of all a reader of the text and has to strive by means of the usual procedures of scholarly analysis[29] to understand the text. This analysis deals with the linguistic-syntactic, semantic, and pragmatic characteristics of the text, as well as its genres. Analysis provides answers to questions relevant to translation.[30]

In analyzing the target language and the target group the translator must acquire an image of the peculiar features of the target group for whom the translation is intended, including cultural and linguistic capacities, etc.[31] Analysis provides an answer to the following problems concerning the audience:[32]

---

[25]Sponsored by the Division of Christian Education of the National Council of the Churches of Christ in the United States of America.

[26]One of the mandates of the NRSV translation committee was to eliminate gender-exclusive language as far as was possible without changing those texts that reflect the patriarchal society of the Bible. For example, whereas the RSV reads "brothers" for the Greek ἀδελφοί, the NRSV often reads "brothers and sisters."

[27]The critical edition *The Greek New Testament* (UBS⁴), which cites the 1,440 most important variants (cf. the section on textual criticism), is intended specially for translators.

[28]See the "Guidelines for Interdenominational Cooperation in Bible Study" (note 40).

[29]Cf. the section on semantics in this methodology.

[30]See below.

[31]The Contemporary English Version (foreword) aims to be both "reliable" and "readable" and strives to be suitable for both public and private use. Similar are the aims of the New International Version, though the first concern of this translation was "the accuracy of the translation and its fidelity to the thought of the biblical writers" (from the preface). The Modern Language Bible sought "to achieve plain, up-to-date expression which reflects as directly as possible the meaning of the Hebrew, Aramaic, and Greek" (from the preface to the 1969 edition). The goal of the New Revised Standard Version included "making the Bible available in the form of the English language that is most widely current in our day" (from "To the Reader"); the NRSV also had in mind the Bible's use corporately and individually.

[32]Nida, "Einige Grundsätze," 15.

- Degree of familiarity with religious language and practice

- Degree of readiness for emotional conformity to existing linguistic and non-linguistic models of behavior

- Level of education

- Age

- Use of specialized speech forms

The actual process of translation consists, first, of the intellectual transference of the discovered meaning structures into the language of the audience, and, second, in the reconstruction of the text in the target language. This is done by formulating the message of the text with words, syntactic forms, and textual forms of the target language. The goal is to achieve the closest possible natural equivalent to the original; that is, the target language text should come as close as possible to the original meaning.[33]

For ecumenical translations the "Guidelines for Interdenominational Cooperation in Bible Study" apply with regard to textual foundations, exegesis, and language as well as the carrying out of collaborative efforts.[34]

4. USE OF TRANSLATIONS

Translations can be used in practical work on the Bible, but also in scholarly exploration of the text, where they serve as aids in understanding. Every translation lags behind the potential meanings of the original. This deficiency can be more or less remedied by using several translations for the same biblical passage.

When we compare different translations,[35] it becomes clear what an abundance of meaning lies in the text. Mark 1:15 may serve as an example:

Greek text:	καὶ ἤγγικεν ἡ βασιλεία τοῦ θεοῦ
Modern Language Bible:	and the kingdom of God is near.
King James Version:	and the kingdom of God is at hand.
Contemporary English Version:	God's kingdom will soon be here.
New American Bible:	The reign of God is at hand.

---

[33]Ibid., 13–15.
[34]The guidelines were issued on Jan. 6, 1965 jointly by the World Federation of Bible Societies in London and the Secretariat for the Unity of Christians in Rome.
[35]Cf. the books on methods for practical Bible work.

A glance at this comparison will show the span of meaning covered by the reception of the biblical text in the different translations. The expression βασιλεία is understood as "God's kingdom/reign/action"; ἤγγικεν has been variously understood and translated, both as to its meaning, "is near/will soon be here/is at hand" and as to the verb tense (present, past, future). These variations correspond to the abundance of meanings in the Greek term, for βασιλεία means God's intervention, which can be sensed in the present and will be completed in the future. We are dealing here with God's action as well as with a sphere of dominion.[36]

The use of translations can have yet another function. When a biblical passage is unclear, under certain circumstances comparisons with another translation can be made to explain the difficulty. The "Good News Bible. The Bible in Today's English" in particular can function as a kind of commentary on difficult biblical passages because as "a companion translation" it can provide instructive interpretive assistance.[37]

SUMMARY OF WORKING STEPS AND POINTERS

1. For Translation

   Try to draw up a rough translation with the help of a lexicon and a grammar.

2. Using Translations

   Study various translations (for example, the Modern Language Bible, the New Revised Standard Version, the Contemporary English Version, the New American Bible, the New International Version) in which text translation problems crop up.

   Then determine in which passages translations vary sharply and what differences in meaning result from translating a given passage this way or that. In the beginning the reader can decide intuitively which translation is more pleasing.

   Using translations (the New Revised Standard Version, say) as aids to understanding, work out the meaning of the terms "spirit" and "flesh" in Rom 8:1–13.

---

[36]Cf. the *EDNT* on δικαιοσύνη.
[37]Müller, "Funktion," 244.

Part 3 ❧

Synchronic Reading

THE ANALYSIS OF A TEXT IDEALLY BEGINS WITH AN ANALYSIS that takes its immediate point of departure from the text under discussion, and its structures. This is what happens in synchronic analysis.[1]

THE TEXT AND UNDERSTANDING AS SEEN IN THE MODEL OF SYNCHRONIC READING

Synchronic models see the text as a structured, coherent quantity. The elements of the text are interrelated; out of these relationships there emerges a unity of form. The text, of course, is not a closed system; it can stand in manifold relationships to other quantities. Above all we must consider the text as embedded in a process of communication.

In synchronic analysis the text is analyzed as a structured, coherent totality embedded in a larger process of communication.[2]

This textual model entails also a model of understanding (Diagram 9).[3] The sense of the text is not located "behind" the text in some fashion, but is found in the (intratextual and extratexual) relations between the elements.

Synchronic analysis gives directions on how to find the relations between the elements within the text, and the relations between the text and extratextual elements. In so doing it gives at the same time directions as to how the meaning of the text can be found.

---

[1]On the primacy of synchrony over literary criticism cf. also Theobald, "Primat," 161–86.

[2]The factors operative in the model underlying synchronic analysis were given a detailed presentation in §§2–4.

[3]In connection with Fossion, *Leggere*, 24.

Model 1:   Model 2:
Meaning behind the Text   Meaning in the Structures of Texts

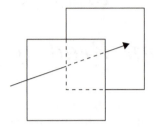
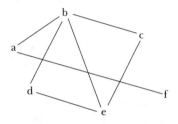

DIAGRAM 9: TWO MODELS OF UNDERSTANDING THE TEXT

PRACTICAL STEPS IN SYNCHRONIC ANALYSIS

After the securing of the form of the text through a first orientation on the text and through translation (§§5–7), the individual methods of synchronic analysis are applied to the chosen text.

> In synchronic reading the following methodical steps are carried out: linguistic-syntactic, semantic, narrative, and pragmatic analysis, and the analyses of textual genres.

The methodical separation and ordering of the practical steps has an objective basis and has come into general use with the advocates of this method.[4] It is based on the relational levels in

---

[4]According to C. W. Morris, one of the founders of modern semiotics, semiotics (the science of signs) is divided into the fields of semantics, syntactics, and pragmatics. On this subject cf. Schober, *Funktionen*, 11, who sums up Morris's concept as follows: "Semantics deals with the relation of signs to 'things'; syntactics with the possible combinations of signs, independently of the things signified as well as of the behavior of their users; and pragmatics with the relations between signs and users, that is, with the goals and effects of signs in behavior." The division into the three fields of syntactics, pragmatics, and semantics is supported by, among others, Akmajian, Demers, Harnish, *Linguistics;* *Funk-Kolleg Sprache;* Kalverkämpfer, *Orientierung;* Plett, *Textwissenschaft;* Sowinski, *Textlinguistik* (instead of syntactics, he speaks of textual grammar and textual stylistics). In the area of exegesis the division into syntactic, semantic, and pragmatic analysis is defended, for methodological and technical reasons, by: Ritt, *Reden;* Schreiner, Dautzenberg, *Gestalt;* Zimmermann, *Methodenlehre;* Frankemölle, "Kommunikatives," 21–22; Schenk, *Philipperbriefe,* 19–26. In several monographs syntactic and semantic analysis are carried out, but not pragmatic analysis; this is the case with: Olsson, *Structure;* Minguez, *Pentecostés;* Hauser, *Strukturen;* Theobald, *Anfang.* Cf. Egger, *Nachfolge,* 195–207.

which linguistic signs are located: the relationships signs–signs, signs–interpreter, signs–objects.[5] Let me emphazize once more that at every step also of synchronic analysis the cultural world of the texts has to be taken unyieldingly into account.

Actual analysis begins with linguistic-syntactic analysis. Perusing the text with an eye to the linguistic signs used in it and combining these signs is the first step toward grasping the peculiar character of the text, "for all subsequent steps start out from observations that emerge from linguistic analysis of the text."[6]

The second practical step is semantic analysis. Here the question is, what does a word or sentence mean, and to which circumstances does a word/sentence/text refer? Semantics also includes narrative analysis.

The third practical step is pragmatic analysis. This investigates the relationship between text and reader, hence the effect that the text has on the reader, with special attention to the concrete elements of communication and activity in the situation.

In the next step, the analysis of textual genres, we seek to discover to which genre the text belongs. Here we apply the findings of the previous practical steps. By comparing texts (whose linguistic, semantic, narrative, and pragmatic nature must have been explored already) we can scrutinize them for similarity and determine the structural patterns common to several texts.

These methods contribute to a methodological expansion of historical criticism. The historical critical method takes as its point of departure a series of observations about the text, but in its approach certain observations (e.g., tensions in the text) are privileged while others are overlooked. In the synchronic methods, comprehensive systematic observations of textual phenomena become a deliberate research step. Beyond that, the tendency to classify texts on the basis of form, already noticeable in form criticism, is carried further. Thanks to this stronger emphasis on form and the systematic observation of textual phenomena the newer methods turn into a still more suitable instrument for verifying the right understanding of texts and hence for checking exegesis.[7]

---

[5] Plett, *Textwissenschaft*, 52.
[6] Fohrer, *Exegese AT*, 57.
[7] On the integration of the methods, see §1.

§8
Linguistic-Syntactic Analysis

PEOPLE HAVING A CONVERSATION REVEAL A PREFERENCE FOR PAR-
ticular words and phrases; they connect sentences in a certain way,
use specific linguistic devices, etc., in order to influence their interlocutor. In order to understand a statement and correctly integrate
it, we need to consider not just the content of the statement, but also
its individual linguistic character. Ascertaining the linguistic peculiarity of each text will help in linguistic-syntactic analysis.

> In linguistic-syntactic analysis of a text we investigate the concrete
> linguistic form of a text. This means the relations between the linguistic
> devices used in the text and the rules by which the elements of the text
> are linked together.

The analysis of linguistic signs and their connections is the
starting point for all further work. It is the foundation for semantic
analysis, which deals with the meaning of linguistic statements.
Pragmatic analysis likewise presupposes linguistic-syntactic analysis, since by choosing certain linguistic means the speaker/author
wishes to have definite effects on the reader. Knowledge of the
peculiar linguistic character of a text is important both for understanding it and for reconstructing its genesis.

INTRODUCTORY LITERATURE: DE BEAUGRANDE, DRESSLER, *Linguistics*, 50–87;
LOUW, *Semantics*, are helpful as introductions to the linguistic-syntactic
character of texts. In the area of exegesis BERGER, *Exegese* §3 and §4, is
also useful.[1]

---

[1] Further literature: Anderegg, *Stiltheorie;* Guiraud, Kuentz, *Lectures;* Sanders,
Stiltheorie; idem, *Stilistik.* Compare the sections on this subject in: Egger, *Nachfolge,*
60–78; Fohrer, *Exegese AT,* 57–81; Michel, *Methodik;* Plett, *Textwissenschaft,* 56–79; Richter,
Exegese, 72–125; Sowinski, *Textlinguistik;* Zimmermann, *Methodenlehre,* 282–83.

1. LINGUISTIC-SYNTACTIC FEATURES OF TEXTS

In linguistic-syntactic analysis the linguistic character of the text is described: sound, rhythm, vocabulary, syntactic means, cohesion of the textual elements, structure, and arrangement.

> The linguistic-syntactic character of a text is shaped by a "lexicon" of linguistic signs (aggregate of words and sentences) and a "grammar" that regulates the connections between the elements.

1.1 VOCABULARY (LEXICON)

The nature of a text depends upon—among other things—the vocabulary at the author's disposal. A text never uses the entire lexicon of a language, but only a selection from it.[2] This selection is characteristic of the text. The size of the vocabulary can vary. Thus John uses only about 1,000 different words (which he uses altogether 19,000 times). In the case of important words in the New Testament we are struck by the usage typical of certain books, for example, εὐαγγέλιον (12 times in the Gospels, twice in Acts, 47 times in the authentic Pauline letters); ἀκολουθεῖν (60 times in the Synoptic Gospels, 19 times in John, once in the Pauline letters). A summary review of the vocabulary of a text, even of a segment of a text, provides a first view of the theological emphases of the biblical text in question (which must be deepened through semantic analysis) and also allows us to draw conclusions, through diachronic analysis, about tradition and redaction.[3]

1.2 KINDS AND FORMS OF WORDS (GRAMMAR)

Texts furthermore offer a choice from the grammatically possible word-types and word-forms in the grammar. Paying attention to the parts of speech, such as substantive/noun, article, pronoun, verb, adjective, adverb, preposition, as well as forms of words, such as verb tenses (aspect, mood, etc.), guides the observer to the key points of the text.[4] Texts with many imperatives contain directives. Texts with many personal pronouns (I, you, she) are chiefly concerned with

---

[2] On the frequency analysis of words, cf. Guiraud, Kuentz, *Lectures*, 222–24. Statistics on the vocabulary of the New Testament are mentioned in n. 23.

[3] On analysis of vocabulary as a practical step in the redaction critical method, see §14.

[4] Cf. Richter, *Exegese*, 88–92. Guiraud, Kuentz, *Lectures*, 214–22, shows by means of examples from French and German that German authors, on the average, use more pronouns and fewer substantives, fewer adjectives and adverbs than French authors do.

questions of communication (cf., e.g., Gal 1:1–5). Furthermore attention should be paid to such things as a preference for certain kinds of sentences (declarative sentences, imperatives, etc.), the use of verbal and nominative sentences, the position of subject and predicate,[5] the use of synonyms (Luke especially likes to vary expressions), the frequency of certain phrases, the frequency of change in verb tense (e.g., shifts between aorist, imperfect, and historical present; in the short passage Mark 1:40–43 we find used for the main verb first a present, then an aorist, three aorists, and a present).

1.3 LINKS BETWEEN WORDS AND SENTENCES

The linking of words to different sorts of clauses (nominal and verbal) and the connection between sentences have characteristic patterns in different texts. Authors are naturally bound to follow certain rules dictated by the grammar of their language; in the New Testament that would mean Koine Greek and the influence of Semitisms, Aramaisms, and Hebraisms.[6] But every grammar also allows certain options for connecting the various elements. The linguistic links within texts and hence their cohesion can have different degrees of "thickness." There are texts in which each text is also linguistically connected with the others, and texts in which asyndeta (unconnected sentences) accumulate.

Some linguistic means of creating cohesion in texts are repetition as well as use of proforms[7] and conjunctions.[8] In repetition (partial or complete recurrence) an element (word or group of words) is inserted at various points of the text; for example, in the parable of the prodigal son, Luke 15:11–32, vv. 18–19 are picked up in a modified form in v. 21; v. 24 is also repeated in v. 31, and v. 13 in v. 30.[9] Repetition can take place through verbal or periphrastic resumption of elements.

---

[5]Although word order in German is much more fixed than in Greek, in German too the position of the verb can be stylistically meaningful: if the word order of verb-substantive in Mark 1:15 is preserved, the dynamic character of the event is more strongly stressed: "Erfüllt ist die Zeit, und nahegekommen ist die Gottesherrschaft" ("Fulfilled is the time, and come near is the kingdom of God").

[6]Cf. Beyer, *Syntax;* Voelz, "Language"; Wilcox, "Semitisms." Cf. also Berger, P.–R., "Aramäisch"; and the reply by Black, "Erwiderung."

[7]Proforms are "economical, short words, empty of their own particular content, which stand in the surface text in place of more determinate, content-activating expressions" (de Beaugrande, Dressler, *Linguistics,* 60, cf. Dressler, *Einführung,* 25–26). The most common proforms are pronouns. Proforms can function anaphorically as well as cataphorically [Ed.].

[8]Cf. the lists in de Beaugrande, Dressler, *Linguistics,* 49; Fleischer, Michel, *Stilistik,* 190–207; Plett, *Textwissenschaft,* 62; Berger, *Exegese,* 13–17; Schenk, *Philipperbriefe,* 22–23.

[9]Cf. Berger, *Exegese,* 14. On analysis of the text in Luke 15 cf. also F. Schnider, *Söhne.*

The most important means of connection includes the use of proforms.[10] A clause or sentence is connected with the preceding one by a pronoun ("he" perhaps), thereby referring to a previously mentioned person. The Synoptic Gospels characteristically begin pericopes not with the name of Jesus but with the pronoun. Since pronouns stand not just for names but for whole groups of words (e.g., "He went away; they were distressed by it"), we also speak of proforms (instead of pronouns). The definite article used with a noun can also have this sort of referential function, since the definite article is employed only when the person or thing being talked about is known.

A second important means of linking the text together is the use of particles and conjunctions. "Particles" means words that accentuate the modality of a clause, modal particles, for instance, such as ἄν, γέ, or interrogative particles such as πότερον . . . ἤ; ἆρα; or particles of assurance such as εἰ μέν.[11] Conjunctions are words that join individual parts of a sentence or complete sentences with one another. The linkage of elements can be coordinating or subordinating.

Among the coordinating conjunctions are the copulatives καί (with many subspecies: adversative, consecutive, introductory, etc.)

> τέ, οὔτε, οὐδέ
> the disjunctives ἤ, ἤ—ἤ, εἴτε—εἴτε
> the adversatives δέ, μέν, ἀλλά, πλήν
> consecutive-coordinating conjunctions such as οὖν, ἄρα,
> τοιγαροῦν, διό
> causal-coordinating conjunctions such as γάρ

Among the subordinating conjunctions are:

> comparative conjunctions, such as ὡς, ὥσπερ, καθάπερ,
> καθώς
> hypothetical conjunctions, such as εἰ, εἰ μήν, εἰ δέ
> temporals, such as ὡς
> causal conjunctions, such as ὅτι, ἐπεί, and others[12]

The most important conjunctions for the New Testament are καί (9,164 times), δέ (2,801 times), γάρ (1,042 times), and ἀλλά (638 times).

---

[10]On the problem of "reference in texts," cf. Kallmeyer, *Lektürekolleg*, 177–257.
[11]BDF, §§442–457.
[12]Ibid.

1.3.1 Lack of Coherence

With New Testament texts we have to observe not only the coherence factors but also indications of breaks in the text. With some sentences a connection has been established with other sentences by using many linguistic means; in others such a connection is lacking. By making this sort of observation we can determine to what extent the author of a New Testament text has set out to make a specific segmentation of the text.[13] In that case the lack of coherence can also be a clue to the history of the origin of the text.[14]

1.4 STYLISTIC FEATURES

In stylistic analysis in the narrower sense both "forms of expression that are preferred and peculiar to the text"[15] and phrases that deviate from normal linguistic use are the subject of observation.

Expressions that deviate from normal linguistic usage have been the particular concern of stylistics under the heading of "tropes (artistic alteration of the meaning of an expression) and [other] stylistic figures" and of rhetoric. Particularly important stylistic figures are substitution, addition, omission, and arrangement.[16]

Figures of substitution include, among others:

• litotes (instead of making a positive statement, one negates its contrary): "I would not have you be ignorant" (Rom 1:13)

• personification: "For our gospel came to you not only in word, but also in power and in the Holy Spirit and with full conviction" (1 Thes 1:5)

• irony (assertion of a fact to express the opposite, e.g., in reproof): "For you gladly bear with fools, being wise yourselves!" (2 Cor 11:19)

• comparison and allegory

• substituting the abstract for the concrete: "gospel of the circumcision" for "the circumcised" (Gal 2:7)

---

[13]On the connection and lack of connection between the sentences with the Sermon on the Mount as an example, cf. Egger, "Bergpredigt."

[14]Cf. literary criticism.

[15]Fohrer, *Exegese AT,* 68.

[16]On the following topics see especially Fleischer, Michel, *Stilistik,* 151–87. On the individual figures of speech and examples: Bühlmann, Scherer, *Stilfiguren;* Alonso Schökel, *Alte Testament;* Rehkopf, "Parallelismus"; Di Marco, "Chiasmus"; Zimijewski, *Stil.* Meynet, *Initiation,* discusses many phenomena of language under the heading of "rhetoric" that this book treats under the heading of "style." On the figures of speech of classical rhetoric see Lausberg, *Handbuch;* idem, *Elemente.* On biblical rhetoric, see Bultmann, *Stil;* Schneider, "Rhetorische."

- hyperbole (exaggeration)

Figures using addition (an expression made more precise through further expressions) include:

- antitheses: "Not that we lord it over your faith; we work with you for your joy" (2 Cor 1:24)

- synecdoche (instead of a single expression the parts are named that "compose" the whole): "flesh and blood" = human being(s) (in the Old Testament sense) Gal 1:16

- repetition of the sentence structure as in parallelism: "Do not be anxious/look at: why you are anxious?/consider: do not be anxious/seek" (Matt 6:25–33) and chiasmus (x–shaped sentence structure)

- framing/inclusio (repeating at the end of the text a phrase used in the beginning). Thus the key words "blessed" and the "kingdom of God" in the Beatitudes (Matt 5:3–10) and the key words "Law and the Prophets" frame the core of the Sermon on the Mount

- pleonasms (decorative adjectives)

Also stylistically effective is the omission of elements, e.g., anacoluthon (not finishing a sentence, e.g., Gal 2:4f.) or the re-arrangement of elements (e.g., placing the verb at the beginning, as in Mark 1:15 in the Greek πεπλήρωται ὁ καιρός, "fulfilled is the time").

From the linguistic-syntactic standpoint texts sometimes reveal tensions or stylistic breaks. Such tensions include[17] disturbing reduplications and repetitions, contradictory information, different designations for the same persons and things.[18] These kinds of stylistic breaks should not be read in the first instance as clues to the genesis of the text but as a means chosen by the author to get the reader's attention.

1.5 STRUCTURE AND ORGANIZATION OF THE TEXT

In analyzing structure and organization we also investigate the arrangement of the elements. This is especially important for poetic texts, but it also plays a part in prose texts.

Distinctive organizational features include:

---

[17]Cf. the list in Strecker, Schnelle, *Einführung*, 41. See also the section on diachronic analysis.

[18]Variations in expression, of course, can also be a stylistic instrument.

- repetition of words and series of words in a sort of "refrain"

- framing, or bracketing

- chiasmus, such as, for instance, A B A' or, more artistically, a concentric structure, such as A B C B'A'

The organization of a text is seen above all by the use of the following linguistic means:[19]

- a change from narration to direct discourse

- a change of subject (often signaled by a formula such as "finally," 1 Thes 4:1; 2 Cor 13:11)

- change in place and time (often announced by particles)

- introduction of new persons

- accumulation of systematic, stylistic, and semantic features, such as the strikingly frequent use of words in some sections of the text. Thus Matthew often employs μακάριος in Matt 5:1–11; ἐγὼ δὲ λέγω ὑμῖν in Matt 5:18–48; negations in Matt 6:19–7:6, etc., as a way of giving indications of the arrangement[20]

- formulations as introductory clauses, "Which of you . . . " (Luke 11:5, among others)

- particles (Mark begins practically all pericopes with καί); adverbs and temporal indications ("at that time," Matt 11:25); the expression "finally" as the introduction to the paraenesis (1 Thes 4:1; 2 Cor 13:11; 2 Thes 3:1)[21]

- headings and governing principles: Matt 6:1 as an introduction to 6:2–18; Matt 5:17 and 7:7–14 as a kind of heading and a confirming summary[22]

2. DOING LINGUISTIC-SYNTACTIC ANALYSIS

Linguistic-syntactic analysis should be applied in an open fashion. No method can guarantee completeness in analysis or claim to be the only approach. Analysis is never complete; its goal is an ever more exact description of the text.

---

[19]On the organizational features see Berger, *Exegese*, 4; Gülich, Raible, "Text-analyse," 73–126, esp. 75–99.
[20]Cf. Egger, "Bergpredigt," 184.
[21]Cf. Egger, *Exegese*, 17–27.
[22]Egger, "Bergpredigt"; on the headings see also Berger, *Exegese*, 24.

Another recommended starting point is an orientation to the conspicuous linguistic elements of the text. This guards against any schematic-formal inventory of all possible stylistic elements.[23]

Linguistic-syntactic analysis is constituted by, among other things, lists derived from basic grammatical concepts, by simple statistical methods, and by a comparison with other texts.

To describe the linguistic character of a text, one must first of all draw up a list of all its basic elements with the help of basic grammatical terms such as substantives, articles, pronouns, verbs (tense, mood), adjectives, adverbs, connectives (prepositions, particles, conjunctions, relative constructions).

In general, simple statistical checks are helpful.[24] One can start out by determining the frequency of the linguistic means used. Numbers on the frequency of the words (in the partial text or book of the New Testament) provide initial access to the peculiar nature of the text (cf., e.g., the distribution of expressions like βασιλεία τοῦ θεοῦ or τῶν οὐρανῶν, εὐαγγέλιον, δικαιοσύνη in the individual books of the New Testament). We can also count the frequency of certain clausal introductions, the frequency with which verb tenses are used, such as, in narratives, imperfect, aorist, and historical present. Likewise the frequency of changes in tense can be typical of one author, as can the frequency of use of parts of speech (articles, nouns, pronouns, verbs, adjectives, etc.).

Statistical surveys are also helpful in ascertaining the linguistic peculiarities of texts, that is, the features which distinguish one book of the New Testament from another. Of special importance here are editorial preference words, or words that appear with particular frequency in one New Testament author compared with others, taking into consideration the length of their writings.[25]

As a third method of working within the New Testament, synoptic comparison is a promising instrument. By comparing texts

---

[23] Fleischer, Michel, *Stilistik*, 340.

[24] On this point cf. Reiser, *Syntax;* Dschulnigg, *Sprache,* 74–83; aids for statistics include Morgenthaler, *Statistik;* idem, *Synopse;* Aland, *Konkordanz,* II, 1–305; Neirynck, van Segbroek, *Vocabulary.*

[25] Berger, *Exegese,* 213. For Hawkins, *Horae,* 3, 10, 15, preference words are words that are used at least four times (three times in Mark) and are either not found at all in the other Synoptics or are found at least twice as frequently as in the other two Gospels together (for Mark, more frequently than in the other two together). Cf. too the criteria in Dschulnigg, *Sprache,* 75–76.

There are a particularly large number of studies on the language and style of Mark: Cancik, *Markus-Philologie;* Neirynck, *Duality;* Reiser, *Syntax;* Dschulnigg, *Sprache.*

SUMMARY AND POINTERS

The following questions are designed to help the reader discover the vocabulary and grammar, that is, the linguistic-syntactic means used in a text. These observations then serve also to work out the effect that the author is trying to achieve with linguistic and stylistic means.

On Vocabulary

Determine whether expressions and clauses are repeated, whether there is any preference for certain phrases.

Determine what words, if any, are typical of the vocabulary of the author in question (use a statistical study of the vocabulary and, for the comparison of the New Testament books, a concordance).

On Parts of Speech and Word Forms

List the most important parts of speech and word forms (in grammatical categories: substantive, verb, etc.).

On Connection

- Underline the pronouns and conjunctions.
- Draw up a list of the conjunctions used.
- List the most important means used in the text for sentence connection, as well as the forms of parataxis and hypotaxis, especially καί, δέ, γάρ, etc.
- Determine whether there is any preference for specific introductory formulas.
- Note subjects and objects as well as their reappearance.
- Collect the verbs that occur, noting any repetition of them.
- Determine the order of subject and predicate.
- Describe the use of verb tense.
- Determine the kinds of clauses used most often in the text under investigation.

On Style

Referring to the list cited in 1.4 note the stylistic figures used in the text.

On Structure and Organization

- Determine whether there are repetitions of word order (refrains, etc.), inclusions, and chiasms.
- Determine to what extent narrative and dialogue are used.
- Determine where changes in person, place, and time occur.
- Compare the divisions of the text in the New Revised Standard Version and another edition of the Bible. Try to explain whatever differences turn up.
- On the basis of what has been observed, suggest a plan for dividing up the text under investigation.

one can quickly grasp the stylistic differences and hence the unique features of each text.[26]

Similar advantages derive from comparing Hellenistic literature (e.g., Mark with *The Greek Alexander Romance*).[27] Comparing the New Testament letters with epistolary literature[28] is especially instructive from the standpoint of rhetoric.[29]

3. EXAMPLES

3.1 MATT 18:15–17

Analysis of this text shows linguistic-syntactic analysis helps focus more closely on the meaning of a text, even of one that is familiar.

In various editions of the Bible we find the following heading assigned to the passage Matt 18:15–17:[30] A Brother Who Sins Against You (NIV; cf. NAB), When Someone Sins (CEV), Disciplining Members of the Church (*HarperCollins Study Bible*, New Revised Standard Version).

Syntactically-grammatically speaking, the text consists of the repetition of a single sentence structure with a directive to an action: a subordinate clause introduced with ἐάν and a main clause whose verb (with one exception) is in the imperative. The particle δέ contributes to the linkage of the clauses.

ἐὰν δὲ ἁμαρτήσῃ	ὕπαγε ἔλεγξον
ἐὰν σου ἀκούσῃ	ἐκέρδησας
ἐὰν δὲ μὴ ἀκούσῃ	παράλαβε
ἐὰν δὲ παρακούσῃ	εἰπέ
ἐὰν δὲ καὶ παρακούσῃ	ἔστω σοι

Judging from this linguistic structure, therefore, the text is not in the first instance about "a brother who sins against you," or "when someone sins," but above all about care for the holiness of the church. Through admonition and, where necessary, exclusion (these are the directives in the imperative) the holiness of the church must be preserved.

We can find a similar text in 1QS 5.25–6.1. What concerns Qumran in this passage is a warning about hatred and about protec-

---

[26]Synoptic comparison is, of course, also productive on the other levels of analysis (semantics, pragmatics, textual genres, history of origins). On comparing the vocabulary of the Synoptics, see Neirynck, van Segbroek, *Vocabulary*, 203–436.

[27]Reiser, "Alexanderroman," 131–63.

[28]Cancik, *Senecas;* Thraede, *Grundzüge;* White, "Literature."

[29]Bultmann, *Stil;* Stowers, *Diatribe;* Betz, *Galatians.*

[30]Literature: Pesch, *Matthäus;* Thompson, "Advice."

tion for the sinner whose offense must not immediately be brought to the community's notice. A comparison of Matt 18:15–17 and its characteristic sentence structure with the directives given in 1QS 5.25–6.1 makes the thrust of the Matthew text still clearer.

3.2 MATT 28:18–20

Our understanding of Matt 28:18–20[31] will be deepened if we pay attention to the linguistic peculiarities of the text. The three sentences of the text are tightly bound together by the conjunctions οὖν (v. 19) and καὶ ἰδού. The text receives its shape primarily through the verb forms: in v. 18 the verb is in the aorist indicative; in vv. 19–20a one verb is in the aorist imperative whereas three verbs are in the participial form (one in the aorist, and two in the present). The fact that ἐδόθη (v. 18) stands at the beginning of the statement stresses the dynamic nature of the event mentioned. The order given here thus depends upon the fact that all power has been given to the speaker. The order itself is expressed by the imperative, while the carrying out of the order is described by the participles. In the concluding formulation, which commands attention with the introduction, "and see," Jesus' helping presence is promised.

Accordingly the text possibly breaks down thus:

> All authority in heaven and on earth has been given to me.
> Going then,
> make disciples of all nations,
> baptizing them
> in the name of the Father and of the Son and of the Holy Spirit,
> teaching them
> to obey everything that I have commanded you;
> and see, I am with you always, to the end of the age.

An abundance of tie-ins with the Gospel as a whole reveals not only the evangelist's compositional interests but also his effort to summarize the essential content of his Gospel.[32] Such links are, first and foremost, the place references, "Galilee" and "mountain," the motifs of doubts (cf. 14:28–31) and adoration,[33] the objective link between the promise and the name "Immanuel" in Matt 1:23, as well as with the promise of Jesus' presence in Matt 18:20.

---

[31]Literature: Trilling, *Israel;* Hahn, "Matthäus 28, 16–20"; Friedrich, "Struktur," 137–83 (with an extensive survey of the current state of the research); Frankemölle, *Kirche,* 42–72.

[32]On the following questions see esp. Hahn, "Matthäus 28, 16–20," 29–30; Friedrich, "Struktur."

[33]Matthew 13 times; Mark twice; John 11 times; Acts 4 times.

Ascertaining the formal structure of the text is also significant for establishing its genre, since doing that requires texts with a
similar linguistic-syntactic structure. In this regard, from both a
formal and material standpoint, the Johannine "I am" sayings constitute a parallel since they too consist of self-revelation, challenge,
and the pledge of a promise.[34]

3.3 MARK 1

Although Mark 1 has for the most part been assembled from originally isolated individual pericopes, the editor has shaped this segment into a unified whole. This can already be seen from the
linguistic-syntactic shape of the text.[35]

One characteristic feature of the chapter is its preference
for certain words: thus the elevenfold use of the adverb εὐθύς in
such a brief text.[36] Besides this, there is a series of words for which
Mark shows a preference: "unclean, enter, teaching, terrify, πάλιν,
πολλά, ask, manifest."[37] Mark likes to employ certain combinations of words and clauses; doublings of various expressions can
be found in 1:14–15, 32, 45;[38] the sentences are paratactically
linked together by καί; even new sections begin with καί;[39] in the
use of tenses the aorist alternates with the historical present, along
with *conjugatio periphrastica*. The placement of the verb in the
sentences changes (verb before subject or after subject).[40] As for
pronouns as connectives, it is obvious that the name "Jesus" stands
at the beginning of pericopes only in 1:9 and 1:14. Mark's style is
also characterized by graphically picturesque details (1:33) and
supplementary explanations (1:19).

The framework for the chapter is provided by three "conflated accounts" with the key word κηρύσσειν, which uses an *inclusio*
to gather the chapter's material into a coherent unit: 1:14–15 —
1:39 — 1:45. Verses 1 and 14 specify this kerygma as the preaching
of the "gospel." Mark 1:4–5 (effectiveness of the Baptist: preaching
and thronging of the people) and 1:45 (preaching, thronging) can

---

[34]On particular points see Friedrich, "Struktur," 161–70. Friedrich refers to
similar structures in the Old Testament: Gen. 17:1–2; 26:24; 46:4; Ex. 3:6–20; in the
New Testament he refers to the open letter of Revelation.

[35]See the commentaries; in particular, Egger, *Lehre*, 39–43.

[36]All told, 41 times in Mark.

[37]εὐθύς (Matt 18; Mark 41; Luke 7; in Matt independently of Mark 5 times,
in Luke once; πάλιν (7 - 28 - 3), πολλά (as an adverb; 0 - 9 - 0).

[38]Cf. Neirynck, *Duality*, on these passages.

[39]Apart from the textually uncertain v. 14.

[40]Parataxis, word order, use of verb tense, pleonasm, lexical monotony, and
narrative technique frequently correspond to the popular Hellenistic novel of Alexander: Reiser, "Alexanderroman"; idem, *Syntax*.

be looked on as a great *inclusio* of the chapter. By means of these narrative collections Mark defines the content of the chapter as proclamation even when seen from the point of view of the external shape of the text. Alongside this framing in 1:4–5 and 1:45 we find still smaller framings, such as 1:21–22 and 1:28 ("teaching"); 1:14–15 and 1:39 ("preaching") and a chiasmus in 1:32–34.

The manifold individual narratives are variously inter-connected. The chapter reveals Mark's typical episodic narrative mode:[41]

vv. 1–8:	preparing for 9–14, referring to 15
vv. 9–13:	structured by the double use of εὐθύς
vv. 14–39:	refrain in 1:14 and 1:39; vv. 21–38 are connected as a description of the "day of Capernaum," especially through verbs of movement and indications of place and time
vv. 40–45:	loosely linked; v. 45 is the semantic high point of the chapter[42]

The unity and the well-rounded form of the chapter is also shown by the fact that in the five subsequent scenes of controversy (Mark 2:1–3:6) we find sketched out a counter-image of this unlimited sphere of activity and this thronging of the enthusiastic multitude; now comes Jesus' confrontation with his adversaries.[43]

3.4 PHILEMON

Because it is so short, the letter of the apostle Paul to Philemon can be analyzed in its entirety, not just in excerpts. Thus it is particularly suited for carrying out the individual methodological steps.[44]

Philemon reveals a clear structure: address with benediction (vv. 1–3), thanksgiving (vv. 4–7), request/directive (vv. 15–21), final greetings and benediction (vv. 23–25).[45] Admittedly, in the request section there is a caesura between v. 20 and v. 21;

---

[41]Breytenbach, "Erzählung," 137–69, esp. 157–61.

[42]Of course Mark 1:45, in keeping with the terminology and semantics of Mark, has to be translated as "proclaimed and spread the word"; the Contemporary English Version obsures this nuance ("talked about it so much and told so many people").

[43]On the semantic character of Mark 1 see later.

[44]See the commentaries. Philemon is discussed from the methodological viewpoint in: Church, "Structure"; Groupe de Montpellier, "Epître"; de Gaulmyn, "Réflection"; Lähnemann, Böhm, *Philemonbrief;* Zimijewski, "Struktur."

[45]The arrangement of the conclusion to the letter is disputed. Lohse, *Colossians,* takes vv. 21–25 together; likewise Stuhlmacher, *Philemon;* Gnilka, *Philemonbrief,* divides the letter up in accordance with the standpoint of ancient rhetoric: prescript (vv. 1–3), proemium (vv. 4–7), argument (vv. 8–16), epiloque (vv. 17–22); postscript (vv. 23–25).

nevertheless, vv. 21 and 22 have to be counted in this part since
v. 21 strengthens the object of the request-section, and v. 22 adds
on a further imperative (cf. the imperatives in vv. 17–18). The
address and conclusion of the letter serve to bracket the letter
because they deal with the theme of coworkers and offer a benediction. Furthermore, the thanksgiving section and the request
section are slightly dovetailed by the reappearance of important
words and themes of the thanksgiving section in the request section, in this case, however, as a concrete expression of the general
statements in the thanksgiving section.[46]

As for the parts of speech, it is striking how few adjectives
are used. We find pronouns in every sentence, with ἐγώ in several
passages pointing emphatically to the sender: vv. 13, 19 (twice), 20.[47]
The verb tenses are rich in variety: present for the verbs that
introduce the parts of the letter; (epistolary) aorist for events that
concern the act of writing and sending (vv. 21 and 12). Imperatives
do not occur until vv. 17–18 and then v. 22.

Cohesion in the letter is guaranteed by the presence of a
pronoun in every sentence.[48] Conjunctions function in the same way;
especially noteworthy is the linking conjunction διό at the beginning of the thanksgiving section and γάρ in v. 15. Less closely linked
are vv. 20–21, 23–24, and 25.

An especially strong inner connectedness is achieved in this
letter through recurrence and paraphrase of expressions.[49] This
applies especially to the sections vv. 4–7 and vv. 8–22, but to the
other verses as well:

> ἀγάπη in vv. 5, 7, 9, 16
> ἀγαπητός in vv. 1, 16
> Ἰησοῦς in vv. 1, 3, 5, 9, 23, 25
> Κύριος in vv. 3, 5, 16, 20, 25
> Χριστός in vv. 1, 3, 6, 8, 9, 20, 23
> κοινωνία in v. 6
> κοινωνός in v. 13
> σπλάγχνα in vv. 7, 12, 20
> ἀναπαύομαι in vv. 7, 20
> ἀδελφός in vv. 1, 7, 16, 20
> ἀδελφέ in v. 2
> δοῦλος in v. 16 (twice)

---

[46]Groupe de Montpellier, "Epître," 19.
[47]There is a striking frequency of the use of ἐγώ in the Pauline letters: Rom
20 times, 1 Cor 30 times, 2 Cor 20 times, Gal 10 times, Phil 6 times, 1 Thes twice.
[48]Cf. Zimijewski, "Struktur," 282.
[49]See ibid., 277–85.

προσευχαί in vv. 4, 22
Παῦλος in vv. 1, 9, 19[50]
δέσμιος in vv. 1, 8
δεσμοί in v. 10
συνεργός in vv. 1, 24
as well as compounds with
σύν
συστρατιώτης in v. 2
συναιχμάλωτος in v. 23
πίστις in vv. 5, 6
παρακαλέω in vv. 8, 10
ἔχειν in vv. 7, 8, 17; and its compounds
κατέχειν in v. 13
ἀπέχειν in v. 15
ποιεῖν in vv. 14, 21
χάρις in vv. 3, 25
ὅς in vv. 9, 14, 16, 17.

Other linguistic uses include:[51] antithesis: v. 11 ("useless/useful"); v. 14 ("by compulsion/of your own free will"); v. 16 ("slave/brother"); parallelism: v. 13 (parallel clause formation); synecdoche: v. 16 ("in the flesh and in the Lord"); specification: v. 12 ("I am sending him back to you, sending my very heart"); v. 19 ("to say nothing of . . . "); intensification: especially v. 16; more detailed description of persons through apposition, with all individual names mentioned in the letter receiving appositives.[52]

---

[50]Apart from the headings "Paul" is found only in 1 Cor 1:12, 13 (twice); 3:4, 5, 22; 16:21; 2 Cor 10:1; Gal 5:2; 1 Thes 2:18.

[51]Cf. Zimijewski, "Struktur," 283–85.

[52]On the semantic and pragmatic analysis of Philemon see later on.

§9
Semantic Analysis

WHEN SOMEBODY ASKS, "WHAT IS THE MEANING OF THE WORD YOU just said?" or "What do you mean by that?" she is asking about the meaning[1] of a linguistic sign or a series of signs. She is interested in the content side, in the expressive content of the word or statement. In everyday life there are ways of clarifying the meaning of a statement, e.g., asking questions of the speaker. With ancient texts like those of the Bible this possibility does not exist, and yet the danger of misunderstanding is especially great here because of the temporal and cultural distance. Thus the search for the sense and the significance of the biblical texts is an especially difficult task—the task of semantics.

> Semantics is the study of the meaning of linguistic signs and sign sequences,[2] that is, of the relations between the form and content of signs in words, sentences, and texts. Semantic analysis of a text seeks to answer the questions, what is a text trying to say, and what is meant by specific phrases and sentences used in a text?

A methodology for semantics gives instructions for ascertaining the meaning of words, sentences, and texts. Granted, individual expressions have their meaning only in the context of sentences and texts; still several key points can be addressed separately: word-concept semantics and actual text-semantics, as well as the semantics of narrative structures.

Verbal semantics is concerned with the meaning of a word, text-semantics with the meaning of an entire text. No text can be understood unequivocally without a knowledge of the verbal meaning; and neither can an individual word's meaning be ascer-

---

[1]Leech, *Semantics*, refers to Ogden, Richards, *Meaning*, 186–87, who cite twenty-two definitions of the "meaning" of meaning.
[2]Ulrich, *Wörterbuch*, 138.

tained without a knowledge of the textual meaning. Here, too, understanding is circular.

First Section: Textual Semantics

Even at the first reading of a text the reader will get a certain notion of the content and meaning of the text. The reader will be able to say roughly what the text is about. She can summarize the text. Semantic analysis of a text is designed to help readers deepen their first understanding of the text, to overcome possible misunderstanding, and to justify their notions of the meaning of the text.

INTRODUCTORY LITERATURE: BALDINGER, *Semantics,* provides an in-depth discussion of semantic theory. LOUW, *Semantics,* discusses semantics in a different way in relationship to New Testament texts. NIDA, *Analysis,* covers a wide range of topics on semantics. PATTE, *Exegesis,* provides an introduction to structural exegesis. PATTE, *Critics,* takes the reader through the steps of structural exegesis. BOERS, *Mountain,* applies a structural analysis to John 4:4–32. Introductions to the method of textual semantic analysis can be found in several studies of specific texts: HAUSER, *Strukturen,* 51–177; MINGUEZ, *Pentecostés,* 71–150; EGGER, *Nachfolge,* 79–136.[3]

1. THE MODEL OF READING AND THE TEXT UNDERLYING TEXTUAL SEMANTIC ANALYSIS

The textual model underlying semantic analysis corresponds to the structuralist idea of the text, as presented in §2.

> From a semantic standpoint the text is the aggregate of relations (structure) between the elements of meaning in the text. The text is a whole, a sort of "semantic micro-universe."[4]

The various meaning-contents can be more or less closely connected (or not at all) with one another, as Diagram 10 shows.

---

[3]For an actual semantics of the text we have to refer to Greimas and his school (the authors already mentioned also take many suggestions from Greimas); Courtés, *Introduction;* Greimas, *Semantics;* idem, *Meaning; Initiation;* Groupe d'Entrevernes, *Analyse;* idem, *Signes;* Fossion, *Leggere.*

[4]Lack, *Letture;* Minguez, *Pentecostés,* 74, 145–50, speaks of an "universo significativo" and a "sistema semantico," which consists of interrelated semantic contents.

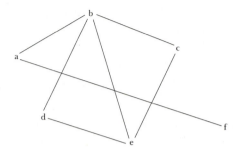

DIAGRAM 10: STRUCTURE OF THE MEANING-CONTENTS

Reading and decoding meaning correspond to the production of a text. For the production of texts, from the semantic point of view, the composition of an essay can provide a pattern. First only the topic is given; this is then developed as various aspects of the topic—that is, the meaning-contents found in the topic—are individually presented and put into a certain order. Development of the topic takes place above all through redundancy (repetitions) of meaning-elements; for the sake of elucidation, contraries can also be introduced, etc. The unity of the text from the semantic perspective is determined by the unity of the objects and circumstances it designates.[5] The semantic coherence of a text can have varying degrees of solidity.

In reception the reader takes the reverse path by trying to see the meaning-elements scattered through the text in their coherence and thereby decode the text.[6] Since reading is understood as decoding, as discovering the meaning-correlations between the elements of the text, reading is in principle never finished. The reader can always discover new meaning-correlations. In this view, therefore, because of both the structure of the text and the peculiar nature of the act of reading, the text is not the bearer of a single, unequivocal meaning, but the "locus of possibilities of meaning."

> The text with its meaning-elements is the "locus of multiple senses."[7] The text itself is also a reference system: Every element refers to another element.[8]

---

[5]Plett, *Textwissenschaft*, 102.
[6]Cf. the discussions of reading.
[7]Barthes, "L'analyse," 188: "le lieu des sens, le lieu des possibles du text."
[8]Barthes, "L'analyse," 185; cf. Egger, *Nachfolge*, 81.

Finding the sense or meaning of the text is no mechanical procedure; it also depends on the reader's personal character and knowledge of culture. Without access to cultural knowledge, readers cannot decode texts, above all texts from the distant past. The additional information needed for understanding can either be worked up anew each time from the texts of the culture in question, or it can be collected (in summary form) from monographs and lexicons. For work on biblical texts one must, at the very least, consider the most important parallels from the Old Testament and the Hellenistic milieu.

2. DOING TEXTUAL SEMANTIC ANALYSIS

At the first reading the reader stands before a multitude of "lexemes"/ words.[9] To ascertain the subject and sense of a text, one can of course also rely on feeling. Reading becomes scholarly by making certain that it is correct.

Understanding a text consists in classifying the great multitude of elements that constitute the text and that the reader encounters, and in seeing them in their context.[10] Semantics gives instructions on how to recognize this multitude as an ordered multiplicity whose elements stand in specific relationships to each other.

To ascertain the meaning of texts, one detailed, time-consuming analytic procedure and several abbreviated ones will be

---

[9]Words are called lexemes insofar as they are the structural elements of vocabulary that as entries in a lexicon exist independently of texts. [Actually in linguistic-semantic usage "lexeme" refers to the minimal meaningful units within words, also referred to as monemes; lexemes are also referred to by some as morphemes, but more precisely by others as grammemes. Baldinger {*Semantic Theory,* 18; see also Greimas, Courtés, *Semiotics,* s.v. Grammeme, Lexeme, Lexia, Moneme, and Morpheme}, following A. Martinet, gives the following example:

"farmer" = farm + -er
word or *lexie* = meaningful unit + meaningful unit
lexeme + morpheme

The monemes farm {lexeme} and -er {morpheme} are the minimal units of meaning in the word or lexie farmer. What Egger refers to as a lexeme is what Baldinger refers to more distinctively as a lexie. B. Pottier introduced what may be even more useful terminology in which a moneme became a morpheme, distinguished as either lexical, a lexeme, or grammatical, a grammeme. In either case lexeme represents the lexical feature of a word's or lexie's meaning, whereas grammeme {or phoneme in Martinet's and Baldinger's terminology (Baldinger is aware of Pottier's terminology)} expresses its grammatical meaning. What Egger refers to as a lexeme, thus, linguistically/semantically speaking, is better referred to as a lexie. In this translation lexeme will continue to be used in the way in which Egger uses the term. Ed.]

[10]That is how Marguerat, *Strukturale,* 64, describes Barthes's intent.

presented; attention will also be called to the relevance of supplementary information.

2.1 PREPARING A SEMANTIC INVENTORY

A first procedure in ascertaining the sense of the text is to prepare an inventory of its meaning-features.[11] The expression "inventory" stems from the language of economics, where it characterizes the aggregate of objects present and their order according to groups. Such a stock-taking can also be done with texts, with an eye to content and meaning. This takes place in several steps.[12]

In the first step, meaning-related lexemes/words are gathered into groups.

In every text we find expressions and meaning-contents that are related with respect to meaning. An extreme example of this is a weather report, which is made up of little else but a list of terms for meteorological phenomena. Much of the same is true, to take another example, of an essay on spring. And this is the case with every coherent text. Thus we find in the text on the calling of the rich young man in Mark 10:17–31, alongside other groups of words related by meaning, a group of verbs of movement: set out on one's way, run, come, follow, go away, enter (the kingdom), arrive (in the kingdom), etc. A second group is made up of words about poor/rich. This is the sort of grouping that must be done to get an "inventory" of the text. A careful inspection of the text in Mark 10:17–31 will show that almost all the lexemes in it belong to one of the three following paradigmatic classes:[13]

Doing	Capacity	Eternal Life
what to do	human power	inherit eternal life
sell	divine help	treasure in heaven
give to the poor	difficult	enter into God's dominion
leave one's house	possible/impossible	be saved

Thus the first step consists in determining what elements of a text belong together on the level of meaning. In this way

---

[11]Barthes, "L'analyse," presents the method and puts it into practice on Acts 10–11; cf. also Greimas, *Semantics,* 169–205; in addition ibid., 269–308, offers an analysis of the semantic universe of Bernanos.

[12]The methodical steps are presented in Minguez, *Pentecostés,* 73–85; Hauser, *Strukturen,* 51–59; Fossion, *Leggere,* 67–74; Panier, "Introduction," 3–31.

[13]On Mark 10:17–31 cf. Egger, *Nachfolge,* 84–120.

groups of meaning-related expressions are formed. These groups of allied elements will be mentioned in the lines of meaning that follow.[14] The phrase "meaning lines" is a metaphor: this sort of line runs through a text like a red thread. In extreme cases such as weather reports or lists, the text contains only one line of meaning; in most cases, however, the text contains a variety of lines of meaning.

A complete inventory of a text strives to determine all the lines of meaning in the text, that is, to find the meaning-connected elements for every element of the text, beginning with the first word.[15] This sort of complete inventory of all lines of meaning prevents the reader from noticing only certain elements, but it also takes a lot of time and under certain circumstances it might be confusing. Hence beginners are advised to work out only the most important meaning lines. Of course this immediately raises the question of what they are.

To cut the material under investigation down to size, criteria have to be observed.[16] Such criteria for sorting out the more important meaning-bearing items could be: Granting a privileged status to autosemantic expressions (those that carry a specific sense within themselves), since they contribute more to the meaning of the text than the "function words" or synsemantic lexemes (prepositions, conjunctions, negations, etc.).[17] This analysis more or less eliminates from most texts a large group of words as less relevant.[18] In constituting the meaning of the text, noting expressions that appear many times in it is especially important. This can be established by word counts.[19] Just applying this method will bring out the presence of key points in the text. Words can acquire weight (even if they appear only once) through their position in the sentence, parallelism, etc.[20] In analyzing text segments attention must be paid to the preferred vocabulary that characterizes the author.[21]

---

[14]The terms for groups of elements that belong together because of meaning have not been standardized. In this context scholars speak of "isotopy" or "wordfield," but these don't cover the same aspects as does the term "meaning line," proposed above.

[15]I have tried to draw up a fairly complete inventory for Mark 10:17–31: Egger, *Nachfolge*, 84–120.

[16]On the criteria: Greimas, *Semantics*, 169–205; Minguez, *Pentecostés*, 77–85; Hauser, *Strukturen*, 54–55.

[17]Minguez, *Pentecostés*, 75; Hauser, *Strukturen*, 54–55.

[18]"Verba dicendi" do not automatically belong to the synsemantic expressions (see the remarks on the verbs of saying in the narrative analysis).

[19]Minguez, *Pentecostés*, 81–82; Hauser, *Strukturen*, 46–47, 54.

[20]Hauser, *Strukturen*, 55.

[21]Minguez, *Pentecostés*, 78–79.

> In the second practical step the semantic contraries, that is, the
> oppositions that exist between meaning-contents, are worked out.

In this way it becomes clear what sort of change is important
in the text, which applies not just to narrative texts. For Mark
10:17–31 the following oppositions, among others, can be established:

rich	⟷	poor
to be rich	⟷	to follow
to follow	⟷	to go away
to follow	⟷	to grieve
to be poor	⟷	treasure in heaven
ties to Jesus	⟷	ties to wealth
earthly family	⟷	brothers
human	⟷	divine
on earth	⟷	in heaven
first	⟷	last

> In the third step the meaning lines and oppositions are arranged in
> overlapping groups.

For Mark 10:17–31:[22]

rich	⟷	poor
wealth		
human		
first		
		divine
		the reign of God
grieve	⟷	treasure in heaven
		brotherhood
last	⟷	first

To conclude, we have to mention that unity of meaning
("seme") which runs through the entire text and that explains the
transformations cited in the text. One device well suited for illustrating this situation is the "semiotic square." This is a graphic
presentation that, in a modification of the logical square, shows the
relations between the meaning-elements.[23]

---

[22]Cf. Egger, *Nachfolge*, 153–54.

[23]Greimas, *Meaning*, 49. Cf. the presentation in Egger, *Nachfolge*, 19–27. For
an orientation in semiotic exegesis this semiotic square is an essential tool: *Initiation*,
39; Groupe d'Entrevernes, *Analyse*, 129–35; idem, *Signes*, 23–24. On Hos 4:1–14, Lack,
Letture (see above, n. 4), 146. offers this sort of square with the categories "life vs. death."

Starting out from a binary semantic category of the type "black vs. white" (s1 vs. s2), the semiotic square has the form exhibited in Diagram 11.[24]

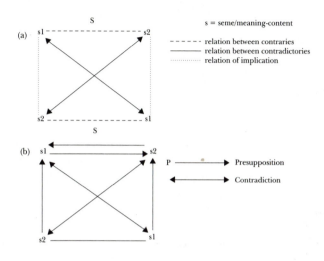

DIAGRAM 11: THE SEMIOTIC SQUARE

This square shows the meaning-structures within a semantic universe. The use of this square demands a very precise analysis and involves a whole series of premises which we cannot discuss here. The semiotic square for Mark 10:17–31 is represented in Diagram 12.[25]

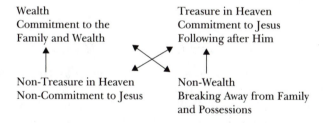

DIAGRAM 12: THE SEMIOTIC SQUARE FOR MARK 10:17–31

Taking stock of the semantic features requires more time because some connections reveal themselves only after extended

[24]Greimas, *Meaning*, 49 (Model 1); 50, 51 (Model b).
[25]Egger, *Nachfolge*, 159.

reading. As such a complete inventory is very time-consuming, let us present a few abbreviated procedures of semantic analysis.

2.2 Brief Procedures of Semantic Analysis

In addition to the time-consuming procedure, which is not equally productive for all texts, there are also several abbreviated modes that allow a certain amount of checking on the interpretation of the text.

2.2.1 Rewriting the Text

We can get to an overview of the meaning of the text when the text is written out in a new arrangement, as, for example, when all the words that belong to a specific class of words are placed under one another in columns, thereby grouping together all subjects, predicates, objects, circumstances.

2.2.2 Declaration of Contents

With longer texts it is advisable to begin by making a matter-of-fact list of the contents, perhaps according to the following framework:

what is happening
who (is speaking or acting)
to whom
when
where
why, etc.

2.2.3 Redaction and Comparison of Headings

The heading or title given to a text has the purpose of providing the reader with a first approach to the text. All texts from our time have a heading. Modern Bible translations also generally supply headings for the individual pericopes. A heading should be both faithful to the text by summarizing its message and offer the reader help through the way it formulates it. The redaction of headings is useful not only as a method of practical Bible work;[26] in actual exegetical work this method also helps the reader grasp the contents and intended meaning of a text. The headings can be

---

[26]The instructions for the redaction of headings run as follows: "For any biblical text try to find a heading that summarizes the message/appeal of the text." As a check the headings can be discussed in a group. Cf. on the method employed here: Egger, *Gemeinsam*, 35–36.

kerygmatic by summarizing the message of the text: Jesus the light of the world (for John 9), or paraenetic (admonitory), by aiming an appeal to the reader: Controversy over Jesus (also in the case of John 9). Comparison of headings given to a text in editions of the Bible also offers a first access to the understanding of the text. This method, which derives from practical work on the Bible, helps us reflect on our first understanding of the text.

2.2.4 Choosing of the Most Important Verse

This method consists in the reader's picking out the verse that strikes her as the most important in a text. The choice must then be justified.

2.2.5 Comparison of Related Texts

Comparison of texts makes it clear to what degree various accents have been placed on the material. One could compare, for instance, the prescripts in the Pauline letters or parallel texts in the Synoptic Gospels.[27] This sharpens the eye and enables it to better recognize what the text under investigation, or its elements, is trying to say.

2.3 ACQUIRING SUPPLEMENTAL INFORMATION

In reading ancient texts, it must be acknowledged that supplementary information is absolutely necessary for understanding the text, owing to the temporal and cultural distance.[28] With biblical texts this is even more true because of the limits of the textual corpus available to us. When beginning scholarly work, the interpreter can draw additional data from specialized literature. For actual scholarly work, parallels can be drawn to the history, especially the religious history of the contemporary world of the New Testament.[29] Needless to say, the rule holds that meaning disclosed and demonstrated from the text can neither be confirmed nor refuted by knowledge about extratextual data.[30]

---

[27]On the Synoptic comparison see §12.
[28]Titzmann, *Textanalyse*, 262–322.
[29]Müller, "Methode."
[30]Titzmann, *Textanalyse*, 275–76: "Whatever can be demonstrated about the 'text' with sufficient knowledge of the sign-system and by compliance with the theoretical rules of the discipline can neither be confirmed nor refuted by knowledge of extratextual data."

SUMMARY OF WORKING STEPS AND POINTERS

The working steps that grow from this method may be
summarized briefly.

1. Preparing a Semantic Inventory

The drawing up of a complete inventory of the meaning-
elements takes place in accordance with the following rules.
For every element of the text, beginning with the first word,
those elements that belong together with regard to meaning
should be identified.

First, collect into groups (meaning lines) the lexemes in the text
that appear more than once in the text, and the lexemes related
to them by meaning.

Then ascertain the (explicit and implicit) oppositions between
meaning-elements in the text.

As soon as you have prepared the inventory of the meaning-
elements that belong together and those that are opposed to
each other, collect the lines of meaning and oppositions into
larger groups and designate the meaning feature that appears
most frequently.

2. Abbreviated Procedures

The presentation of the method has already given the necessary
practical pointers for listing the contents, redaction of the
headings, and choosing the most important verse. For the
synoptic comparison of texts, which is also helpful for semantic
analysis, see the section on synoptic comparison.

3. Additional Information

To avoid misunderstandings, enlist the necessary information
from a theological dictionary of the New Testament for the major
terms of the text.

3. EXAMPLES[31]

3.1 LUKE 4:16–30: PLACE AND TIME OF THE OFFER OF SALVATION

The semantic inventory of the section on the "Rejection of Jesus
at Nazareth" (NRSV) contains the following meaning lines, i.e.,

---

[31]As an example of a carefully conducted semantic analysis of an Old
Testament text see the analysis of Gen. 11:1–9 in Fossion, *Leggere*, in four practical steps:

groups of elements that belong together because of meaning, and because of oppositions:[32]

VERBS OF MOVEMENT:
Came, went, stood up, sat down, got up, drove out, hurl off, passed through, went on.
The most important oppositions are: come ⟷ went on, (stand) ⟷ sat down, might hurl off ⟷ passed through the midst of them.

WORDS FOR "SALVATION":
Good news, release (of captives), sight, free, year of the Lord's favor, gracious words, doctor, (deeds in Capernaum), (satisfy hunger), clean of leprosy (Naaman).
The oppositions: help in Israel or only outside (for the widow of Zarephath and Naaman the Syrian).

PLACES CITED:
Nazareth, synagogue, Capernaum, hometown, (the heathen) Zarephath in Sidon, Syrian (from heathen Syria), town.
The oppositions: Nazareth ⟷ Capernaum, Israel ⟷ outside Israel (Zarephath/Sidon, Syria).

INDICATIONS OF TIME:
Sabbath, year of the Lord's favor, today, the time of Elijah, the time of Elisha.
The oppositions: earlier ⟷ today.

VERBS OF SAYING:
Read, (proclaim), (provoke).

WORDS OF RECOGNITION AND REJECTION:
Speak well, (criticism), rage, intention to destroy.

(a) Discovery of the lexical fields ("inventory of the semantic features"). Such fields are: "build" and similar (nouns and verbs), speech, totality, acting persons, place, etc.
(b) Discovery of the semantic oppositions: e.g., people/lord; build/stop building; be a people/be scattered, make a name/be scattered.
(c) Ordering the oppositions by column:
　　people ⟷ Lord
　　　earth ⟷ heaven
　　human ⟷ divine
　　　below ⟷ above
(d) Interpretation: Fossion proposes as the most important categories for grasping the story: totality/lack and self/otherwise (name oneself/be named; in the Italian translation available to me the terms were "auto-denominare/denominare").
　　[32]Grässer, "Jesus"; Meynet, *Initiation*, 28–54; Baarlink, "Jahr"; Albertz, "Antrittsrede"; Aletti, "Jésus."

After the meaning lines and oppositions have been determined, they can be grouped.

PLACES	Nazareth/synagogue/ hometown	presence of Jesus outside Nazareth
	Israel	heathen
TIMES	earlier	today
	sabbath	year of favor
OFFER	prophetic message	message of salvation, salvation (Isa 61)
REACTIONS	reject	(accept)
	destroy	(recognize)

The result of semantic analysis: The text concerns the question whether Capernaum will become a place of salvation and the Sabbath a "today" of grace and the inauguration of the Lord's year of grace. Thus salvation is now offered to the people who are part of the group standing outside, like the widow and the Syrian.[33]

3.2 MARK 9:14–29: THE POWER OF FAITH[34]

The meaning lines prove to be:

VERBS OF MOVEMENT:
Came, cast out, etc.

EXPRESSIONS FOR PHENOMENA OF "POSSESSION":
"Able to," "believe."

Oppositions:

crowd	⟷	disciples
could not (cast out)	⟷	able
(evil) spirit	⟷	Jesus
convulse (till "as if dead")	⟷	lift up
possessed	⟷	able to stand
crowd	⟷	private

---

[33]The subsequent narrative analysis brings clearly to light the decision-character of the narrative: Salvation is offered; the people of Nazareth reject it; others (and Luke describes this extensively in Acts) accept it. Analysis of textual genre establishes that this is a story of decision, of the sort Luke often tells: The Jews reject the offer of salvation, the gentiles accept it: Acts 13:14–52 (13:46 expresses this point with particular clarity); 14:1–7; 17:1–15; 28:23–28 (as a conclusion to the whole book of Acts). On the concluding narrative of Acts in the light of textual semantics, see Hauser, *Strukturen*, 81–110.

[34]Lang, "Gratia"; Carmignac, "Mc 9, 23."

The grouping of the lines of meaning and oppositions produce:

possessed boy	⟷	healing
disciples	⟷	Jesus
(evil) spirit		
cause to convulse	⟷	lift up
powerlessness	⟷	power
unbelief	⟷	faith

The key saying proves to be: "All things can be done for the one who believes." The text is a semantic unfolding of this statement: Everything (leading up to ἤγειρεν αὐτόν, καὶ ἀνέστη; as opposed to the tormenting by the demon) is possible (δύνασθαι) for the one who believes. Power/powerlessness is the element that runs through the entire text: Believing is miraculous faith; faith is understood as trustful prayer. The possessed boy is under the power of the demon, a power broken by Jesus. The disciples stand by like unbelievers, to whom no power has been granted. The change of roles is represented by the father.

3.3 Gal 1:1–5: God's Saving Action

Linguistically-syntactically Gal 1:1–5 is a single sentence. The basic structure generally found in epistolary addresses, "Paul to the communities of Galatia: grace and peace," is expanded by many elements: by appositions (v. 1), prepositional expressions, participial constructions (vv. 1, 4), and relative clauses (v. 5). It is clear already from a linguistic standpoint that we are dealing with a variety of qualifications.

From a semantic viewpoint the grouping of the elements can be undertaken without too much difficulty: A word count shows that of 75 lexemes there are 32 function words (prepositions, articles, etc.), 34 autosemantic words, and 9 pronouns. Especially remarkable is the fact that 18 substantives and all the pronouns refer to persons. There are only three verbs.

The meaning lines are as follows: In the meaning line "bearers of the action" we find cited: Paul, human beings, Jesus Christ, God the Father, the brothers with me (coworkers), communities in Galatia, us. For such a short text, then, there are very many active persons. The relations between them will be explained.

The meaning line "action" implicitly includes the expressions: resurrect, give oneself, the will of God (substantive), (called as an apostle); requests (in the benediction), and praise (in the doxology).

Along with these clearly graspable groups there are some individual elements that are not so easily grouped at first glance: grace and peace, sin, the present evil world, honor.

The integration of acting persons and expressions of activity reveals the semantic structure:

God the Father	raise up
	will
	(give: grace and peace)
	called to be an apostle
	our
Jesus Christ	call to be an apostle
	to give himself
	for our sins
	to save from the evil world
Paul	(grants grace and peace)
	(conversation partners in
	the churches)
the brothers with me	(coworkers of Paul)
	(conversation partners in
	the churches) "we" set free
churches	(addressees)
	(recipients of the blessings)

The oppositions are numerous:

Paul	$\longleftrightarrow$	recipients (epistolary situation)
God and Jesus	$\longleftrightarrow$	Paul
as commissioners	$\longleftrightarrow$	as commissioned
grace and peace	$\longleftrightarrow$	sin and evil age

From a semantic standpoint the text thus proves to be a statement on a variety of relations between persons: on the one hand, "God the Father and Jesus Christ"; on the other, "we," comprising Paul, his coworkers, and the communities. Within this "we" there are still more differentiations. The individual active persons are more closely described by declarations about salvation history: God's salvific acts and the redemption of Christians.[35]

---

[35]Pragmatic analysis further clarifies this: By shaping the beginning of the letter Paul aims to attune readers to the reading. The readers are to accept the letter as an apostolic communiqué (hence the emphasis on authority), and they are to find in the letter an answer to the question of salvation (Law or Grace) that moves them.

Analysis of the textual genre reveals the similarity in the beginnings of Paul's letters. Deviating from the letter form (on this point, however, cf. Rev 1:4–6), Paul shapes the beginning of the letter into a song of praise to God. Thus the desired effect of the text, reshaping of its genre, and semantic lines all fit together: it is a eulogy of God's saving action by which God's activity is praised and the Galatians are called to be trustful.

3.4 MARK 1: THE RAPID SPREAD OF THE GOSPEL

The inventory of the most important semantic lines of the text lets us see its key thematic points:[36]

- The christological expressions, "Jesus Christ, Son of God" (1:1); "Holy one of God" (1:24); "because they knew him" (1:34), make the reader focus on the nature of Jesus, which must then of course remain concealed (1:45).

- The emphasis on "gospel" (1:1, 14, 15) and the verbs of proclamation (1:4, 7, 14, 38, 45) and of teaching (1:22, 28) set up a second focal point.

- Several groups of semantic elements lend the text a strong dynamic: through verbs of movement (and sending): v. 2; way: vv. 2, 7, 9, 14, etc.; through indications of time: 1:32, 35, immediately: 1:10, 12, 18, 20, 21, 23, 28, 29, 30, 42, 43; through indications of place: at the Jordan, Galilee (1:9, 14, 16, 28, 39), from all sides (1:45).

The chapter gets an inner dynamism through the indications of time (especially from the "at once"), through the indications of place, from the verbs of movement, and from the verbs and substantives of proclamation. The pattern illustrates how quickly the spread of the gospel occurs, and how broad is Jesus' sphere of influence. Thus the inner structure of the chapter is shaped by the thought of the epiphany-like coming of Jesus and the lightning speed of the dissemination of the gospel. Verse 45 gathers together the semantic lines: The kerygma is continued; Jesus is known everywhere, so that people come from all over; Jesus, however, must now guard his secret (which is linked to the gospel's messianic theory).

3.5 PHILEMON: HOUSE-CHURCH AS A PLACE OF INTEGRATION[37]

The various lexemes of the text can be grouped with relative ease as series of meaning-related elements. The most important lines of meaning turn out to be:[38] Lord Jesus Christ. Despite the brevity of the text, this element occurs 11 times. A series of expressions belongs together, since they share the semantic feature "association and relationship": brother, companion,

---

[36]Linguistic-syntactic analysis was already presented in §8. On semantic analysis cf. Egger, *Lehre*, 39–43.

[37]On linguistic-syntactic analysis and the bibliographical entries see §8.

[38]See above, the list of their occurrence.

association through participation, house(-church). This feature of
"connectedness" is also found in the lexemes fellow worker/war-
rior/prisoner: vv. 1, 2 (13, "serve me"), 23, 24. The theme of
belonging together is strengthened by the appearance of "love"
(vv. 1, 5, 7, 8). Several terms refer explicitly or implicitly to places:
house-church, prison; others refer to absence: separated, to keep
with me, guest room.

The oppositions between the semantic elements of the text
show that Paul is essentially concerned with a transformation of
circumstances. Some of the most important oppositions in the text[39]
concern the first series: the relationship between Philemon and
Onesimus:

δοῦλος	⟵⟶	ἀδελφός
		σύν (coworker, etc.)
χωρισθῆναι	⟵⟶	προσλαμβάνομαι
strangers	⟵⟶	house community
Philemon's claim	⟵⟶	renunciation of the claim
to owe something (vv. 18–19)	⟵⟶	write off/replace (vv. 18–20)
compulsion	⟵⟶	voluntarily

The following oppositions affect Paul:

prison	⟵⟶	freedom
Paul's absence	⟵⟶	prepare guest room
ἐπιτάσσειν	⟵⟶	παρακαλεῖν
(authority of the apostle)	⟵⟶	(renunciation of rights)

The text presents the changes that must be carried out:
from the absence/separation of the slave Onesimus and the indebt-
edness arising from that, to his presence with Paul, to a new
(for Paul, "forever" lasting) presence with Philemon and the
"house-church."

The presentation through the semiotic square in Diagram
13 allows us to elucidate the process as change, as movement from
one "place" to another.[40]

The "course" of the process is sketched out as follows: from
A (slavery and its peculiar qualities) to non-A (separation, provisional stay with Paul and provisional service for the gospel) to B
(brother). The negation of B in non-B can lead only to A.

---

[39]On this point see especially Groupe de Montpellier, "Epître."
[40]As opposed to the sketch of a semiotic square for Philemon, ibid., 14–17
(not completely worked out) and de Gaulmyn, "Réflection," 25, only the expressions in
the text itself are used in the analysis presented here. This heightens the precision of
the analysis.

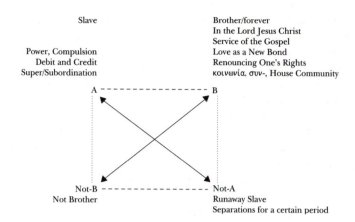

Slave

Brother/forever
In the Lord Jesus Christ
Service of the Gospel

Power, Compulsion
Debit and Credit
Super/Subordination

Love as a New Bond
Renouncing One's Rights
κοινωνία, συν-, House Community

A — — — — — — — — — — — — — — — B

Not-B — — — — — — — — — — — — — — Not-A
Not Brother

Runaway Slave
Separations for a certain period

DIAGRAM 13: THE RELATION OF THE SEMANTIC CONTENTS IN PHILEMON

The characteristic feature running through the entire text is "integration and renunciation of rights." The text wants to move Philemon and the house church to accept Onesimus as a brother who has been integrated into the house church. The house church is therefore the place where social contrasts are overcome. Paul himself can procure the admission of the slave since he himself already has ties to Philemon. The bond between Paul and Philemon is now to lead to a bond between Philemon and Onesimus. This integration is possible only if Philemon renounces his rights. Thus, to make this renunciation easier for Philemon, Paul, as his writing strategy, chooses to renounce his own apostolic authority.

Second Section: The Semantics of Word (Term), Motif, and Word Field

Right from the start, in everyday life understanding depends upon words being heeded in their context. The meaning of a word in many cases depends on the context in which it is used. This is especially important with ambiguous (polysemous) words: the wing of a castle is something different from the wing of a bird or a political party or a hockey team. And the wings of fantasy are something else again.

But even with words that are univocal (monosemous), certain emphases can become more prominent, according to the
context. For example, in the sentence "Don't be a child," the
allusion is not so much to physical age as to the level of intellectual
development. Only the context makes words unequivocal. Since
words in this connection are viewed above all as elements of the
vocabulary (lexicon), they are from this perspective often called
"lexemes." The meaning of lexemes is the object of the branch of
semantics that will be designated in what follows as the semantics
of word, motif, and word field. The semantics of words is primarily
concerned with the meaning of individual lexemes (always taken,
of course, in their own context). The semantics of word fields
addresses the meaning of words that are used in fixed combinations. With regard to motifs the issue may be either individual
lexemes or groups of lexemes.

In the semantics of word, motif, and word field the question is, What does
a lexeme mean in general and then in a specific context?

With regard to biblical expressions, because of the temporal and cultural distance of the texts, special attention has to be
paid to semantics so as not to fall prey to misunderstanding. An
introduction to semantics also provides a glimpse of how biblical
dictionaries are drawn up and what are the functions and possible
uses of lexicons.

INTRODUCTORY LITERATURE: NIDA, *Analysis,* is a groundbreaking study con-
cerning the components of meaning of individual words. LOUW, NIDA,
Lexicon, demonstrate how the components of meaning of individual words
can become the foundation of a lexicon of New Testament Greek. NIDA,
LOUW, *Semantics,* discuss the principles involved in their lexicon. *Funk-Kolleg
Sprache* II, 13–101, offers a first introduction into the semantics of words.
Several essays by NIDA, as well as KEDAR, *Biblische Semantik,* provide a biblical
semantics.[41]

---

[41]The literature on textual semantics has already been mentioned. The
following works offer a presentation of semantics, primarily insofar as it deals with
lexemes/words: Barthes, *Semiology;* Berruto, *Semantica;* Blanke, *Einführung; Funk-Kolleg
Sprache* II, 23–39; Mounin, *Introduction;* Kallmeyer, *Lektürekolleg,* 97–176; Leech, *Semantics;* Sowinski, *Textlinguistik,* 79–106.
On the biblical semantics of words see the criticism of *TDNT* by Barr, *Semantics,*
206–62, and the response by Friedrich, "Problem"; idem, "Prehistory," 10.659–60.
Further literature: Berger, *Exegese,* 20–22; Kedar, *Semantik;* Nida, *Semantic;* idem,
Analysis; idem, "Signs." Ossege offers a concrete semantic analysis in "Aspekte."

1. THE MODEL OF THE LEXEMIC
MEANING-STRUCTURE WHICH UNDERLIES ANALYSIS

The semantic analysis of expressions is based on a specific notion of how the meaning of an expression comes about.

1.1 MEANING: DEPENDENT ON THE CONTEXT

> Every lexeme receives its precise meaning through the relations it finds itself in, that is, through the context.

These relations are, as Diagram 14 shows, of two kinds: syntagmatic and paradigmatic.[42]

	Paradigm 1	Paradigm 2	Paradigm 3
Syntagm 1	a	b	c
Syntagm 2	a1	b1	c1
Syntagm 3	a2	b2	b3

DIAGRAM 14: SEMANTIC RELATIONS

Syntagm means the linear connecting of lexemes into a meaningful chain of words, e.g., "the house is large," "the man tells a story." In many cases the meaning of a word is specified through its syntagmatic relations, e.g., "he lives on the second story," "he tells a story." Only by coming to the end of both word chains is the meaning of "story" unmistakable in each case.

But words also stand in a paradigmatic relationship, i.e., certain words can be joined together in paradigmatic classes. This refers to a group of expressions that at a certain place in a word chain can be exchanged for one another and still yield meaningful statements. Thus in the word chain, "He tells a story," the lexeme "story" can be replaced by "joke, lie," etc.

> The exact meaning of a word depends on the syntagmatic and paradigmatic relations that are peculiar to it.

---

[42]Barthes, *Semiology*, 53–78, esp. 60; see also *Funk-Kolleg Sprache*, I, 119–24.

The relations between expressions differ in their "solidity," with respect to both paradigms and syntagms. From the paradigmatic standpoint "man," "woman," and "child" are more closely related to one another than "man" and "house." "Man," "woman," and "child" belong to the paradigmatic class "human being." "Man" and "house" cannot be combined in the group "things," but only in the group "beings." Likewise from the syntagmatic standpoint some lexemes are more closely and frequently connected with one another than others are, and hence enjoy a "solidarity." Thus the relation between "dog" and "bark" is closer than that between "dog" and "run." The verb "to bark" is characteristic (except in metaphors) of dogs.

In two cases context plays an especially large role in the meaning of lexemes: with motifs and word fields. By "motif"[43] is meant an individual lexeme or combination of lexemes that owing to frequent use in certain contexts has acquired an additional meaning. For example, "mountain" is this sort of motif: "mountain" as the site of revelation and the giving of the Law. Similarly the "disciples' failure to understand" is a motif in the Gospel of Mark: the overall context of Mark gives the individual passages the meaning that faith comes hard to the disciples and that a gradual introduction to the nature of Jesus is necessary for them.

"Word fields," which are also called "semantic fields," are understood either as "regularly recurring combinations of words"[44] or else as classes of paradigmatically associated words, for example, "clever, wise, sly," etc. An especially distinctive word field is the one used in apocalyptic texts. It includes, among other terms, "oppression, rage, persecution, joy, temptation."[45]

1.2 Meaning: The Sum of Semantic Features

Many lexemes have meaning elements in common with other lexemes. Thus "man" shares the feature "human" with "woman," "child," "old person," etc. But in addition the lexeme "man," as Diagram 15 shows,[46] has features that distinguish it from the other terms mentioned: vis-à-vis "woman" this would be "gender"; vis-à-vis "child" the feature would be "grown up," etc.

---

[43] As Berger remarks in *Exegese*, 169, the term is for the most part used very imprecisely. One exception is Fohrer, *Exegese AT*, 99–106.

[44] Berger, *Exegese*, 138.

[45] Cf. ibid., 143.

[46] Leech, *Semantics*, 95–125; Berruto, *Semantica*, 77–115; Nida, "Signs," 47–90.

> The meaning of a lexeme is made up of smaller meaning-elements, which are often called "meaning-components" or "semantic features."[47]

	Masculine	*Feminine*
Grown up	Man	Woman
Young	Boy	Girl

DIAGRAM 15: THE DISTINGUISHING SEMANTIC FEATURES
OF THE LEXEME "MAN," ETC.

Since according to this interpretation the meaning of a lexeme is the sum of its semantic features, it is imperative, if we wish to determine the exact meaning of a word, to break down a lexeme (word) into its component parts.

2. DOING SEMANTIC ANALYSIS
OF WORDS AND MOTIFS

Of the many possible kinds of semantic analysis the following sections will deal with those practical steps that correspond to the previously mentioned models of the meaning structure of lexemes.

2.1 ASCERTAINING THE SYNTAGMATIC AND
PARADIGMATIC CONTEXT

Even for the use of a lexicon one needs to pay some elementary attention to the context of a passage in order to find the right translation. Which of the dictionary entries for λόγος should be selected will be decided by the context: word, conversation, account, the rational grounds, the (eternal) Logos.

In most semantic investigations the linguistic competence of the reader is readily assumed. With ancient texts, however, this is not the case. Thus we have to use the concordance and word counts to see in which syntagmatic and paradigmatic relationships a word can actually be. And so we can determine whether there is solidarity among certain expressions. For example the phrase βασιλεία τοῦ θεοῦ is often linked with verbs of coming, but also with verbs of "entering into." These fixed combinations lend the term "kingdom

---

[47]Leech, *Semantics*, 96.

of God" the meaning of something dynamic that breaks in, but also the sense of a domain into which a person must enter.[48]

2.2 ANALYSIS OF COMPONENTS

"Componential analysis" is based on the notion of meaning as the sum of meaning-elements. Providing this method is not used exclusively, it is a good heuristic device for working out the semantic features of words.[49]

To work out the meaning of a word, the meaning content of the word has to be broken down into its component parts. This "breakdown" is carried out primarily with the help of comparison with other words. One necessary presupposition for this work is the linguistic competence of the person investigating the terms. Specifically, the method consists in the following practical steps: To determine the meaning-components of a word, one first cites words whose meanings are related or opposed. For instance, the word "run" is related to the words "go, dance, crawl, saunter, hurry" and opposed to the words "stand, sit." [50] Then one formulates sentences in which the word under investigation appears, and sentences in which the words chosen for comparison appear, or one simply asks, "How is running different from crawling?" etc. Certain features can be integrated into the words mentioned, as, for example, "movement" applies to "going"; "movement" also applies to "running," and so does "fast movement." "On all fours, on the ground" applies to "crawling." In this way one gets a list of semantic features.

For the analysis of biblical expressions the concordance provides every word with a series of sentences or clauses in which it is used. One must also consider the textual genre in which a lexeme appears. This provides an early overview of the semantic features of a word. The result of the work is presented on a matrix with the help of semantic descriptors.[51] In addition to such a list of features one can also choose to paraphrase.[52]

Since according to component analysis every expression (term) consists of the sum of its semantic features, we must at least

---

[48]Cf. Merklein, *Jesu*, 23–24. Merklein draws tradition historical conclusions from the fact that the "kingdom of God" is coupled with these two more specific terms.

[49]The method is also interesting because major translation projects, such as the "Good News Bible: The Bible in Today's English," and similar efforts in other languages work with this method. On this point cf. §7 (translations).

[50]Nida, "Signs," 47, starts off his explanation with the example: run, go, hop, dance, crawl.

[51]*Funk-Kolleg Sprache*, II, 26–29, 58–61. On this point cf. the example above.

[52]Kallmeyer, *Lektürekolleg*, 133.

work out the most important meaning components in order to grasp the exact sense of an expression.

2.3 ANALYSIS OF MOTIFS AND WORD FIELDS

For the analysis of motifs, principles similar to those governing the analysis of individual lexemes are in effect. In order to highlight word fields in the sense of recurring word combinations, it is advantageous to draw up a matrix on which one enters expressions related to the lexeme.

SUMMARY OF WORKING STEPS AND POINTERS

To determine the semantic components of a word, the following steps should be carried out:

- With the help of the concordance prepare a list of passages where the word in question occurs.
- Determine in which context the expression is used.
- Group the texts in which the word occurs by textual genre.
- List the expressions with which the word is often coupled.
- Prepare a list of words that are related or opposed in meaning to the word under investigation.
- Draw up a matrix on which the common and different semantic features of the words under comparison are entered.
- Now list the semantic features belonging to the word being studied and look for an English word that reveals a similar wealth of semantic features.

3. EXAMPLES

3.1 "APOSTLE"

The term "apostle" in the New Testament, as Diagram 16 shows, is not characterized by monolithic features. In the individual books of the New Testament one finds different features.

Semantic Features	Acts 1:21–22	Mk 6:7, 30 Lk 6:13	1 Cor 9:1 1 Cor 15:8	Phil 2:25
Sent	+	+	+	+
By Christ	+	+	+	–
By the communities	–	–	–	+
Fellowship with the earthly Jesus	+	+	–	–
Encounter with the risen Lord	+	+	+	–
Identical to the circle of the twelve	+	+	–	–

DIAGRAM 16: SEMANTIC FEATURES OF "APOSTLE"

These data explain the difference between the title of "apostle" in Paul and Acts.[53]

3.2 Παιδίον IN THE NEW TESTAMENT

All people associate the term "child" with certain meaning-contents that bear the stamp of personal experience and of the social and cultural environment. To understand the word in the New Testament sense, look for help from the various practical steps of word and motif analysis.[54] Statistically speaking, the New Testament uses the lexeme παιδίον 58 times. The lexeme is found with special frequency in the Synoptics: 18 times in Matthew, 12 times in Mark, 13 times in Luke, 3 times in John, 3 times in Hebrews, twice in 1 John, once in 1 Corinthians.

3.2.1 "Child" and Related Expressions

Diagram 17 provides a first overview of the meaning of "child" and related expressions. The allotment of the semantic features in the case of the following expressions can vary according to context. The siglum ± means that either the one feature or the feature opposed to it (masculine-feminine) must be present. The sign *p* indicates that in some contexts the feature in question is possible.[55]

---

[53]Cf. the commentaries on Acts.
[54]The following remarks present the verbal semantic analysis underlying the article on παιδίον in *EDNT* 3.4–5. The methodological premises can be more clearly worked out in the light of this lexicon article. See Patte, "Kingdom."
[55]Cf. the appropriate entries in the *EDNT*.

Semantic Features	παιδίον	βρέφος	κοράσιον	παῖς	υἱός	θυγάτηρ
Masculine	±	±	–	±	+	–
Feminine	±	±	+	±	–	+
Age	+	+	+	–	–	–
Relative	±	–	–	±	+	+
Service relationship	–	–	–	P	–	–
Metaphor	P	–	–	–	P	P

DIAGRAM 17: SEMANTIC FEATURES OF "CHILD"

3.2.2 "Child" in the Light of the Generic Context

For the meaning of the word in the New Testament the textual genres in which this lexeme is used play a special role. A glance at the concordance will show that the term occurs with particular frequency in the infancy narratives of Matthew and Luke. Jesus is characterized as a "child" (9 times in Matthew, 3 times in Luke), as is John the Baptist (3 times in Luke). In these texts "child" means first of all a designation of age, with "grown-up" necessarily serving as its contrary. But the term gets its special coloring from the kind of text in which it is used. Mattew 1–2 and Luke 1–2 are infancy narratives, that is, kinds of texts in which the significance of a great man is indicated by the fact that even his childhood is shown as under God's particular, miraculous guidance.[56] In this way "child" acquires from its generic context, among other things, the feature of "miraculous anticipation of later life."

The word then can also acquire certain semantic features from being used in images. According to Matt 11:16–17 (Luke 7:32), the comparison to children is supposed to lead to new behavior. Jesus' listeners should *not* be like children who refuse to play along, who in their listlessness turn down invitations to the games of a pretended wedding or funeral. The listeners are supposed to recognize the auspicious hour. In this context, therefore, "child" stands for "uncooperative, negative behavior."

A brief comparison may also be found in Mark 10:15, where entrance into the kingdom of God depends upon the condition of "accepting (the kingdom) as a child" would. The point of this comparison is still disputed in New Testament scholarship. The logion itself emerges from a formal and historical background: Matt

---

[56]On the infancy narratives see esp. Zani, "Influsso."

10:15 is a paradoxical challenge. Jesus takes up the form of the entrance requirements [into the kingdom of God] common in contemporary Judaism according to which a certain outcome is attributed to doing a certain thing. But instead of mentioning the expected lawful conduct, Jesus speaks of "children," that is, persons who simply cannot fulfill the Law. Thus, although the form is retained, the connection between doing and outcome is shattered. The sentence gives no immediate information about what is to be done, but challenges the audience to rethink the doing-outcome connection by asserting that doing is not decisive.[57] Expressions from the Gospel tradition that have a similar orientation are "publicans and sinners," who do not observe the Law. "Child" acquires a further metaphorical meaning in Matt 7:27–28, where only the children, not the dogs, have a claim to nourishment from the table of the father of the family. Thus "child" has the semantic feature of "entitlement."

3.2.3 "Child" in the Context of a Word Field

In Mark 10:14 the kingdom of God is awarded to children: To such belongs the kingdom of God. The children are thereby counted among that group for whom the Beatitudes are intended. Those to whom God's kingdom is promised in the New Testament include minors, children, and "little ones" (Matt 18:1–14), the poor, mourners, the powerless, the meek, the hungry, peace makers, those persecuted for the sake of justice (Sermon on the Mount). The opposite concept is expressed in the "wise" (Matt 11:25).[58] Children also belong to the group of people for whom the disciples must care (Mark 9:37). This group includes tax-collectors and sinners (cf. Luke 15), the sick, the hungry, etc. (cf. Matt 25).

Consideration of the narrative structure, for example, in Mark 10:13–16,[59] opens up yet another approach to the understanding of "child." The text deals with alterations: children are given the blessing; they have the right to obtain the kingdom of God. At first the disciples are opposed to all this.[60] The relations between persons change in the course of the action. Divisions are

---

[57]"The parallel passage in Matt 18:4 turns the provocation into a teaching by interpreting 'being a child' as humility, and by placing the whole discourse on the household of God under the banner of the child (18:1f.)" (Egger, *EDNT*, 3.4).

[58]On the word field pertinent to this, cf. Frankemölle, *Handlungsanweisungen*, 80–108, esp. 89–90, 99–100.

[59]Patte, "Pronouncement," esp. 4–11.

[60]On the oppositions see ibid., 22–38, 39.

overcome, closeness and sympathy created.[61] This narrative context further clarifies the meaning of "child."

Third Section: Narrative Analysis

Another part of the territory of semantics belongs to "narrative analysis," which deals with the peculiar nature and function of stories.[62] Narrative analysis could also be discussed under the heading of textual semantics since it deals above all with two meaning-lines of the text, namely, with the actions (meaning-line of the "do" words) and with the acting persons. Because of its importance for New Testament texts, which over broad stretches are made up of narrative, and because of the specific problems of story-telling texts, it will be better to present narrative analysis in a separate section on semantics.

As an analysis shows, narrative is closely tied to textual pragmatics and can also be presented in relationship to it. Narratives report changes of situation: a condition is altered through the influence of various forces. Events/actions that follow in a certain order and are interconnected are described, and action-bearers through whose activity changes take place are brought forward. Like the actions, the action-bearers are also related to one another. In the representation the narrator can make use of a variety of linguistic means to make the narratives effective, in keeping with her concerns (her "pragmatic" purpose).

Narrative analysis investigates texts with an eye to actions and their consequences, to the action-bearers and the relations between them. Beyond that, narrative analysis aims to make clear the linguistic means that the narrator utilizes in the biblical texts.

In view of recent efforts of narratology to work out the basic structures of stories, analysts of narrative texts in the Bible have the responsibility of exploring the nature of these texts, with regard to both the sequence of the actions and the forces at work. They have to draw up a narrative theory appropriate to the biblical texts, one

---

[61] Patte, ibid., 24–25, defines the opposition "connection/separation" on the basis of internal textual analysis. The oppositions he notes between "holy/profane" and "active/passive" need to be studied more carefully.

[62] Greimas, *Semantics*, contains very wide-ranging discussions of narrative texts.

that corresponds to the specific character of the New Testament (and the Bible as a whole).[63]

There are, it is true, a number of carefully worked out narrative theories. But since these often have a high degree of complexity, a methodology designed to introduce the subject can refer to only a selection from these sorts of methods.

INTRODUCTORY LITERATURE: ALTER, *Narrative*, is a basic text on narrative in the Hebrew Bible. KERMODE, *Secrecy*, concerns himself specifically with the narrative of Mark. GERHART, WILLIAMS, *Narrativity*, contains a number of essays on the gospel genre. GÜLICH, RAIBLE, *Textmodelle*, 192–314, offer an overview of models of narrative analysis. Articles by HAUSER, MINGUEZ, and EGGER provide narrative analyses of biblical texts. PROPP, *Morphology*, remains a fundamental work.[64]

First of all something must be said to clarify the terminology, on which there is still no general agreement. What is the difference between narrative, story, and report?[65] In the pages that follow "narrative" will be understood as a text whose elements include actions and action-bearers. The relation to reality (and to questions of historicity) are not taken into account.

The necessity of more precisely grasping the character of narratives grows from the significance they have in many respects: A basically narrative structure is characteristic of the biblical message.[66] From an anthropological perspective narrative is "a fundamental need, a social activity that serves the processing of experience and aims to constitute social identity."[67] Narratives take place in many everyday conversations. Many aspects of life cannot be communicated except through stories. This is especially true of experiences and a person's life story as well as the history of the family and society in which such an individual lives. Stories help us find our way in the world, enabling us to behave in appropriate ways. And so the church understands itself as a "narrative community" in which the words and deeds of Jesus continue to be recounted.[68]

---

[63] Egger, "Nachfolge," 3.

[64] Gülich, Raible, *Textmodelle*, 192–314; Propp, *Morphology*. Further literature: Barthes, "Introduction"; Bremond, *Longique;* Haubrich, *Theorien;* Kahrmann, *Erzähltextanalyse;* Kanzog, *Einführung;* Lämmert, *Symposium;* Ehlich, "Alltägliches." Exegetical works: Calloud, "L'analyse"; idem, *Analysis;* Egger, *Nachfolge*, 6–48 (survey of narrative theories); Güttgemanns, "Einleitende"; idem, "Analyse"; Marguerat, *Strukturale.*

[65] Kremer, *Lazarus*, 28, prefers the term "narrative" for the Lazarus pericope (John 11), since "narrative" is characterized by a more defined structure than "story" is.

[66] On the basic narrative structure of the biblical message, cf., inter alia, Arens, "Theologie."

[67] Lewandowski, *Linguistisches.*

[68] In this perspective the following articles have had a particularly great effect: Weinrich, "Theologie"; Metz, "Apologie."

1. THE MODELS OF THE TEXT WHICH UNDERLY NARRATIVE ANALYSIS

Both the historical-critical method and theories of narrativity propose models of the text, that is, specific notions about the character
of narrative texts. In part these theories limit their purview to some
factors involved in communication through narrative texts. Narrative texts too have to be considered in a total context of communication: There is the narrator, who composes a text for the listener
in order to influence the reader in a certain way. To what extent the
narrative text is related to the real world or to a "told world" has to
be looked into one case at a time.[69] Similarly, the question must be
answered, to what degree the real narrator coincides with the "narrated narrator," or the real listener with the "narrated listener."[70]

Of the many different analytical procedures, only a few can
be presented within the framework of this introductory methodology.[71] The approach chosen by V. J. Propp for his analysis of
fairy tales about magic[72] has been widely influential. For Propp
narratives are established combinations of actions and action-bearers.
In Propp's view of the magic fairy tale an essential part is played by
the "functions," i.e., the actions of the persons in the story viewed
from the standpoint of their connection with the course of the
action. Propp says that the number of the functions is restricted,
amounting to thirty-one.[73] They always follow the same order.[74] All
magic fairy tales are developments and variants of the same, single,
basic formula. The number of persons acting in these fairy tales
amounts to seven. These persons stand in a fixed relationship to one
another;[75] and there is a specific connection between functions and
action-bearers.[76] This approach, namely, the inventory of the actions

---

[69]Cf. Anderegg, *Fiktion.*

[70]Cf., among others, Iser, *Reading,* 27–38 (concepts of the reader and the
concept of the implicit reader); Fowler, "Reader," 38–49 (see above §1, n. 1).

[71]Treated in greater detail in Egger, *Nachfolge,* 8–48: on Propp, Dundes,
Bremond, Greimas, Güttgemanns, Barthes.

[72]In the following section the Italian edition of Propp's *Morphology of the
Folktale* will be cited, because in it difficult passages from the original edition are partially
explained with the help of Propp's correspondence. Cf. the comments by the editor on
the method of translation, ibid., 229–30. The original Russian edition appeared in
Leningrad in 1928; the German translation, *Die Morphologie des Märchens,* in Munich in
1972. The German edition contains the article by Meletinskij, "Strukturell." An introduction to Propp's life and work is provided by Breimeyer, "Propp." Further bibliography
in Egger, *Nachfolge,* 7.

[73]Propp, *Morphology,* 64.

[74]Ibid., 22–23.

[75]Ibid., 79–86. Propp mentions villain, donor, helper, princess, dispatcher,
hero, false hero.

[76]Ibid.

and agents and the structures existing between them, has been used as the basis of many modern analyses of narrative texts.[77] Such theories often strive to reduce the multitude of actions and to determine more precisely the relation between the acting persons.[78]

The following section will present several models, developed in connection with Propp, that can serve as a foundation for analyzing narrative texts. For the sake of a clearer overview a distinction will be made here between models that attend more to the sequences of action and those that look more to the bearers of the action.

1.1 MODELS FOR THE ANALYSIS OF ACTION-SEQUENCES

1.1.1 Narrative as the Opening Up of Possibilities

C. Bremond[79] in his analysis of narrative texts focuses particularly on the crucial points in the story: in every narrative there are "nodal points" at which alternatives for further development open up. Consideration of such decisive moments is important for the understanding of narratives. Granted, the story tells only one of the possible alternatives; still, we can determine from logical reflections, generalized experiences, and comparison with other narratives at which points in the narrative alternatives open up. The basic scheme presented in Diagram 18 is what Bremond calls the "elementary sequence."[80]

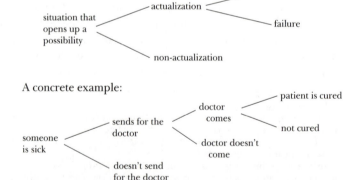

DIAGRAM 18: THE ELEMENTARY SEQUENCE ACCORDING TO BREMOND

---

[77] De Pomero attempts a precise application in *Analisi*.

[78] Especially Güttgemanns, "Einleitende," has carried this approach further and drawn up a transformed repertory of functions. What Propp calls the constants of a narrative, namely actions and action-bearers, are also essential for analyzing biblical narrative texts.

[79] Bremond, *Longique*. Cf. Egger, *Nachfolge*, 28–34.

[80] Bremond, *Logique*, 131.

This model invites us to reflect on what would happen if one of the action-bearers had decided otherwise. The presentation of the alternate actions offered by the text is done with the help of a logic tree. An analytical procedure oriented in this way is especially suitable for texts that deal with decisions. It clarifies the meaning of alternatives and shows the consequences of a decision. Since the "doing-outcome" connection belongs to the fundamental structures of biblical narratives and biblical orders, this view is well suited for biblical texts, and Bremond himself takes many of his examples from the Bible.[81]

1.1.2 Narrative as a Combination of Motifs

Classical form criticism has already addressed the question of the course of action, especially in miracle stories. Attention must be paid to the small units of action from which narratives are composed. A narrative is a more or less fixed combination of motifs (as the smallest narrative elements are called). Depending upon the kind of combination, we can also distinguish the various classes and subclasses.[82]

1.2 MODELS FOR THE ANALYSIS OF ACTION-BEARERS

Different models have also been proposed for the analysis of acting persons.

1.2.1 The "Actants" Model

Continuing the approach of Propp, Greimas[83] defines more closely the relationship between the acting persons. Greimas speaks of "actants," by which he means the acting persons in their relations

---

[81]Ibid., 234, 236, 244–45, 257, among others.

[82]The motif analyses of miracle stories presented in form history were carried further particularly by Theissen, *Miracle*, and then by Pesch, Kratz, *Synoptisch*, 3; and Léon-Dufour, "Structure." Theissen's list in *Miracle*, 71–83, comprises four groups of motifs. They include (1) coming of the wonder-worker, (2) appearance of the crowd; appearance of (3) people in need, (4) representatives, (5) legations, (6) opponents; (7) motivation of the appearance of antagonists; the expository motifs include (8) characterization of the emergency; approach to the wonder-worker with (9) impediment, (10) falling down, (11) cries for help, (12) pleas and expressions of trust; drawing back with (13) misunderstanding, (14) skepticism and mockery, (15) criticism, (16) counter-attack of the demon; conduct of the wonder-worker with (17) pneumatic excitement, (18) exhortation, (19) argumentation, (20) withdrawal; the central motifs include (21) preparing the scene: the miraculous act with (22) touching, (23) healing word, (24) miracle-working word, (25) prayer, (26) verification of the miracle; the final motifs include: (27) demonstration, (28) dismissal, (29) command to maintain secrecy, (30) admiration, (31) acclamation, (32) disapproving reaction, (33) spread of the cry.

[83]Greimas, *Semantics*, 197–221.

with one another (the concrete acting persons he calls "actors"). Greimas reduces the number of actants to three pairs: subject-object, sender-receiver, helper-adversary. The first pair shares the level of willing, the second the level of communication; the third pair belongs to the circumstances of an action. Diagram 19 shows the pairing of the actants.

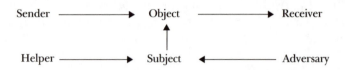

DIAGRAM 19: THE ACTANTICAL MODEL ACCORDING TO GREIMAS

By way of explaining the narrative relationship of the acting persons, in other words the interactions, in a narrative, we can use a simple model of interactions (Diagram 20).

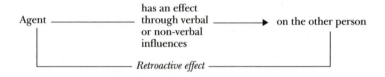

DIAGRAM 20: A MODEL OF INTERACTION

The influence which the sender has on the receiver can be defined more precisely by means of a list of the so-called speech acts: ask, answer, assert, describe, explain, interpret, know, hope, wish, conceal, reveal, command, demand, advise, appoint, thank, etc.[84]

The relations between persons can be explained by means of simple questions: How does A relate to B? How does B relate to A? etc. This sort of simple model or question grid helps us describe the relations between the acting persons and understand the essential interactions involved in human action.[85]

---

[84]This analysis refers to the narrated (thus, internal textual) events. In pragmatic analysis the speech acts are dealt with once again.

[85]Only passing reference can be made here to a further model that helps explain the relations between the acting persons, namely, the "field of characters," discussed by Theissen in *Miracle*, 43–46.

2. DOING NARRATIVE ANALYSIS

The models just presented are appropriate for use in analysis as grids that enable us to understand narrative structures more precisely. Of course, not every grid is suitable for every text. Testing the grids will show whether they will furnish insights. In general, not every form of narrative analysis is fruitful for every biblical text in the same way. In analyzing narrative texts the text must first of all be transformed into a homogeneous object of investigation.

2.1 THE TRANSFORMATION OF THE TEXT INTO A HOMOGENEOUS OBJECT OF INVESTIGATION

Since narrative analysis methodically limits itself to actions and action-bearers—in other words, it analyzes only the structures of action and ignores other structures (although naturally the narrative text must also be explored with the methods of linguistic-stylistic, semantic, etc. analysis)—the narrative text must be transformed into an object of investigation suited for such analysis. The transformation of longer narrative texts into an abbreviated version, which is necessary for analysis, is by and large not needed for biblical narratives, since they are short texts the narrative elements of which can all be taken into consideration. Two kinds of transformation are, however, necessary.

2.1.1 Transformation of Direct and Indirect Discourse

Since narrative analysis studies only actions, direct discourse, which is often found in narratives, is not its immediate object. The verbs of saying which introduce direct discourse may not, however, be excluded from narrative analysis,[86] since as a means of interpersonal influence they imply action and hence are important precisely for narrative analysis. In this context linguistics uses the expression "speech act."[87] When someone says to somebody else, "Do that," it is a speech act of "demanding." When someone says, "If you do that, you have to bear the consequences," it is a speech act of "warning." So, in order to make implicit the active nature of verbs of saying fruitful for narrative text analysis, the verbs of saying, together with the subsequent direct (or indirect) discourse, must be replaced by a "doing" word that expresses the corresponding speech act. Such speech acts can be: asking, answering, asking, commanding,

---

[86]As Minguez, *Pentecostés*, 81, proposes.
[87]See later (pragmatics).

appointing, advising, threatening, warning, promising, finding, re-
buking, etc.

2.1.2 The Transformation of the Sequence of Actions

In the presentation of actions the narrator is not bound to
chronological or causal sequence. The narrator can, in keeping with
narrative techniques, hold back the reasons for the action until
afterwards. For narrative analysis, however, the sequence of the
actions has to be arranged according to chronological, causal, and
logical connections. This means that the events/actions must be
ordered so that they follow one another temporally. It means likewise that causes have to be set before effects, and that contradictory
or contrary polarities (such as the opposition between the initial
situation and the final result) have to be clearly worked out.

2.2 THE ACTUAL ANALYSIS

In the actual analysis the text can be examined from the standpoint
of the sequence of actions and from that of the action-bearers.

2.2.1 Determining the Nodal Points

The passages of a narrative at which the action might have
proceeded other than as told are the nodal points. Some nodal
points are important, others less so. They can be represented in the
manner of a genealogical tree.

2.2.2 Determining the Relation between the Action-Bearers

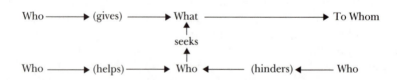

DIAGRAM 21: DETERMINING THE ACTION-BEARERS
ACCORDING TO THE ACTANTIAL MODEL

In order to establish the position of the individual action-
bearers, one must first establish the list of the action-bearers. In
defining the relationship between the acting persons the questions
noted in Diagram 21 will be of help.

SUMMARY OF WORKING STEPS AND POINTERS

After linguistic-syntactic and semantic analysis of the text under study has been dealt with, the following steps in narrative analysis must be carried out:

1. Preparation of a Homogeneous Object of Investigation

(a) First the "doing" words in the text are underlined.

(b) Then the verbs of saying and the direct and indirect discourse connected with them must be replaced by verbs that express the kind of interpersonal influence going on and imply the same content as that of the replaced discourse.

(c) Finally the actions must be arranged in a logical, chronological, and causal sequence; and one has to specify the opposition that exists between the initial situation and the final result of the narrated sequence of action.

2. Use of Grids for the Sequence of Action

In the practical carrying out of narrative analysis Bremond's model of nodal points and G. Theissen's inventory of motifs* will be especially useful. The issue of which grid is best suited for a given text can be settled only by the actual application of the grid itself.

(a) Analysis of a Narrative according to Bremond's Model

List the nodal points of the story, that is, those passages at which a decision occurs that crucially influences the further course of the narrative. Cite the alternative that could open up at this juncture. Try to enter the elements of the action into Bremond's grid:

```
                                        ----------------------

                ----------------------

----------------------                  ----------------------

                ----------------------
```

Tell the story in an alternate version: If at this point of the action one of the acting persons had acted otherwise, the story would continue as follows: . . . .

---

*Use of the other models presented would require a broader theoretical foundation, which cannot be provided in this context.)

(b) Inventory of Motifs

Using the framework of motifs worked out by G. Theissen, determine which of the motifs he lists appears in the narrative being studied.

3. Use of Grids for the Action-Bearers

Once again only the use of grids for action-bearers on a concrete text will show whether and to what extent such grids are suited for analysis.

(a) On Greimas' Actantial Model

Draw up a list of the acting persons and arrange the list according to the action-bearers who belong together or stand in opposition.

Try to answer the following questions by means of the text: Who is seeking what? Who gives what to whom? Who is helping/aiming to hinder?

Should it be possible to answer these questions (which need not be the case with every text), fill out Greimas' grid:

-----------------------   -----------------------   -----------------------

-----------------------   -----------------------   -----------------------

(b) On the Model of Interaction

Determine which forms of influence are narrated in the text through actions and through speech-acts.

Clarify the relations between the acting persons by means of questions: How does A relate to B, B to A, etc.?

This model is particularly suited for narratives dealing with the obtaining of things. In narratives stressing interpersonal relations this grid is scarcely usable. For the latter case a general model of communication and interaction will be more appropriate.

3. EXAMPLE: MARK 10:46–52:
MIRACLE NARRATIVE AS FAITH HISTORY[88]

Narrative analysis must be preceded by linguistic-stylistic and semantic analysis. On these two working steps only a few important observations about the text may be mentioned.

---

[88]Stock, *Umgang*, 85–93.

From the stylistic-linguistic point of view all the sentences have been paratactically connected with καί; only vv. 48 and 50 are linked with δέ. The verbs are all in finite forms, with the exception of a few participles (vv. 46, 47, 49 [twice], 50 [twice]). Twice in the narrative Mark changes to the historical present: in the introduction in v. 46 and in the description of the calling of the multitude in v. 49. The imperfect, used in verses 46, 48 (twice), and 52, expresses an ongoing attitude. In the direct address of vv. 49b and 52 there are asyndeta.

From a semantic point of view three main groups of expressions are discernible as continuous lines of meaning that leave their mark on the text:

Verbs of movement	(and the opposite of movement):
going	sitting, etc.
Verbs of calling	(and its opposite):
crying out	keeping silent;
Words for well-being/woe:	
blind	see
	save

The most important oppositions in the text are clearly formulated at the beginning and the end: sitting blind by the wayside vs. following with sight. The transition from one condition to another, made possible by crying aloud, makes it clear what "faith" means according to Mark. Mark 10:46–52 is therefore a story about the success of crying out.

After the transformation of the text into a homogeneous object of investigation the various grids presented in the discussion of models are put to use.

3.1 THE TRANSFORMATION OF THE TEXT

The transformation of the text into a homogeneous object of investigation scarcely raises any difficulties: The verbal link of "calling out" + direct discourse (Jesus, Son of David, have mercy [vv. 47–48]) has to be transformed into a phrase that both expresses trust in Jesus as the Son of David and is a plea for compassion. The appropriate choice for this seems to be "trustful plea." The transformation of further word connections may be shown in summary fashion:

v. 49:	Jesus said: Call him	sending for
v. 49:	Calling the blind man and saying: Take heart; rise, he is calling you	bringing
v. 51:	Jesus says: What do you want me to do for you?	inquiring about some-one's wishes
v. 51:	said Rabboni, let me receive my sight	answering trustfully, pleading
v. 52:	said: Go your way; your faith . . .	granting the request

The sequence of actions is chronological and causal, so that they need not be rearranged for analysis. Of course, in this transformation process many aspects are left out of account.

3.2 USE OF GRIDS

Through the use of grids developed for the analysis of action-sequences and action-bearers the narrative character of Mark 10:46–52 can be described in greater detail. In the case of the individual grids the possibilities and limitations of their use will be indicated.

3.2.1 Alternative Versions of the Narrative (Following C. Bremond)

Mark 10:46–52 reveals a large number of nodal points at which the story might have taken a different turn.

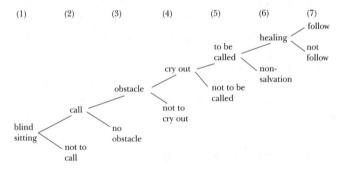

DIAGRAM 22: ALTERNATIVES TO THE STORY IN MARK 10:46–52

In Diagram 22 the individual action-steps have been numbered. The fact that the passages in question are also nodal points in the sequence of actions emerges from general considerations ("here the story might have taken a different turn") and above all from the comparison with other narratives, in which the narrative line does in fact proceed differently (e.g., Mark 3:1–6; 7:27; 8:11; 5:19).

(1) is the opening situation (blind; sitting); the opposites to this situation are (6) (=seeing) and (7) (=going).

(2) means: take the opportunity.

(3) obstacles to a plea occur in so-called standard miracle stories (Mark 3:1–6, e.g.).

(4) The obstacle is overcome; otherwise the blind man would be back in position 1.

(5) Jesus' reaction to the plea. We can find Jesus objecting to a request in Mark 7:27 and to the call for a "sign" as a test (in Mark 8:11–12).

(6) is an expression of the faith that Jesus demands here.

(7) One alternative would be that the man becomes a missionary (as in Mark 5:19–20).

This model allows us to get a good grasp of the alternatives and the decisions about which the text tells us: whoever chooses crying out and faith receives a cure.

3.2.2 The Framework of Motifs

Consideration of the various motifs appearing in the text, as presented in Diagram 23,[89] also sheds light on the action steps.

1. Localized indication of the situation with the appearance of the miracle-worker, his companions (disciples), and a crowd of people (v. 46ab, motifs 1, 3, 4).
2. Appearance of a person in need of help (mentioned by name) with a concise characterization of his need (narrative variant: the miracle-worker comes upon those needing help) (v. 46c, motifs 2, 11).
3. Cry for help (v. 47, motif 14).
4. Command to keep silent (issued by the crowd, motif of impediment) (v. 48a, motif 12).
5. Renewed cry for help (v. 48bc, motifs 14, 15).
6. Establishment of contact, legation (v. 49ab, motifs 7, 10).
7. Encouragement (v. 49cd, motif 25).
8. Preparing the scene (v. 50, motif 29).
9. Exploration (v. 51ab, motif 11).
10. Plea for healing (v. 51cd, motif 15).
11. Healing word: as a liberating command and a confirmation of faith (v. 52abc, motifs 32c, 25).
12. Confirmation of the miracle (v. 52d, motif 39).
13. Demonstration (v. 52d, motif 39).

DIAGRAM 23: THE FRAMEWORK OF MOTIFS IN MARK 10:46–52

---

[89]Pesch, Kratz, *Synoptisch*, II, 79.

According to this model, small individual action units are presented, but opposition and alternatives (in other words, the actual structure) do not become very clear. The result of this analysis is well suited for comparison with other similarly analyzed texts.

3.2.3 The Actantial Model

The acting persons are: Jesus, the disciples, the blind man, and the crowd. The relations between them can be interpreted, in part, according to the actantial model in Diagram 24.

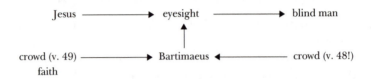

DIAGRAM 24: THE ACTING PERSONS IN MARK 10:46–52

The model clearly shows the conflicts between the acting persons and illustrates well the fact that the crowd is at first an adversary (v. 48), then a helper (v. 49). Faith is a helper too. The model cannot describe in any more detail the interpersonal events that are important for this text.

3.2.4. Interactive Model

The relation between the acting persons may be indicated with key words.

blind man towards Jesus	trusting plea
	following after
Jesus toward the blind man	calling
	healing
"Many" toward the blind man	hindering
	helping

§10
Pragmatic Analysis

Whoever speaks with someone or sends someone a written message wants to influence that listener/reader: She wants to urge on her certain notions, to get her to change her mind or to confirm her in an opinion already held, to move her to share certain feelings, or to lead her to certain ways of behaving. The speaker is interested in "moving the listener with the message to engage in behavior appropriate to the situation. The listener is supposed to react to the text."[1] "Pragmatics"[2] is concerned with the peculiar nature of linguistic statements and texts insofar as they aim to influence the listeners/readers.

> Textual pragmatics deals with the dynamic function of texts,[3] hence with the process of directing action and guiding the reader through texts.[4]

The objects studied by pragmatics are often (oral) user texts from the present for which readers have all sorts of extratextual knowledge. In addressing pragmatic questions to biblical texts allowance has to be made for the fact that we have only the texts, while extratextual knowledge or "everyday knowledge" about communication at the time of composition is scarcely available. Thus what guidance is intended for the reader can be inferred only from the text.[5]

Introductory Literature: Akmajian, Demers, Harnish, "Pragmatics," present a clear introduction to language as communication. *Funk-Kolleg*

---

[1]Weinrich, *Kommunikation*, 11–20, esp. 16.
[2]Greek πρᾶγμα = deed.
[3]Van Dijk, *Textwissenschaft*, 68.
[4]Pragmatics is understood here in a narrower sense than, for example, in Breuer, *Texttheorie*, and Frankemölle, "Kommunikatives."
[5]We can get a certain degree of help from the pragmatic history of the text, insofar as it shows what meaning potential lies in the texts and what effects texts have. In this way the dynamic function of texts can be grasped.

Sprache II, 113–123, and SCHOBER, *Funktionen,*[6] offer an introduction to pragmatics. There are specific New Testament studies in the area of rhetoric (especially for the Pauline letters)[7] and on the use of language in the parables of Jesus.[8]

1. THE TEXTUAL MODEL
OF PRAGMATIC ANALYSIS

Pragmatic analysis of written texts seeks to answer why a piece of writing was composed and to what end.[9] A linguistic statement, or text, is understood as a means used by the author both to establish linguistic communication and to influence the reader in a manner appropriate to the situation, moving the reader to a specific kind of conduct.

Since results can be achieved through speaking and writing, speaking and writing are themselves understood as action, at least in the broadest sense. They bring about, influence, and alter attitudes, feelings, and behavior. Speaking/writing is also an action, inasmuch as it can often go so far as to bring about a change in circumstances, for example, by the drawing up of a will, the making of an appointment, etc. The expression "speech act" was coined to convey this active aspect of speaking. A similar situation obtains for written statements: One could in a certain sense speak of a "writing act."

Pragmatic textual theory views the composition of a text as an "acting through writing," insofar as the text is aimed at influencing and changing the relation between author and reader, as well as the context of the situation—and can, under certain circumstances, actually accomplish this.

---

[6]Along with the articles on textual theory (in this work §2–4) see especially the introductions to pragmatics: Breuer, *Texttheorie;* Funk-Kolleg Sprache, II, 113–123; Kanzog, *Einführung;* Schlieben-Lange, *Pragmatik,* and the sections on the subject in Akmajian, Demers, Harnish, "Pragmatics"; van Dijk, *Texwissenschaft;* Leoni, Pigliaccio, *Retorica;* Plett, *Textwissenschaft,* 79–99. On biblical pragmatics: Arens, *Logic;* Berger, *Exegese,* 14–17; Dormeyer, *Leidens;* Egger, *Nachfolge,* 195–203; Frankemölle, "Kommunikatives"; Lack, *Letture,* 25–28; Meynet, *Initiation;* Schweizer, *Grammatik,* 211–324; Patte, *Paul's Faith;* Reedy, "Concerns"; Theissen, *Miracle,* 219–89 (on the social, religious-historical, and existential function of early Christian miracle stories); Wuellner, "Jakobusbrief"; Zeller, "Pragmatik"; idem, "Wunder"; idem, "Heilung."

[7]On rhetoric in Paul see especially Betz, *Galatians.*

[8]See esp. Arens, *Logic;* Frankemölle, "Kommunikatives."

[9]Cf. Schlieben-Lange, *Pragmatik,* 97: "For what purpose are we speaking, and what do we expect from it?"

1.1 FUNCTIONS (INTENDED PURPOSES) OF TEXTS

Whoever speaks or writes can have different purposes in mind. She might simply wish to express herself and get others to share in her feelings. She might wish to transmit information or move her readers to act. Sometimes writing (for instance, a simple message of greeting) serves the purpose of deepening community,[10] and so on. The goals of speaking need not always be conscious. Often intermediate goals are pursued. The goals of speaking, in fact, are often of a vague, rather nebulous nature.[11]

Pragmatic analysis thus starts off with the observation that linguistic statements—and hence texts as well—must not be viewed exclusively from the standpoint of their contents but also from that of their intended purpose.[12] Depending on the context of the situation in which a statement is made or destined for use in a text, one and the same statement can have different effects. The sentence "It's raining" can in one context be the answer to a question about the weather; another time it can be a way of turning down an invitation to take a walk.

Pragmatic analysis distinguishes between the contents (proposition), purpose (function), and effect of a text.

Different models have been proposed to systematize the different functions of statements or texts.[13] In accordance with the model of communication presented in the section on the "Theory of the Text," which distinguishes the factors—author, reader, and text (as a structured quantity with a subject), code, channel, and situation context—the intended purposes can be distinguished depending on which factor is more strongly stressed:[14]

---

[10]Cf. the brief letter from Hermopolis, first century A.D.: "Philia greets the highly esteemed Apollonios. As often as I find people who are traveling to you, I sense the necessity of greeting you and . . . (here the papyrus breaks off)," from Hengstel, *Papyri*, 85.

[11]Schlieben-Lange, *Pragmatik*, 70.

[12]Although the terminology changes, a distinction is often made between the making of the statement, the contents of the statement (proposition), the intended purpose (illocution), and the effect achieved (perlocution). Cf. the summary in Ulrich, *Wörterbuch*, on "speech act." Illocution (e.g., a promise) can sometimes be specified by a so-called performative verb (e.g., "I promise you").

[13]Bühler's organon model of speech has been significant and influential. See his *Sprachtheorie*, 28–29: The functions of language are expression (symptomatic power of dependency on the sender, whose inward nature it expresses), appeal (as control over the conduct of the listener), and presentation (by virtue of coordination with objects).

[14]The model of communication with different factors and the functions of language correspond to one another in the model of Jakobson, "Statements," 350–77;

- the expressive (emotive) function, when the main thing at stake is expression of the sender's feelings

- the directive (conative) function, when the point is appeal to receiver

- the referential function (information), when the point is presentation of a subject

- the contextual function,[15] when the issue is consideration of the situational context (e.g., "Read the following note")

- the poetic function, when the linguistic form arouses particular interest

- the contact (phatic) function, when the contact between sender and receiver becomes the primary problem (cf., for example, the use of "hello" on the telephone)

- the metalinguistic function, when the text itself becomes the topic (as in "What does this word mean?").

Granted, more than one intended purpose can be in operation at the same time; nevertheless, one or the other can predominate.

Examples of the different functions of language can be found above all in the Pauline letters:

- the contact function of speech: the address in the letters, the concluding greetings (especially strong in Rom 16); Gal 4:20: "I wish I were present with you now and could change my tone" (NRSV)

- the expressive function, such as the indignant self-portrait in 2 Cor 11

- the directive function: the manifold orders issued to the communities, especially in the sections introduced by "I beg you, I admonish you"

- the referential function: presenting matters of fact

- the poetic function, as seen, say, in 1 Cor 13; Rom 8:31–39

---

adopted from Lack, *Letture*, 25–28. The list presented was prepared in accordance with Dell H. Hymes, *The Ethnography of Communication*, cited by Schober, *Funktionen*, 18.

[15]Jakobson and Lack take presentation of a theme and consideration of the context of a situation as a unit.

- the rhetorical function, which is especially evident in Galatians[16]

- the metalinguistic function: Gal 4:24: "Now this is an allegory [ἀλληγορούμενα]" (NRSV)

1.2 MEANS FOR GUIDING THE READER

With speech acts/writing acts we have to distinguish between instruction and strategy. Instruction is understood as the directions the text gives the reader so that she may orient herself in the text and in the given situation,[17] as well as the directions provided by the text so that the reader can correctly classify it (e.g., "Now this is an allegory," Gal 4:24).

In order to lend effective force to the instruction, a strategy is set in motion, that is, certain means are employed to reach the goal. Oral discourse can also be accompanied by extralinguistic means (gestures, such as begging motions, etc.). With texts only linguistic means are available to the author. The choice of such means depends on—among other things—the linguistic virtuosity of the author, the existing communication situation, formulas of politeness, conventions, etc. Thus a command can be formulated as a wish or question ("Could you . . . ").

The application of linguistic means to obtain an effect is called strategy.

Instructions are most unmistakable when they are given in the imperative, e.g., "Close the window!" Yet one and the same order can be expressed in different ways, for example, in propositions with varying contents, such as the comment "It's drafty," or "The window's open!" or "Don't you see that the window's open?" Since the linguistic shape of the instructions can be manifold, additional information is often necessary to grasp the exact meaning of the instruction. With linguistic statements the context is important: When an authority structure is present, a request can be a disguised command.[18] As an example for guiding the reader by linguistic means we may cite the Sermon on the Mount. Here

---

[16]Betz, *Galatians*, in his consideration of ancient rhetoric pays special attention to rhetorical means.

[17]Cf. Weinrich, *Textgrammatik*, 213.

[18]Eighteen variations on "Monica, shut the window!" in *Funk-Kolleg Sprache*, II, 113–14.

we find provocation, pointed language, examples, reference to experience, formation of series.[19]

1.3 CONDITIONS FOR SUCCESS IN LINGUISTIC ACTION

> If action through speaking/writing is to achieve the effect it aims for, a series of conditions must be met each time.

A meaningful command presupposes that the speaker is in a certain situation, namely, that the speaker is set over the person spoken to (the right or power to give orders) and that the speaker has the power to enforce the command through sanctions. Meaningful advice requires certain experiences, familiarity with the action advised and its consequences, knowledge about what is good for the person seeking advice. With genuine advice the person seeking advice must retain freedom of decision. Under certain circumstances such freedom must be explicitly mentioned: "I advise, but I don't command" (cf. 1 Cor 7). In making a promise the speaker must know that she can make good on the promise. She must also know that the listener values getting the thing promised (otherwise it could be at most a threat).

> Acting through speaking/writing is crucially dependent on the context of communication and life, and, here again, to a special degree, on the communication structures existing between sender and receiver.

This has consequences for the analysis of biblical texts, for which there is often no "common knowledge" available about their intended purpose. Knowing the mere form of the linguistic statements, without knowledge of the authority structures and the situational context, is not enough to define the speech act we have before us in the statement. Only when the entire communication and the authority structure are known, does it become clear whether a statement formulated as a request really is a request or a disguised command.

Analysis also seeks to explain which social conditions influence the act of speaking and writing in any given communication and action situation. For this reason pragmatic analysis presup-

---

[19]Cf. Egger, "Auslegung," 135–36.

poses historical and sociological insight.[20] Thus, in a broader sense pragmatics can be understood as a comprehensive vision that does justice to most aspects of a text by considering its rootedness in specific structures of communication.[21] At the same time this approach can be used to draw interpretive lines for analysis of textual genres.

2. DOING PRAGMATIC ANALYSIS

With many contemporary linguistic statements the nature of the desired result can be grasped with no special effort since the communication and authority structures existing between speaker and listener or author and reader are known from extratextual information. With the Bible we have only the text at our disposal. Thus we have to work out from the text what sort of speech act we are dealing with, what intention the author is pursuing, how the writer employs the resources of language to get the reader to react. Various indications in a text will enable us to recognize its dynamic force and motivating intention. This method can *not* be applied mechanically; it merely gives pointers as to how the concerns of pragmatic analysis can be met.

We have immediate access to the guidance intended for the reader when the author himself addresses the subject. In the Gospels this is the case in Luke 1:1–4 and John 20:30–31. According to John 20:30, the reader's response sought by the author is a confession of Jesus as the Messiah and Son of God. In the Pauline texts, under certain circumstances, the peculiar nature of the speech act itself is mentioned, e.g., "I beg, admonish, encourage you," which is the sort of thing we read in the exhortatory parts of the Pauline letters, where Paul also often cites the authority of the Lord and thereby underlines the authoritative character of his admonition.

The instruction (orders) in a text can be gauged simply from its linguistic form if that instruction is expressed in the imperative. Imperatives are an especially clear order to observe certain ways of thinking and behaving.[22] "Let the same mind be in you" (Phil 2:5); "Do not worry" (Matt 6:25). Threats and warnings are also readily understandable as modes of instruction, as is the doing/outcome schema ("whoever does . . . will . . . "; "Whoever does not do . . . will . . . ").

---

[20]Frankemölle, "Sozialethik," esp. 65. Cf. also Venetz, "Beitrag."
[21]Cf. Frankemölle, "Sozialethik," 63–68.
[22]Weinrich, *Textgrammatik*, 213.

The instruction intended by the text can also be recognized by the values presented in it, as well as in the behavior of those persons whose actions the text more or less clearly shows to be a model. Thus John shows us all sorts of figures in whom the reader sees an exemplary faith (John 4: the Samaritan woman who finds faith; John 9: the cured blind man; cf. also Mark 10:46–52, Bartimaeus follows Jesus).

One special problem is the dynamic function of narratives. Admittedly, narratives should not be conceived of as direct guidance. The words that one acting person in a narrative addresses to another are not immediately addressed to the reader of the story. Nevertheless, a narrative presents the reader with many stimuli to a new kind of thinking. In some narratives, however, the narrator passes over the persons named in the text and speaks directly to the reader (John 11:5, 51–52). Narratives present solutions to problems, from which the reader can learn how to behave if such is desired. They likewise present various roles and kinds of behavior, offering the reader a choice of parts to play. A story shows the reader possibilities for which she might decide. Often the narrative (like a drama) stimulates the reader to identify unconsciously with a person or several persons, thereby addressing not just the reader's understanding but heart. The dynamic function of narratives also derives from the fact that they invite us to reflect on our conduct; they suggest alternative ways of living and move us to sympathy, to rejoice in the joy of others, and to action.

A further procedure for grasping the intended effect of the text, in particular from the standpoint of the speech act, is to coordinate the biblical speech acts with those that have been elaborated in other areas. Various authors have developed lists of speech acts that are also applicable to the description of biblical texts. From a list compiled by Jürgen Habermas[23] the following groups of speech acts may be cited.

(a) describe, report, communicate, tell, notice, contradict
(b) maintain, assure, affirm, deny, contest
(c) reveal, disclose, betray, delude, disavow
(d) command, request, beg, desire, admonish, allow, advise, warn, comfort
(e) greet, congratulate, thank, etc.

---

[23]Habermas, quoted in Schlieben-Lange, *Pragmatik*, 48–49.

SUMMARY OF WORKING STEPS AND POINTERS

The following questions should help to find indications in the text about what sort of guidance the author intends for the reader.*

1. On the Process of Communication

With what sort of communication process are we dealing?

Which norms of linguistic and social behavior are presupposed in the text?

2. On Guiding the Reader

What explicit indications of the purpose of the speaking/writing can be found in the text?

Which direct and indirect instructions for the reader's thinking and acting can be found in the text?

To what extent do problems with the relation between author and reader become explicit?

Which values does the text present to the reader?

Specifically, on Guidance Given the Reader by Narrative Texts

With what persons in the text does the text sympathize?

To what extent does the text reveal to the reader its addressees?

What possible solutions does the text offer for specific problems of the community (or reader)?

With which persons does the reader sympathize (or identify)?

3. On the Speech Acts

The following questions are more appropriate for Pauline texts; for the speech act of "narrating," the questions posed above are also relevant.

Who is speaking/writing, and how much credibility does that one have?

By which norms of behavior is the intended audience governed?

What hints does the text give about the authority structure that exists between the author and the readers?

Using a list (the one compiled by Habermas, say), enumerate some speech acts, for example, "command, advise, explain," that might arise in the text being studied.

What conditions have to be fulfilled so that the speech act under consideration attains its goal?

---

*Cf. Breuer, *Texttheorie*, 212–20.

3. EXAMPLES

3.1 1 Cor 7: A Nuanced Conversation with the Community

First Corinthians 7 is one of those texts[24] in which the relationship between Paul as author and the members of the community of Corinth is several times made explicit, and in which Paul himself comments on the modes of influence he has chosen by naming the speech acts that he uses (concession, command, request, opinion, advice, etc.). In this way we can define more closely the intention underlying the text, as well as the proposed instructions and the response desired from the reader.

3.1.1 The Addresses

Paul distinguishes precisely between the various addressees he has in mind in the individual sections of 1 Cor 7. After his remarks on the danger of licentiousness (vv. 1–7), he turns to the unmarried and the widowed (vv. 8–9),[25] whom he advises to remain celibate. Then he turns to married people, repeating the prohibition against divorce for married Christians (vv. 10–11), while making a concession for couples, if one of the members is pagan (vv. 12–16). Thereupon he addresses "everyone" (vv. 17–24), advancing the basic principle, "Let each of you lead the life that the Lord has assigned";[26] after that he speaks to the "brothers" (vv. 25–30), promoting celibacy, though reminding married persons of the ties to their spouses and allowing marriage for the unattached. Finally he turns to groups with specific problems (vv. 36–40).

3.1.2 Paul's Speech Acts and Their Roles[27]

In this section Paul explains the importance of his statement by spelling out which speech acts he means. In v. 6 he speaks of a concession, which is contrasted to a "command." In vv. 10 and 12 he distinguishes sharply between the command of Jesus (which has special authority) and a ruling he himself has issued for difficult marriage cases. In v. 17 he explains the command that each should lead his life in accordance with his allotted vocation. This is meant not only for the community in Corinth, but for all the churches ("valid for Christians in general").

---

[24] Egger, "1 Kor 7"; Baumert, *Ehelosigkeit.*
[25] According to Baumert, *Ehelosigkeit,* 49–52, vv. 6–9 belong together.
[26] Ibid., 99.
[27] On the explanation of individual speech acts, cf. the commentaries on this passage, above all Baumert, *Ehelosigkeit.*

On the question regarding the "virgins" in v. 25[28] Paul is not aware of any commandment from the Lord. In justifying his preference for celibacy he cites himself. He can advance an "opinion/notion" as someone who "by the Lord's mercy is trustworthy." So alongside the speech acts of "concession, wish, order from the Lord, special ruling," there has now been introduced the speech act of "notion, opinion." In v. 26 the notion that the celibate life is preferable is expressly qualified as an opinion. In v. 32 the point is made that Paul wants his addressees to be without care. In v. 35 he lets it be known that his invitation to a celibate life is not intended for every Christian. Again and again Paul refers to the fact that the individual "should find the standard of right behavior in the light of his spiritual 'call' and hence of his natural talents and special circumstances."[29] He would like not to imperil anyone, but to help. In v. 40 Paul calls the suggestion to live a celibate life (directed in this case to widows) a notion that gets its significance from his own experience. From the context of the letter, the word "opinion/notion" acquires the sense of "advice," since these are remarks in which Paul states how one should (not "must") behave in certain cases.

The text of 1 Cor 7 acquires its character from these specifications about the obligatory force of his words and about his speech acts. What we have here is a highly nuanced or differentiated conversation of Paul with his community. Just as Paul knows how to distinguish between his addressees, he distinguishes between the consequences of his various statements. And so his notion of the superiority of celibate life does not lead him to lay down his instructions as absolute or to turn them into a command.

3.2 PHILEMON: A GUIDE TO BROTHERHOOD[30]

The context (situation and action) which the letter to Philemon aims at influencing is a society in which slavery was taken for granted. Still there were in this society slave-owners who had become Christians, as well as Christian house-churches.

3.2.1 Instructions in the Text

Paul gives some of his instructions in the imperative (vv. 17–18). The personal relations between Philemon and Paul are to be extended to Onesimus. The letter does not deal with the abolition

---

[28]According to Baumert, *Ehelosigkeit*, 162–64, this is a concrete group within the community.

[29]Ibid., 338.

[30]On the linguistic-syntactic analysis of Philemon, see §8.

of slavery but with a fraternal relationship both within the social world and in the eyes of the Lord.[31] Apart from the imperatives Paul also gives instructions by presenting the new system of values obtaining in the group of Christians.[32] The new relations and communication structures are made clear by the reference to both the Paul-Onesimus connection and to Jesus Christ. The command that Onesimus should now be a beloved brother must be thought of not as a purely religious statement in the sense that all people are equal before God, but as a directive for social change. More detailed material about such changes set in motion by the Christian message can be found in Gal 3:28, 1 Cor 7:21–24, and 12:13. There is no longer Jew and Greek, slave and free, man and woman. While Paul's thinking about the integration of Jews and gentiles as the overcoming of division in favor of fellowship at table becomes clear, as does his notion of the overcoming of differences between rich and poor (1 Cor 11:11–20), and while the surmounting of the social roles of man and woman can be seen in the role allotted to women in the communities, not much is said on the topic of social change with regard to Christian slaves. The context of the letter to Philemon indicates that Paul sees the solution to the problem coming through integration into the house-church and through personal solidarity between slave-holders and slaves.

3.2.2 The "Writing Acts"

The "writing acts" that Paul puts in this text are described by Paul himself: this is a request. Paul expressly avoids invoking his apostolic authority (vv. 8–10). Of course, he can invoke the "authority" that is due him as an old man who is in prison for Christ. The request is accompanied by so many reasons that the recipient of the letter can hardly resist it. Thus the speech act approaches the genre of request-cum-listing-of-many-convincing-reasons. This speech/writing act acquires its character and power especially from the fact that it is presented before the household and thus is, in a certain sense, public. This makes it still more difficult for Philemon not to respond to the request.

To assure the success of the speech act, "publicly presented request, mentioning the appropriateness of compliance," the following conditions must be present: Paul's wish, Philemon's willingness to listen, support from the household for the request, convincing (based

---

[31]The most appropriate translation for "in the flesh and in the Lord" is probably: "In the social conditions of life and in the new realm of life opened up through faith." Linguistically it is a so-called merismus: a totality is expressed through two parts.

[32]On the system of values in the Pauline letters with regard to the question of slavery, cf. Gayer, *Stellung*.

on personal ties or specific circumstances) grounds for the appropriateness of compliance.

The letter becomes urgent and effective above all thanks to the references to the heartfelt connection between Paul, Philemon, and Onesimus.

The strategy of reader guidance used in the letter makes it a small masterpiece of nonaggressive guidance.

§11
Analysis of Textual Genres

To HANDLE FREQUENTLY RECURRING CONVERSATION AND COMMUNI-cation situations every linguistic community develops certain rules according to which statements can be made. Thus the forms for making contact in a conversation (e.g., when exchanging greetings) are by and large fixed. Letters are written in accordance with a specific pattern. Wedding and death announcements follow a prescribed scheme. From such schemata we can also draw conclusions about the social and cultural context of the texts (wedding customs, etc.). "In all these cases similar experiences and intentions at work in a spatially and temporally identical speech area create similar linguistic forms that are typical for each situation."[1]

Groups of texts with common features are called in linguistics "textual genres." In literary scholarship the problems that arise on this score are dealt with under the heading of "genres." Historical-critical exegesis treats them under "forms and genres" or "form criticism and tradition history."

> In analyzing textual genres the point is to sort out the texts that appear in the New Testament and to group them in groups with similar structures to determine their peculiar nature and to grasp the social milieu and the areas of interaction in which the texts are rooted.[2]

Since research concerns essentially the same problems, despite different approaches and many unresolved questions, no

---

[1] Fohrer, *Exegese AT,* 83.

[2] Lohfink, *Bible* (see below, n. 6), 35, describes in different words (and with different terminology, in which "formal criticism" means something like "analysis of the textual genres") the same concern: "Form criticism is nothing but discovering, describing, and finally determining the linguistic intention and Sitz im Leben of fixed forms (of the sort described) in everyday life or in literature, in oral or written statements of men and women." Of course, as Strecker and Schnelle rightly stress in *Einführung,* 70, in the coordination of texts and genres the elements not typical of a genre that indicate the peculiar quality of the individual piece must not be overlooked.

distinction will be made in the pages that follow between "types of texts" and genres;[3] and for simplicity's sake the term "textual genres" will be used. The genres will be dealt with first of all from the synchronic standpoint.[4] While in traditional form criticism often no precise distinction is made between "form" and "genre,"[5] "form" here refers to the individual shape of a particular text, "genre" to the common ground shared by several texts.

INTRODUCTORY LITERATURE: BEARDSLEE, *Criticism,* discusses a number of "literary" genres. McKNIGHT, *Form,* provides an introduction to form criticism. TALBERT, *Gospel,* focuses specifically on the gospel genre. HEMPFER, *Gattungstheorie,* and GÜLICH, RAIBLE, *Textsorten,* deal with textual genres. BERGER, *Formgeschichte,* and LENTZEN-DEIS, "Bestimmung," deal with questions of biblical genre theory.[6]

1. THE MODEL OF TEXT AND READING UNDERLYING ANALYSIS OF TEXT TYPES

In keeping with the theory of the text advanced here, also text types/genres will be addressed within the framework of a theory of communication and action. The traditional historical approach has already stressed that speakers/writers and their theological ideas were dependent on their particular situation and were influenced by their particular communication groups.[7]

---

[3]On making types of texts and genres equivalent see Raible, Lockmann, "Textsorten." The fact that we are dealing with the same problems can also be seen in the discussion of kinds of texts in Hempfer, *Gattungstheorie* (see below, n. 6), ch. 4; cf. also the lists in Berger (see below, n. 6).

[4]In some books on methodology this distinction is not made with precision; thus in Zimmermann, *Methodenlehre,* ch. 3, genres are discussed under the heading of "form critical method"; in Strecker, Schnelle, *Einführung,* under the heading of "form criticism."

[5]Zimmerman, *Methodenlehre,* 133, understands by "genre" the overarching form, by "form" the smaller—fixed orally or in writing—unit, citing as "genres" the Gospels, Acts, Letters, and Revelation, as "forms" the tradition of sayings and stories.

[6]Hempfer, *Gattungstheorie;* Gülich, Raible, *Textsorten;* Berger, "Hellenistische"; idem, *Formgeschichte;* Lohfink, *Bible;* Lentzen-Deis, "Bestimmung." The classical authors on form criticism are Bultmann, Dibelius, and K. L. Schmidt.

Further literature: Gülich, Raible, "Textanalyse"; Raible, "Gattungen"; Isenberg, "Grundfragen," 303–42; idem, "Texttypen," 261–70; Kalverkämpfer, *Orientierung;* Hellholm, *Hermas;* Koch, *Growth;* McKnight, *Form;* Richter, *Exegese,* 72–152 (form, genre); Schelbert, *Formgeschichte,* 11–39; Strecker, Schnelle, *Einführung,* 67–90; Zimmermann, *Methodenlehre,* ch. 3; Zimmerman, "Formen."

[7]Cf. Frankemölle, "Sozialethik" (see above, §10, n. 20), 65. Berger, *Exegese,* 134, calls for a certain caution toward a sociological classification.

1.1 THE MODEL OF THE TEXT: TEXT TYPES AND THE LIFE OF THE COMMUNITY

Text types are understood to be groups of texts that share certain common features.[8]

As in every linguistic community, so too in the early church frequently recurrent situations led to the emergence of fixed models for language. Particular situations called for appropriate linguistic treatment. Thus in the confrontation with Judaism certain modes of argumentation proved to be appropriate and thus became fixed "forms."

Thanks to the similarity, not only in content, but also linguistic form, intended effect, and the social environment they come from, New Testament texts can now be sorted and gathered in groups. In so doing, for the sake of exact description, we must consider not only internal textual viewpoints, but also—in keeping with the communications theory approach—viewpoints external to the text, related to the communication situation.

The similarity, based on common features, that characterizes texts of one and the same type must be given on the linguistic-syntactic, semantic-content, pragmatic level of the text. Texts of a single type are rooted in a similar life situation.

Texts, then, belong to one and the same genre when they are similar to each other in the following respects:[9]

---

[8]Stammerjohann, *Handbuch,* 496, defines text types in this way: a "partial aggregate of texts that can be described by certain relevant common features and can be demarcated from other partial aggregates of texts." Cf. Fohrer, *Exegese AT,* 84: "Disregarding the individual character of units, the typical structural features common to them are defined in a process of abstraction and described as hallmarks of a genre."

[9]Cf. the relevant lists. As an example the list following Zimmermann's *Methodenlehre,* ch. 3, III B, may be cited:
1. The various genres of the New Testament Scriptures include: Gospels, Acts of the Apostles, Letters, and Revelation.
2. The "forms" include: (1) THE GOSPELS: (a) *the sayings tradition:* prophetic sayings, wisdom sayings, sayings about the law, parables, "I" sayings, sayings about following, composite sayings; (b) *the stories tradition:* paradigms, disputes, miracle accounts, historical narratives, the passion narrative, composite narratives. (2) THE LETTERS: (a) *traditional liturgical material:* hymns, confessions, eucharistic texts; (b) *traditional paraenetic material:* catalogues of vices and virtues, domestic tables, catalogues of duties; (c) *the formulas:* homology, formulas of faith, formulas of praise and glorification.

- They display a similar linguistic-syntactic structure. This can be a matter of similar linguistic elements, such as "Whoever of you . . . ," a similar sequence of elements, and a similar construction.

- They have a similar semantic and narrative structure, such as accounts of healing or exorcism.

- They try to achieve a similar effect.[10]

- They feature a similar life situation, that is, they grow out of a similar social environment, and hence a similar communication, action, and life situation, which they mirror. Texts can become effective in a series of typical situations. These are, for example:

  - mission

  - confrontations with the other Jewish groups and breaking away from Judaism

  - minority situation

  - controversial integration of Jews and Gentiles

  - necessity of organization and of maintaining unity within the group

  - competing Christian groups

  - the scandal of Jesus' shameful death on the cross

  - adoption of the structure of the Jewish Diaspora situation

  - problems with wandering charismatics

  - relations with pagan public opinion

  - the Lord's Supper

  - baptism

  - introduction of newcomers, etc.[11]

---

[10]Berger, *Formgeschichte*, 18–19, divides the genres according to the functions of the text: "symbuleutic texts: they aim to move the listener to act or refrain from acting; epideictic texts: the reader is supposed to feel admiration or horror; his sensitivity to values is addressed in the pre-moral realm; dikanic texts [from δικανικός = 'judicial']; their goal is to get the reader to make a decision on a controversial matter, or to recommend one."

[11]The list has been taken, slightly altered, from Berger, *Exegese*, 113–14.

1.2 READING AS THE DISTINGUISHING OF TEXT TYPES

Upon the very first reading, the reader of a text does an amount of differentiating between text types. For modern texts everyday knowledge often provides the prerequisites for classifying the text properly, and often this classification takes place by itself. Things are different with ancient texts. Since text types always grow out of particular situations and are used to cope with them, comprehensive cultural knowledge is the prerequisite for grouping texts from the distant past according to text types.

With texts from the distant past classification by type especially presupposes in a special way specific cultural knowledge.

If we are to have differentiation on a scholarly basis then the criteria for such differentiation have to be spelled out. The division into genres by form criticism and history of tradition, however, often lacks uniform criteria for differentiation. Accordingly, the terminology is also variable. Along with content-oriented designations (such as "miracle account," "passion story"), formal designations ("parables," "acclamation," "song") are also used.

For distinguishing between text types a single criterion (grouping all texts by length, or some such approach) is just as inadequate as a mere summary list of criteria. Instead we have to pay attention to the relations between criteria.[12] We can differentiate between text types only after considering the linguistic-syntactic, semantic, and pragmatic characteristics in their relationships to each other and to what we assume was the social environment. In this process the pragmatic function of the texts and their relationships to the "life situation" takes on particular significance, because here the active nature of speaking/writing is expressed with special clarity.[13]

To differentiate between text types, we have to consider, along with linguistic-syntactic and semantic characteristics, above all the pragmatic function of the text as a directive for action (in the broadest sense) and the Sitz im Leben as a communication situation and realm of interaction. The connection between directions for action and typical situations must be made clear.

---

[12]Berger, *Formgeschichte*, 19; Hempfer, *Gattungstheorie*, 137–39. Criteria internal and external to the text have to be observed; cf. Gülich, Raible, *Textsorten*, 151.

[13]The linguistic shape and the semantic substance are not as important in determining genre as pragmatic function and situation.

1.3 NAMING TEXT TYPES AND LISTS

Because of the great variety here it is scarcely possible to draw up a "typology of the text" in which all text types are catalogued from a unified perspective. There is more promise in an approach that more simply registers information about the genres.[14] The drawing up of such lists is best done with an eye to the aspect under which the similarities between the texts were determined, e.g., "series" (sequences of similar sentences), "miracle story" (content-semantic aspect, with shades of difference such as "healing miracle story," "exorcism story"), "admonition" (pragmatic function), "macarism" (introductory formula). The terms, of course, should not be too general, and if possible should make apparent their situation-typical use.[15]

An overview of the genres that appear in the New Testament, insofar as they have been defined by research, can be found in the scholarly works on this subject.[16]

2. DEFINING TEXT TYPES

The traditional procedures for defining text types all operate, in the final analysis, by examining a group of texts for elements common to the entire group.[17]

To define text types similar texts are compared. Such a comparison naturally requires that the individual texts to be compared first be studied from a syntactic-stylistic, semantic (content), and (where appropriate) narrative and pragmatic viewpoint.[18] As soon as these kinds of characteristics of the individual texts have been established, comparison of the chosen texts will make it possible to establish the elements that are common to all texts. The common features of the texts that have been identified then form the distinguishing characteristics of the type in question. In defining the text type, therefore, a summary is drawn

---

[14]This was the argument proposed against Isenberg by Gülich (working paper at the Convention of the Institute for German Language on "Textual Genres" in Mannheim, in 1985).

[15]Cf. Fohrer, *Exegese AT,* 92–93.

[16]Particular reference should be made to Bultmann, *Synoptic;* Zimmermann, *Methodenlehre;* Berger, *Formgeschichte;* idem, "Hellenistische"; Berger, Preuß, *Bibelkunde.*

[17]Cf. Hempfer, *Gattungstheorie,* 136–37.

[18]Richter, *Exegese,* 138; Fohrer, *Exegese AT,* 86.

up from the observations on the individual texts by means of linguistic-syntactic, semantic, narrative, and pragmatic analysis. Under certain circumstances defining the textual genre also contributes to a better knowledge of the pragmatic function of the individual text.[19]

It is relatively easy to recognize the common syntactic-stylistic, content-semantic, narrative, and pragmatic features that are shared by the texts. It is harder to do this with the Sitz im Leben, that is, the social environment out of which the text type grows, and the interactions the text is intended to achieve. We get clues for defining the Sitz im Leben (life situation) primarily when the text mentions specific institutions or behavior of a community, such as in the Pauline letters problems with apostolic authority (Gal 1–2) or Paul's coworkers (Phil 2:19–30), among other things,[20] or the issue of Jesus' circle of disciples in the Gospels.[21]

Listing the text types is best done, unless there are particular reasons against it, by making use of the lists prepared in the scholarly literature.[22]

To save labor, beginners, as a rule, ought to take a different path to define text type; namely, after analyzing the linguistic-syntactic, semantic (perhaps narrative), and pragmatic structure, an attempt can be made to classify the text as belonging to one of the types defined by previous research.[23] Needless to say, with such an arrangement there is a danger that some characteristics of the text will be overlooked in favor of a quick classification. In the area of defining genres, clinging to rigid criteria can lead to a misunderstanding of the text.

---

[19]Deviations of an individual text from the character of the text type must not be overlooked.

[20]Ollrog, *Paulus;* Funk, *Status;* Egger, "Mitarbeiter."

[21]On Mark: Petersen, *Literary Criticism,* 49–80.

[22]Fohrer, *Exegese AT,* 92–93; Isenberg, "Texttypen" (see above, n. 6), 265–66, takes a different view.

[23]Fohrer, *Exegese AT,* 92.

SUMMARY OF WORKING STEPS AND POINTERS

Every comparison of texts presupposes that the reader has first had an overview of the syntactic-stylistic, semantic-content, narrative, and pragmatic structures of the individual texts. To determine to which type a text belongs, the following practical steps should be carried out:

1. Look for a text similar to the one being studied. In the beginning the most easy to find similar texts will be texts with a similar content, for instance, miracle accounts (especially accounts of healing and exorcism), stories of calling (Mark 1:16–20). References to similar texts (parallel passages) can be found in many editions of the Bible and, above all, in commentaries on the individual books of the New Testament.

2. Determine, working at first on the linguistic-syntactic and semantic levels, the common features of similar texts. These common features may relate to the introductory and concluding formulas, the sequence of elements, acting persons, etc. Prepare a list of the features shared by similar texts.

3. Then (still working on the linguistic-syntactic, semantic, and narrative levels) expand the comparison to other similar texts. This comparison will give rise to the characteristic schema for the text type in question.

4. Designate the pragmatic function peculiar to this text type. The following questions can be useful: "Who is speaking here? Who are the listeners? What mood dominates the situation? What effect is being sought?"*

5. Designate the Sitz im Leben, that is, the social environment out of which the text has developed, and the situation in which this text was used and in which it is designed to be effective. The following questions will direct the reader's attention to the Sitz im Leben: Which institutions mentioned in these texts played a role in the early church? What community behaviors are presupposed for this sort of text?

---

*Fohrer, *Exegese AT*, 94, raises these questions in order to grasp the Sitz im Leben; these questions are also effective for grasping the pragmatic function.

3. EXAMPLE: THE SUMMARY REPORTS OF JESUS' ACTIVITY IN THE GOSPEL OF MARK[24]

In his Gospel the evangelist Mark offers at various points brief summaries of Jesus' activity. Such narrative texts which gather together various items and generalize features of Jesus' activity, stressing them as characteristic of him, have been called, since K. L. Schmidt introduced the term, "conflated accounts."[25] The list from Mark includes 1:14–15, 1:21–22, 1:32–34, 1:39, 1:45, 2:1–2, 2:13, 3:7–12, 4:1–2, 6:6b, 6:30–34, 6:53–56, 10:1. By means of summary and generalization these texts point to a greater temporal and geographical range for Jesus' activity than is possible to establish from individual narratives.

Thanks to a series of special features these texts stand out as a unique kind of group, different from the individual pericopes and the notes on Jesus' itineraries. On the one hand, they lack the individuality of the separate pericopes; on the other hand, they contrast with mere introductions or conclusions to stories owing to a certain rounded-off and closed form which they have and to their content, which is understandable in itself.

3.1 Linguistic-Syntactic Character

Generalization is first achieved through linguistic-syntactic means:[26] Often the expressions πάντες, πάλιν, πολλοί are used. The verb is often in the imperfect, the tense that expresses repetition and ongoing activity. The effort to provide summarizing descriptions has the stylistic effect of having the conflated accounts strike the reader as weightier than the individual stories, since the declarations are piled up together.

As far as structure goes,[27] every conflated account contains—see Diagram 25 (page 149)—as a rule three elements: an indication of Jesus' coming to a precisely named place, the description of how the people gather around Jesus, and the report of Jesus' activity.

These three elements are most often cited in the same sequence. The three parts are also matched by a different use of tense: in the note on the coming of Jesus the verb is usually in the

---

[24]The textual examples for tradition criticism will also be dealt with under the aspect of text types in §13.

[25]For specifics cf. Egger, *Lehre*. There are fundamental observations on the conflated accounts in Schmidt, *Rahmen*.

[26]See Egger, *Lehre*, 1–2.

[27]Ibid., 27–31.

aorist (or the historical present: Mark 1:21; 10:1); the behavior of the people is described in different tenses (present, aorist, imperfect, periphrastic construction); the activity of Jesus is recounted in the imperfect (or a participle tantamount to the imperfect).

3.2 SEMANTIC CHARACTER

From the content-semantic standpoint,[28] the conflated accounts provide a generalized view of Jesus' activity. The similarities between the conflated accounts, with regard to the contents (and the corresponding vocabulary) are very strong. The presence of Jesus is announced in a place; the text in each case speaks of his coming, with the words ἐλθεῖν (1:14, 39), εἰσελθεῖν (1:21; 1:45; 2:1), εἰσπορεύεσθαι (1:21), ἐξελθεῖν (2:13; 6:54). To describe the coming of the people the text uses verbs of movement, and Jesus is described as the goal of this thronging: πρὸς αὐτόν (2:13; 3:8; 4:1; 6:30; 10:1). In keeping with the activity of Jesus that is narrated, the conflated accounts can be grouped under the following headings: conflated accounts of cures (Mark 1:32–34; 6:53–56); conflated accounts of preaching (1:14–15; 1:39); doctrinal summaries (1:21–22; 2:1–2; 2:13; 4:1–2; 6:6b; 6:30–34; 10:1); generalized statements on Jesus' secrecy (1:45; 3:7–12).

3.3 PRAGMATIC FUNCTION

The conflated reports take on their pragmatic function only from the total context.[29] In the first instance they function to continue the flow of the action. The conflated accounts in Mark 1:14–15, 21–22, 39, 45 present the rapid spread of the gospel. The conflated accounts of Mark 3:7–12 and 4:1–2 show the sort of dialectic of revelation and concealment that runs through the Gospel. The doctrinal summaries function to remind the reader of a continuous feature of Jesus' activity.

For the evangelist the conflated accounts are an important means for the structuring of his work. This is especially true of Mark 1:14–15; 3:7–12; 6:6b; and 6:30–34. Structuring takes place primarily by the conflated accounts' forging transitions between the blocs of material. They are at once retrospective toward what has gone before and prospective toward what follows. They give the author the opportunity for reflection; and in this way Mark regains an overview of the action.[30]

---

[28]See ibid., 27–31.
[29]See ibid., 162–63.
[30]But this does not hold equally for all conflated accounts, cf. ibid., 162–63.

The important pragmatic function of the conflated accounts lies in the fact that by repeating them and their key words the evangelist presents the reader with the last and most comprehensive interpretation of Jesus' activity:[31] Jesus' work is to announce the good news and his teaching. And the reader ought to receive the gospel as just that.

3.4 THE SITZ IM LEBEN

C. H. Dodd assumed that the conflated accounts of Mark's Gospel were a traditional sketch of Jesus' life and work. He thought this sketch had a kerygmatic function and a corresponding Sitz im Leben.[32] But the conflated accounts are in essence (as the analysis of redaction criticism has shown) the products of editing.[33] They are anchored in the Gospel as a whole and not in the context of communication in the primitive church. The social environment or the life situation of the conflated accounts must be seen in connection with the Gospel as a whole. Their place has to be looked at in the communication and life situation in which the Gospel as a whole directs its message to the reader. The evangelist is concerned with linking the tradition of Jesus with the message of death and resurrection. The realm of interaction and the historical setting of the Gospel are a community in which the tradition of Jesus is deepened in the light of the kerygma about his death and resurrection. Mark fashions this deepening in a kerygmatic and didactic manner.

---

[31] Ibid., 165–67. On the thematic complex of the teaching in Mark cf. also Dschulnigg, *Sprache,* 359–60.

[32] Dodd, "Framework." On Dodd and the discussion of his thesis see Egger, *Lehre,* 13–17.

[33] Cf. the introductions to the New Testament.

DIAGRAM 25: OVERVIEW OF THE STRUCTURE OF MARK'S CONFLATED ACCOUNTS

VERSE	COMING OF JESUS — Time	Place	Tense[a]	BEHAVIOR OF THE PEOPLE	Tense	JESUS' ACTION	Tense
1:14-15	afterwards	Galilee	A	—[c]	—	κηρύσσειν	P[b]
1:21-22	sabbath	Capernaum	P		—	διδάσκειν	I
1:32-34	evening	"around the door"[d]		carry gather	I I	θεραπεύειν, ἐκβάλλειν οὐκ ἀφιέν	AA I
1:39	—	all Galilee	A			κηρύσσειν, ἐκβάλλειν	P[b]
1:45[e]	—			(proclaim)	A	ἐπ᾽ ἐρήμοις τόποις ἦν	I
2:1-2	again, after some days	Capernaum	A	gather	A	λαλεῖν τὸν λόγον	I
2:13	again	sea	A	come	I	διδάσκειν	I
3:7-12		sea	A	follow come call (demons)	A A I	εἶπεν ἐπετίμα	A I
4:1-2		sea		gather stand on the shore	P I	ἤρξατο διδάσκειν διδάσκειν	A I
6:6b		villages	I			λέγειν	P[b]
6:30-31[f]			A	(disciples)	I		
6:32-34		lonely place	A	come together	AAAA	see-compassion ἤρξατο διδάσκειν	P AA
6:53-56	(after lake crossing)	Gennesaret	A	run together	AAII	σῴζεσθαι	A
10:1		Judea	P	come together	P	διδάσκειν	I

[a] The only tenses cited are those of the predicates in the main clauses: P(resent), I(mperfect), A(orist), P(articiple).

[b] As individual analysis shows, this corresponds to an imperfect.

[c] The three elements of the conflated accounts are contained here, but in a different sequence: the marveling of the people comes as a choral finale.

[d] Because of the narrative connection the place has to be the same as Mark 1:21.

[e] Different narrative order: coming together of the people as choral finale.

[f] Mark 6:30-31 is at once an introduction to Jesus' withdrawal and a transition from the activity of the disciples (Mark 6:7-13) to the pericope on the multiplication of the loaves and fishes. The crowd is also mentioned in 6:30-31.

Part 4 ▓

Diachronic Reading

THE PROCEDURES OF SYNCHRONIC ANALYSIS OPEN THE WAY TO THE meaning of the text by showing the structures present there. Diachronic analysis, by contrast, opens an access to the text by shedding light on its innertextual prehistory. Consideration of the dialectic relation between textual phenomena and the sources of the text leads to a deeper understanding of the text,[1] which a person who thinks historically cannot ignore. Beyond that, insight into the genesis of the New Testament texts gives us a glimpse of the religious life of the first Christian communities and their efforts to interpret the meaning of the Good News for new situations.

Information about the prehistory of the New Testament texts has to be garnered, essentially, from the texts themselves. There are other accounts (from Papias of Hieropolis, etc.), but these witnesses raise many questions and require an especially close scrutiny in conjunction with the biblical texts.[2] The methodical approach to the New Testament texts consists of gathering observations from which inferences about the history of textual origins can be made.

THE TEXTUAL MODEL OF DIACHRONIC ANALYSIS

While the procedures of synchronic analysis view the text as part of a communication process taking place at a distinct point in time, as part of a complex net of (simultaneous) relations, diachronic analysis views the text as it comes into existence.

The methods of diachronic analysis basically match, as Diagram 26 shows, the stages in the genesis of the text:

---

[1]Babilas, *Tradition*, 60.
[2]Cf. the introductions to the New Testament.

Oral Tradition
(before and after Easter)
    Jesus' logia
    Narratives about Jesus   } Traditions criticism
    Creeds and confessions of faith

Writing Down (in Stages)   Literary criticism

                                  Redaction criticism

DIAGRAM 26: STAGES IN THE EMERGENCE OF
THE TEXT AND EXEGETICAL METHODS

The New Testament texts are the result of a long-term process of oral and written editing and transmission.[3]

THE METHODS OF DIACHRONIC ANALYSIS

Proponents of the historical critical method have worked out the methodological steps that are currently considered classic: textual criticism, literary criticism, form criticism and tradition history and criticism, redaction history and criticism. The argument of this section will tie in with these methodological steps.[4] The following presentation, however (unlike the usual historical critical method), will limit itself strictly to the diachronic side, that is, to the reconstruction of the genesis of the New Testament texts.[5] Some practical steps, though, that are more synchronic in nature have already been presented in the synchronic analysis. Because of its special position textual criticism has already been treated in the second part.

With respect to the technical terminology, which is sometimes inconsistent, the following should be noted: The goal of diachronic analysis is the reconstruction of the historical course along which the texts reached their definitive forms. The composite terms, "tradition and redaction history," characterize this historical

---

[3] See §4.

[4] It would admittedly be possible to integrate the historical-critical methods more forcefully with modern analytic procedures. But for didactic reasons the traditional methods of the historical criticism will be treated separately to provide the beginner with access to this sort of research. The historical critical method distinguishes between synchronic and diachronic aspects insofar as a distinction is frequently drawn between genre criticism and genre history, redaction and composition criticism, on the one hand, and redaction history on the other.

[5] The synchronic side of text types was given a separate presentation.

course. In order to reconstruct it, "critical" observations about the text are necessary, as suggested by the preferred current terms, "literary criticism," "tradition criticism," and "redaction criticism."[6] Those terms are not always understood to mean the same thing in scholarly research, and so the concepts advanced in this methodology will be explained in the pages that follow.

The following working steps accord with the model offered by textual theory:

Literary criticism investigates the text with a view to the establishment of literary (written) sources.

Tradition criticism investigates the prehistory of the biblical texts, insofar as they are based on oral sources. Conclusions about that prehistory and about the Sitz im Leben of the textual units originally transmitted in isolation are based on observations about the context, form, and genre of the New Testament texts.

Redaction criticism investigates how the redactor or editor made a unified work out of the material available. At its outset, form criticism had little esteem for the evangelist as an author. He was looked on simply as a collector of traditions. But even then critics were aware of the evangelists' theological achievements.

As for the sequence of working steps, no step can be taken without the other. Redaction criticism can proceed more analytically and thus stand at the beginning of the steps, or more synthetically and comprehensively and then stand (as it does in this book) at the end of the diachronic procedures.

---

[6] This linguistic description takes as its point of departure the following (colloquially understandable) basic principle: "The tradition/redaction history of the text can be traced by means of critical observations about the text." Thus, "tradition/redaction criticism" in this linguistic usage is not the label of a method; the terms "redaction critical/redaction historical method" are linguistically possible. This linguistic description does not aim at solving the problems raised here, but only at presenting the terminology chosen for this book on methodology.

§12
Literary Criticism
(Quest for the Written Prehistory of the Texts)

THE AUTHOR OF A LITERARY WORK CAN USE DIFFERENT SOURCES AND materials for the composition of her work. If in doing so she gives an indication of the origin of her material—as is done nowadays, for example, in scholarly writing through footnotes—the reader will be alerted to this state of affairs. There is, however, a way of using and editing materials that is not immediately recognizable. Even in works that use sources and materials without indicating this, there are of course often many signs pointing to such use.

Observations made most especially about the Synoptic Gospels, but also about the Gospel of John and some Pauline letters, suggest that the series of "discrepancies" we find in them can be traced back to the fact that in the composition of these books, written (and oral) materials were employed.

> Literary criticism investigates the New Testament texts with an eye to the question whether written sources were used for their composition, and has made it its business to reconstruct these source materials as well as to illuminate their theological emphasis and Sitz im Leben.

The task of literary criticism is manifold. In the case of the Synoptic Gospels it attempts to clarify the relations of dependency among the Synoptics and to reconstruct the sources. With the Gospel according to John it is the stages of redaction (editing of sources, strata, and materials) that need clarification. With the letters that have been handed down under the name of Paul, the point is to investigate whether some letters are in reality compilations from originally separate letters (1 and 2 Cor; 1 Thes; Phil); and, on the other hand, the issue is a possible literary dependency of later letters on earlier ones (Eph on Col; 2 Thes on 1 Thes). The rule that applies to Johannine literary criticism also holds good for other investigations: "Literary criticism is not an end in itself, but a device for recognizing the genetic process of this work and thus at the same time to get insight into the theological history of the Johannine communities."[1]

The distinction between literary criticism and tradition criticism corresponds to the theoretical model of the origin of texts, but the separation of the two steps methodologically cannot always be maintained. Literary criticism can be done more easily with longer, coherently edited texts. This is related to the fact that with longer texts the indications of "writtenness" are easier to determine. Indications of "writtenness" are the weaker linkages of a text to a strict form and the connection between a short text and an overarching unit (e.g., the reference to the death of Jesus as early as Mark 3:6, among others).[2]

INTRODUCTORY LITERATURE: BEARDSLEE, *Criticism,* discusses a variety of literary-critical features of New Testament texts. MOORE, *Criticism,* provides a thoroughly literary criticism of the gospel. BOISMARD, LAMOUILLE, *Werkstatt,* offers an introduction to the methods of literary criticism by means of many examples. PESCH, KRATZ, *Synoptisch,* is meant for intensive and more exact study of the Synoptic Gospels.[3]

1. THE MODEL OF THE TEXT AND OF READING UNDERLYING LITERARY-CRITICAL ANALYSIS

The problem of the use of written sources affects, as has already been said, numerous books of the New Testament. Various models have been developed to try to explain the literary evolution of these writings.

1.1 MODELS OF THE TEXT

The most important theories on the Synoptic question are well known through introductions to the New Testament. The classic Two Source theory is rated as so certain by many authors that they never compare it in detail with other theories. But people do argue for other theories: the theory of multiple sources, the theory of the "conflation" of Mark out of Matthew and Luke.[4] In addition, there are special theories on the origin of the Gospel of Mark that have

---

[1]Becker, "Literatur" (on Johannine literary criticism), esp. 301.

[2]The problem of orality/"writtenness" is still as open as ever; cf. Güttgemanns, *Questions.*

[3]Boismard, Lamouille, *Werkstatt;* Pesch, Kratz, *Synoptisch.* Cf. too Richter, *Exegese,* 50–72; Fohrer, *Exegese AT,* 5. On the Pauline letters see, among others, Merklein, "Einheitlichkeit"; Murphy-O'Connor, "Interpolations"; Pesch, *Entdeckung.* Klauck, "Frage," offers a methodological reflection by means of a concrete text.

[4]Cf. the introductory works.

to be looked into.[5] For the Gospel of John it is almost universally accepted that there were several stages in the literary development of the text. As to the sources, scholars widely agree on the existence of a "Semeia" or Signs Source and a Passion Narrative.[6]

With regard to the Pauline letters a great number of scholars have long seen in 2 Corinthians and perhaps 1 Corinthians as well a compilation of several letters.[7] Recently similar assumptions have also been made for Philippians and 1 Thessalonians.[8] In the case of 2 Thessalonians one obviously has to reckon with the fact that it is dependent, as literature, on 1 Thessalonians.[9]

The textual theories mentioned also offer many refinements of each of the models. The differences in the theories are based on the degrees of importance that are assigned to the individual elements in the texts.

1.2 THE MODEL OF READING

Reconstructing the source materials used for the preparation of a text is useful not only because it lets us know the genesis of the text, but also because such a reconstruction answers the questions that pose themselves when a text is read. Sometimes a reader gets the impression that a text is overburdened with repetitions, that its train of thought is hard to follow, that its logic is not readily understandable, or that the text lacks coherence. As always in exegesis, this is where careful reading proves to be extremely helpful, insofar as a careful reading allows observations on the character of a text to be gathered and assessed.

The literary-critical model of reading is not in and of itself the model of an actual reader, since a reading in layers or strata is not truly possible. An appropriate model for reading instead starts out from the experience of the reader who perceives the difficulties mentioned above and then contemplates them.[10]

2. DOING LITERARY-CRITICAL ANALYSIS

In order to work out more precisely an author's written sources, to determine their theological accents and the Sitz im Leben of a

---

[5]Such as Pesch, *Markus.*
[6]Survey of the reasearch: Becker, "Literatur."
[7]For a summary of 1–2 Corinthians see Bornkamm, *Paul*, 244–47.
[8]Most recently Pesch, *Entdeckung.*
[9]Cf. Trilling, *Untersuchungen.*
[10]Frankemölle, "Kommunikatives," 23, in connection with van Iersel, "Exeget," esp. 317.

source, the text is read primarily with a view to whether it contains "tensions," that is, disturbing repetitions, breaks in style, inner contradictions with regard to content, etc.

If we find the text lacking in coherence, this allows us to argue for the existence of earlier patterns. Thus literary criteria are consistently "criteria of incoherence."[11] The "group of criteria that speaks against the unity of the text"[12] may not, however, take its place at the beginning of work on the text, for this sort of "heuristic rule" gives rise to the danger that the only things discovered in the text will be tensions. There is a need for an authoritative system of checking the text, which means we also need to consider its coherence factors.[13]

The research lists those criteria that permit us to determine the presence of earlier sources: interruption of the continuity of a text, doublings and repetitions, tensions and contradictions.[14]

These criteria are rules of thumb, allowing us to make inferences. One individual criterion, however, is generally insufficient. Only by linking together various indications can we make a judgment. Just as the coherence of texts is created by different kinds of factors (on the linguistic-syntactic, semantic, and pragmatic levels, as well as on the basis of text type), incoherence likewise can exist on different levels. But this has to be determined. Mere lack of coherence on one level is not enough to allow us to assume that a text is not unified.[15]

2.1 OBSERVATIONS ON THE INTERRUPTION OF CONTINUITY

"When a coherent text is interrupted by interpolations on a subject foreign to it, one can conclude with some likelihood that the first version of the text has been further revised."[16] Examples of such interruptions are: Acts 5:12b–14 breaks the continuity between Acts 5:12a, 15–16; Acts 4:33 breaks the continuity between Acts 4:32 and

---

[11]Merklein, "Einheitlichkeit," 157.

[12]That is how Richter, *Exegese*, 48, describes the first step of the literary-critical method.

[13]This demand by Merklein, "Einheitlichkeit," 157–58, is met by this methodology by undertaking to determine the coherence factors as the first step in analysis. Richter, *Exegese*, and Fohrer, *Exegese AT*, 25, consider literary criticism a prerequisite for any analysis. Of course, even an analysis searching for coherence factors may not bypass tensions and disturbing repetitions.

[14]Cf. Merklein, "Einheitlichkeit"; Pesch, *Entdeckung*, on 1 Thess and Phil, as well as the books on methodology.

[15]Merklein, "Einheitlichkeit," 158.

[16]Boismard, Lamouille, *Werkstatt*, 34.

34–35. John 13:34–35 breaks the continuity from John 13:33 to 36–38. As a consequence of such an interruption, after the inserted part, the last words of the original text, which anticipate a completion, are sometimes picked up again.[17] Examples of such a "resumption are John 18:33, 37: "Pilate . . . asked him, 'Are you the King of the Jews? . . . So you are a king?' " Mark 7:1, 5: "Now when the Pharisees and some of the scribes . . . So the Pharisees and the scribes . . . "[18] A particularly large role in scriptural research has been played by the interruption between John 14:31 and 18:1. John 14:31 presents itself as the conclusion of the discourse, but it is nonetheless continued in 18:1.[19]

2.2 DOUBLINGS AND REPETITIONS

"Doubling and repetitions" means the repeated appearance of textual units, sections from the text, or combinations of words that are similar in language and content.[20] Such "multiple texts" are especially suited for clarifying the relations between the texts. Methodologically the first step is to establish the agreements and differences in detail. Establishing agreements between the texts serves to demonstrate the presence of earlier source materials. The great degree of congruence between the texts about the multiplication of the loaves and fishes can be explained only if the texts are interconnected. The differences between the texts, then, help us to recognize relations of dependency. The rule of thumb is: That text is younger which, based on the presence of linguistic-stylistic improvements and elucidation of the contents, has to be considered a modification of the other. What needs to be shown is which text reveals intentional changes: The text in which there is demonstrably an intentional alteration of the sequence (e.g., Luke 4:16–30 compared with Mark 6:1–6) or linguistic and material changes (undertaken for the sake of the editorial enterprise as a whole) has to be considered younger (written later). Thus Matt 13:58, "And he did not do many deeds of power there, because of their unbelief," can be understood as a content-oriented improvement of Mark 6:5, 6a: "And he could do no deed of power there, except that he laid his hands upon a few sick people and cured them. And he marveled because of their unbelief." Editing in the opposite direction would be hard to comprehend. In a similar way Matt 19:17 is a smoothing of the content of Mark 10:18.[21]

---

[17] Ibid., 29–34.
[18] Ibid., 29–31.
[19] On this point cf. the commentaries.
[20] Richter, *Exegese*, 51–55; Boismard, Lamouille, *Werkstatt*, 36–40.
[21] Cf. Kümmel, *Introduction*, 61, and commentaries.

With parallel texts, which we can call A and B, we must investigate which change is easier to justify, the change from A to B or from B to A.

The presence of entire texts in duplicate indicates the use of sources. When shorter sections or word-combinations are repeated within a text, this need not always indicate the use of sources because there is a certain redundancy of expression in all texts.

2.3 TENSIONS AND CONTRADICTIONS

An important means for establishing the use of source materials is "tensions and contradictions in the text,"[22] in other words, the lack of coherence within a text. Assuming that an author is concerned with achieving the greatest possible coherence for a text, lack of coherence will be attributed to the fact that the revising of an earlier source sometimes leaves traces behind when the editor did not succeed in fully reworking the original, or did not try to do this.

Needless to say, there is a certain tension in all texts, especially narrative texts, just as texts often contain repetitions. For this reason tensions and repetitions indicate earlier source material only when we find "irreconcilable tensions and disturbing repetitions."[23] Such a tension in a text and a contradiction due to statements that do not jibe is present,[24] for instance, in Mark 6:45 and Mark 6:53: Jesus and his disciples leave for Bethsaida and arrive in Gennesaret. Mark 6:53–56 is a conflated account, and hence a comprehensive description of Jesus' activity. The mere fact that in this account Mark (in contrast to his usual style) provides exact place names suggests the presence of tradition. Tradition is indicated above all by the way this geographical information contradicts the goal of the journey mentioned in 6:45.[25]

Another sort of tension in a text is created by elements lying disconnectedly alongside each other in it. An example of this is Mark 10:23–27. Here we find, to begin with, an "unevenness and doublet," since the statement about the impossibility of a rich man "entering the kingdom of heaven" is bound up with the statement that no one at all can "be saved."[26] The first statement is formulated as an image, the second in technical theological language.[27] A

---

[22] Richter, *Exegese*, 55–59; Fohrer, *Exegese AT*, 45–46; Boismard, Lamouille, *Werkstatt*, 24–27, 40–54.

[23] Fohrer, *Exegese AT*, 46.

[24] Cf. Richter, *Exegese*, 56.

[25] For particulars cf. Egger, *Lehre*, 135–36 (bibl.).

[26] Boismard, Lamouille, *Werkstatt*, 80–82.

[27] Cf. Egger, *Nachfolge*, 191–92.

material parallel to the statement about being saved can be found in Luke 13:23–24: it is hard for anyone to be saved.[28]

Tensions in the text also arise from contradictions in content (e.g., John 13:36: "Lord, where are you going?" as opposed to John 16:5: "None of you asks me, 'Where are you going?'"), as well as from concluding remarks to which the author does not adhere (e.g., John 14:31; 20:30–31).

SUMMARY AND POINTERS ON LITERARY-CRITICAL ANALYSIS

On this subject a preliminary remark has to be made: As a first step the exact data with which one is working have to be established. For the interpretation of this data one must at first disregard any one specific model of the text.

The practical helps are a gospel synopsis, a concordance, and word counts.

Reconstruction of earlier source materials presupposes synchronic analysis of each text in question. Their linguistic-syntactic, semantic, and pragmatic character must be determined, as well as their text type (in each case with the provision that changes may become necessary owing to new insights). Such an analysis already alerts us to breaks and tensions in the texts.

1. Work on the Synoptic Gospels

In determining common features of the texts being studied it can be useful, first of all, to mark individual words with colors:

- underline in blue whatever is common to all three Synoptics
- yellow for what is common to Mark and Matthew
- green for what is common to Mark and Luke
- red for what is common to Matthew and Luke

Then the differences between the texts have to be surveyed: Are we dealing with

- differences only in language, or
- in content as well?

Now the accents in each section can be described:

- with Mark it is a question of . . .
- with Matthew of . . .
- with Luke of . . .

---

[28]Boismard, Lamouille, *Werkstatt,* 82–83.

Finally, we can draw conclusions: Which text do we suspect is the reworking of another? Smoothing of language and accentual shifts in the content are indications of this.

2. Work on Non-Synoptic Texts

After synchronic analysis the text must be studied explicitly for lack of coherence. This means, on the different levels:

- linguistically-syntactically: interruptions in (and resumption of) the text; vocabulary not otherwise used by the author but present in other texts
- semantically: abrupt and unexplained changes of subject; subjects otherwise foreign to the editor, but found in older texts; disturbing repetitions; contradictions in the text
- pragmatically: tension in the pragmatic design of the text
- text type: elements alien to the genre; tensions with regard to the assumed Sitz im Leben

3. EXAMPLE: JOHN 13:34–35:
THE NEW COMMANDMENT

A series of observations leads to the conclusion that John 13:34–35 is not in an original context but has been fitted after the fact into an already existing text.[29]

First of all, John 13:34–35 interrupts the continuity between 13:33 and 13:36. Verses 31–33, 36–38 deal with Jesus' departure and Peter's being with Jesus. Verse 36 connects directly with 33. Also, vv. 36–38 make no reference to the new commandment of vv. 34–35.[30] Linguistically, the phrase γινώσκειν ἐν, which does not otherwise appear in John, points to 1 John, where it frequently occurs.[31] Also the phrase "new commandment" is found only in 1 John 2:7. From the standpoint of thematic content, the meaning of ἐντολή as moral instruction differs from the use in John 14, where keeping the word or the words of Jesus is looked upon as the content of the instruction.[32] The theme of love dominates so thoroughly in 1 John that along with faith it becomes the fundamental admoni-

---

[29]This notion is defended by: Schnackenburg, *John,* 3.53–55; Segovia, "Structure."

[30]Schnackenburg, *John,* 3.53.

[31]1 John 2:3, 5; 3:16, 19, 24; 4:2, 13; 5:2.

[32]Schnackenburg, *John,* 3.53; Segovia, "Structure," 491.

tion.[33] And so John 13:34–35 also differs from the farewell address in John 14 in its "tendency" and pragmatic intention.[34]

Therefore from the linguistic-syntactic, semantic, and pragmatic standpoints there is incoherence. This observation leads to the conclusion that in John 13:34–35 we are looking at a later, interpolated segment. As far as its origin goes, the commandment about love points to the milieu of the community described in 1 John. The fact that the segment could be interpolated here without great difficulty is connected with the "farewell address" text type, in which admonitions to love have their place.

[33]Schnackenburg, *John*, 3.53.
[34]Segovia, "Structure," 492.

§13
Tradition Criticism
(Search for the Oral Prehistory of the Texts)

OBSERVATIONS ABOUT THE NEW TESTAMENT TEXTS, ESPECIALLY THE Synoptic Gospels, suggest that prior to their written composition isolated individual pieces of various kinds, for instance, narratives about Jesus, Jesus' sayings, formulas of faith, etc., first circulated by word of mouth. These individual pieces were taken up into larger collections (e.g., the Gospels) or inserted as quotations into larger context (e.g., that of the Pauline letters).

Tradition criticism tries to gain insight into the oral prehistory of the New Testament texts. The idea is to comprehend the changes that the texts, which originally circulated in isolation, have undergone in the course of oral tradition, as well as the groups responsible for the changes.

"Tradition criticism" here refers to the method; "tradition history" to both the history of traditions, insofar as it deals with the handing down of texts, and the history of tradition, insofar as it deals with an activity of certain groups responsible for the handing down of texts.[1]

---

[1] On the terminology see above. In books on methodology, as a rule, form and genre criticism are linked to form and genre history. They are separated according to the synchronic and diachronic aspect of the question in Richter, *Exegese*, 152–64; Fohrer, *Exegese AT,* 118–36; Berger, *Exegese*, 160–201. [The distinction which Egger makes here between genre criticism and genre history can also be made in English, but not the distinction between "form criticism" and "form history" because in English the German "Formgeschichte," literally "form history," has been translated from early on with "form criticism." This problem poses no difficulty for the discussions which follow because they concern only the distinction between genre criticism and genre history. Ed.] For historical and systematic reasons Berger assigns to tradition history the domain of the Old Testament, the Jewish world, the New Testament, and the early history of the church and sects. Meanwhile the comparison with texts from groups outside this area is assigned to the history of religions. Fohrer, *Exegese AT,* 99–116, esp. 101 and 110, uses the expression "tradition" in connection with motif and tradition criticism, in other words looking more to content: Tradition is a fund of thoughts and themes bearing a certain stamp and available for given linguistic situations, and with a responsible group interested in

The task of tradition-critical analysis is to reconstruct the individual pericopes and brief texts, which originally circulated in isolation, in their oldest form and in the alterations they have undergone in the course of transmission; to describe the character and generic features of these texts in their different phases; to portray the life and community situations in which the texts were used during the various stages; to establish the groups responsible for handing down the traditions, and to describe the regular patterns according to which such texts are shaped and altered.

INTRODUCTORY LITERATURE: BULTMANN, *Synoptic* remains the basic work on the history of the synoptic tradition. DEWEY, *Orality* contains a series of essays concerning the development from oral tradition to written texts. KLOPPENBERG, VAAGE, *Q*, provide articles on the traditions in Q. Similarly KLOPPENBERG, *Formation*. SCHENKE, *Brotvermehrung*, offers a realization of, and a reflection on, the method, using a concrete text.[2]

1. THE TEXTUAL MODEL UNDERLYING TRADITION-CRITICAL ANALYSIS

According to the model that underlies tradition-historical analysis, at the beginning of the development of the text there is a short, relatively unified, self-contained, and coherent textual unit. This textual unit is related to a concrete community situation. The short individual texts with which New Testament tradition begins are thus "utilitarian texts" or texts that were used in specific situations of communication and interaction within the community, in order to realize certain goals. These brief texts are changed by, among other things, the influence of community situations, by the interests of certain groups transmitting them, and by contact with other genres.[3]

> The traditions acknowledged by the first communities find expression in "utilitarian texts." These texts were developed and changed, and they bear the marks of their history on them.

---

transmitting it. There is also a series of works that are important for tradition history; they have already been cited in the chapter on textual genres (see §11, n. 6).

[2]Schenke, *Brotvermehrung*. The classic works of history of tradition are: Bultmann, *Synoptic*; Dibelius, *Tradition*; Schmidt, *Rahmen*. Cf. Schelbert, *Formgeschichte*, 11–39.

[3]Richter, *Exegese*, 164: change in itself or through contact with other genres.

Change and development take place under the influence of various factors.[4] Working with the parables, J. Jeremias established certain regular patterns in the editing of New Testament texts.[5] He argues that the following factors affected the handing down of the parables:

- the translation of the parables into Greek

- transformations of the illustrative material

- embellishments

- influence of the Old Testament and of folk narrative motifs

- the change in the audience

- the use of the parables for paraenesis in the church

- the effect of the church's situation (the delay in the return of Christ, the missionary role of the church, the church's hierarchy)

- allegorization

- collections of parables and fusing of parables

- the framework

2. DOING TRADITION-CRITICAL ANALYSIS

To grasp the development of, and changes in, a text, and so also to prepare a relative chronology of the different strata of tradition, we must first examine the text with an eye to tensions. If tensions can be discerned in a text, especially in the light of the overall genre and the guidance intended for the reader (the purpose of the text), this allows us to infer the existence of strata in the editing of the text.

The stratification of a text, then, can be explained by comparison with other texts. In this case the focus is less on the content than on the formal aspects of the text. The comparison of texts with similar linguistic-syntactic, semantic, and pragmatic structures can be profitable for the history of tradition.[6]

A further way of tracing the developmental history of a text is to attempt to view the genesis of the text in the context of various

---

[4]See above §4.

[5]Jeremias, *Parables*, 23–114.

[6]Berger, *Exegese*, 168, mentions the following elements that may be compared with others: semantic fields, rhetorical and literary forms, all further genre criteria (e.g., the Infancy stories), traditions that can be assigned a fixed time and place.

other factors. In this way, inferences can be drawn as to how the text came into being or received its distinctive character:

- on the basis of a comprehensive picture of the origins and development of the renewal movement engendered by Jesus,[7] or (in the case of the Johannine scriptures) on the basis of a comprehensive picture of a Johannine school[8]

- by considering the great theological themes and traditional groups (Gospels, epistolary literature) of the New Testament scriptures

- sometimes historical reflections (e.g., concerning the twelve apostles in the Gospels) also play a role.

For the sake of getting a better overview, the methodological steps for research on the Gospels and Paul will be presented separately.

2.1 Tradition-Critical Scrutiny of the Gospels

Determining the presence of tensions here serves, first of all, to "isolate" the previously autonomous units, that is, to detach them from the larger contexts into which they have been inserted. The first step, at least so far as the Gospels are concerned, is "disassembly of the framework of the Gospels," as it is called, because the Gospels reveal distinct seams between the individual pericopes. The connections are loose, secured perhaps only by "and," "or," and "then." Sometimes there are no chronological and causal-logical connections. We often find formal introductory phrases or information used to incorporate the individual piece into the total structure of the Gospel. (Such peculiarities in language and content, especially when they appear accumulated at the beginning and end of the pericopes, can in the course of the investigation be assigned to the editorial stage, and hence play no part in the history of tradition.) By means of this "disassembling," the pieces of the text are once again isolated.[9]

In reconstructing the form that the text had in the beginning and over the course of its tradition, the interpreter must examine the inner tensions, and, above all, ask whether the text represents a unified generic model, and whether the text fulfills a single purpose (its pragmatic function).

---

[7]Cf., for example, Theissen, *Followers*.
[8]Cf., for example, Brown, *Community.*
[9]Similar principles also hold for the tradition-critical analysis of Acts and Revelation.

2.2 Tradition Criticism of Epistolary Literature

For epistolary literature it is possible to draw conclusions about the traditions based on the following criteria. Texts with the following peculiar features point to pre-Pauline tradition:[10]

- express comments by Paul that he is speaking about traditions, e.g., in 1 Cor 11:23; 15:1

- introduction of a section with the word "believe" or "confess" (such words typically preface confessional formulas)

- parallelism, relative pronouns and connectives, introductory participial constructions, rhythm, as in Rom 4:25 or 1 Tim 3:16

- loose contexts and tensions in the text, for example, Rom 1:3–4; Phil 2:6; 1 Tim 3:16

- non-Pauline language usage (as determined by word counts)

- verbal and topical parallels, set phrases that are also used in other parts of the New Testament, hence a kind of multiple attestation in the New Testament scriptures

SUMMARY AND POINTERS FOR TRADITION-CRITICAL ANALYSIS

1. Isolation of the Individual Pericopes

Determine how strongly the beginning and the end of a pericope (and possibly other details as well) are connected to what precedes and follows, in other words, the context. After the editorial features have been defined in the light of stylistics and theological trends, we have the pre-editorial state of affairs before us. At this point a glance at redaction-critical analysis is needed to separate tradition and redaction.

2. Reconstruction of the Original Forms and of the Different Versions of a Text

First of all, one must establish the earliest version (from a literary-critical standpoint). Then we need to determine if there are any transformations of the text, looking within the text itself and comparing it with thematically and structurally similar texts. Such transformations may be of the sort mentioned by J. Jeremias and in the generalized list.

---

[10]Bibliographical data will be supplied below in connection with the analysis of Rom 1:3–4.

*3. The Theological Trends of the Renditions of the Text
at the Various Layers*

Which content-oriented theological emphases emerge clearly in the different renditions of the text?

Which Christology is presented in the different renditions?

4. Conclusions about the Intended Purpose (the Pragmatic Function)

To what sort of thinking and behavior did the text, in its different reconstructed versions, wish to lead the communities in which it was used?

What function could the text in the various stages of development and transmission have had in religious life and in the shaping of conduct?

5. Conclusions about the Sitz im Leben, the Socio-Cultural Milieu

What indications do the different renditions of the text contain concerning the development of community life, community discipline, and the events of community life?

What indications does the text contain of different bearers of tradition and of a transformed circle of addressees?

What situations from the world around it and from contemporary history shine through the text?

3. EXAMPLES

Two examples will serve to demonstrate the history, the "destiny," of texts.

3.1 MARK 14:3–9: CONFESSION OF THE DIGNITY OF JESUS

Use of the textual model of tradition-critical analysis on Mark 14:3–9 shows how an originally unified, self-enclosed text with a clear structure and objective is for manifold reasons changed and expanded over the course of tradition.[11]

Tradition-critical analysis presupposes synchronic analysis.

---

[11] März, "Traditionsgeschichte"; Schnider, "Jesuserzählung," as well as the commentaries.

3.1.1 Synchronic Analysis of Mark 14:3–9

The breakdown of the text is clear:
v. 3 narrative (introduced by καί)
vv. 4–5 speech by indignant guests (with δέ recognizable as an objection)
vv. 6–9 Jesus' reply (again with δέ)

The narrative recounts at length the details of the event, after which the narrative elements increasingly recede. The speech in vv. 4–5 still has two narrative verbs; Jesus' reply has only, "he said."[12] While the objection against the woman is formulated briefly and coherently, Jesus' reply has a complicated linguistic-syntactic structure. True, we find a parallel structure in vv. 4b, 5 (a question and a statement of reasons appended with γάρ) and 6d, 7 (statement and justification with γάρ),[13] but then the parenthesis in v. 7b interrupts the justification, vv. 7a, c; v. 8 is a continuation that just doesn't quite fit; v. 8b offers a new justification for the woman, and as compared with vv. 6–7 it has the effect of a later addition; the whole passage is followed by the word Amen in v. 9.[14]

A number of continuous lines are characteristic of the semantic structure of the text: "ointment" (and the description of the ointment), "good work," "do." Above all the text is marked by oppositions:[15]

waste	good work, burial
give to the poor	"to me"
always	not always

It is characteristic of the narrative structure that many elements relate to the actual case. Some elements, however, burst through the framework of a concrete episode and present a much broader sequence of actions: The anointing is related to the burial; the narrative of the event will become part of the proclamation of the gospel.

The pragmatic function of the text is multiple. The deed of the woman is described as a good work, and so the woman is characterized as a model for the reader. At the same time the message of Jesus' death is proclaimed. Beyond that it is then expressly said that this story is worth telling.

---

[12] März, "Traditionsgeschichte," 91.
[13] Ibid.
[14] Pesch, *Markus,* on this passage, by contrast sees no tensions and disturbing doublets at all.
[15] Less clear is the opposition between one/many that Schnider speaks about in "Jesuserzählung," 176–78.

As for the text type to which this text belongs, Luke 10:38–42 may be cited as a parallel. There too we meet behavior to which an objection and a counter-objection are formulated. Linguistically-syntactically there is a similar structure: description of behavior-objection (introduced, as in Mark 14:4, with δέ),[16] reply by Jesus (again, as in Mark 14:6, introduced with δέ).

Also as far as content is concerned, we are dealing with similar material in both texts: two ways of behaving, of which the one is characterized as "the good portion" (Luke 10:42) or "good work" (Mark 14:6). Thus the contrast is not, as in the disputes, between "allowed" and "not allowed," but between "good" and "better."

3.1.2 Tradition-Critical Analysis

Mark 14:3–9 and its parallels are considered a test case for tradition-critical inquiry.[17] In analyzing this pericope, comparison with John 12:1–8 and Luke 7:36–38 is important. On the question of the history of tradition of these texts the following notions have been advanced about their "relative chronology":[18] (a) According to März, Mark 14:3–9, once obviously handed down in isolated form, is a self-contained story that recognizes the dignity of Jesus. Early in the tradition it was linked to the Passion story. John 12:1–8 incorporates a later stage of the tradition. In Luke 7:36–50 the anointing is a later addition.[19] (b) According to Brown, on many points the Johannine tradition is closest to the earliest tradition.[20] (c) According to Daube and Holst, the anointing of Jesus' feet in Luke 7:38, 46 is, from the standpoint of history of tradition, earlier and closer to the historical event.[21]

The interpretation of the history of the tradition of this text depends upon observations made about it, and on the scholar's judgment of the facts as they have been determined. The tabulation of the agreements and differences in Diagram 27 allows conclusions about the history of the tradition of the text.[22]

---

[16]Vis-à-vis the controversies this is another linguistic-syntactic structure; cf. the texts in Mark 2:1–3:6.
[17]März, "Traditionsgeschichte," 89.
[18]Only a few especially pointed conceptions are presented here.
[19]März, "Traditionsgeschichte," 104, 106.
[20]Brown, John, 1.451–52.
[21]Review in März, "Traditionsgeschichte," 105, on Daube and Holst.
[22]See Brown, John, 1.450.

Mark 14:3–9	John 12:1–8	Luke 7:36–38
two days before Easter (v. 1)	six days before Easter	
Bethany	Bethany	(in Galilee)
Simon the leper	—	Simon the Pharisee
	Lazarus	
	Martha	
unnamed woman	Mary	sinful woman
alabaster flask	pound	alabaster flask
ointment	ointment	ointment
νάρδος πιστική	νάρδος πιστική	wets Jesus' feet
		dries them with her hair
pours it on his head	anoints his feet	anoints his feet
some guests	Judas	
more than 300 denarii	300 denarii	
Jesus defends	Jesus defends	Jesus forgives
"Let her alone"	"Let her alone"	
"You always have the poor"	". . . burial"	
". . . burial"	"The poor you always have with you"	
". . . gospel"		

DIAGRAM 27: SYNOPTIC OVERVIEW OF MARK 14:3–9;
JOHN 12:1–8; LUKE 7:36–38

This overview reveals an unusual state of agreement among the texts, even in details; but then again there are also differences and shifts in the elements. The relatedness of these texts is obvious. When we work our way back from the text before us to its earlier version, reflections on redaction and on literary and genre criticism have to play a role, and history too has to be taken into consideration.

On redaction-critical grounds Mark 14:9 must be ascribed to the evangelist's redaction: its vocabulary and subject matter correspond so closely to the peculiar character of the evangelist[23] that this verse was doubtless inserted by him. Likewise in the Johannine version, one should conclude that the elements connecting this narrative to the story of Lazarus must be attributed to Johannine editing. For John the anointing and the entry into Jerusalem are an aftereffect of the Lazarus story and are viewed against the background of the decision by the Jews to put Jesus to death (John

---

[23]März, "Traditionsgeschichte," 102, with reference to Strecker, in Baltensweiler, *Geschichte*, 91–104.

11:49–53).[24] The reference to the Passion story was already established before Mark and before John.

From a literary-critical point of view, we can scarcely assume that John had the Markan text before him as a source. It is true that we find many baffling points of agreement; still, the differences are too significant to accept the notion that John revised the text of Mark. Thus, we have to assume the presence of common traditional material, but it must have been in oral form; into this material the differences we have noted made their way during the course of tradition.[25]

From the standpoint of genre criticism both Mark 14:3–9 and John 12:1–8 are characterized by the fact that neither of these texts reports a closed event, but both place the event against the broader horizon of Jesus' Passion. There is a widely accepted assumption in scholarship on tradition criticism that in the beginning, short, closed individual pericopes were handed down, not yet integrated into a larger context. If this is true, then it has consequences for the story of the anointing. In the beginning there may very well have been a brief narrative about the deed of a woman who honored Jesus by her anointing. In this original version the woman's action, the objections made by some, and Jesus' reply are all reported. Reconstructed in this way, the text is a "self-enclosed story that develops Christology in an early and primitive fashion by cryptically confessing Jesus' special dignity, which shatters all the limits of conventional behavior."[26] As far as genre goes, this text belongs to the genre that is also attested in Luke 10:38–42.[27] To the simple generic structure of narrative, objection, and reply, as found in Mark 14:3–7, Mark 14:8–9 adds some elements foreign to this simple structure: references to the death of Jesus and the proclaiming of the Gospel. When different structural models appear in a text, it indicates that an expansion has taken place in the course of tradition.[28] This sort of reconstruction aptly explains the fact that for Mark the point of the story lies in Jesus' comment, "You always have the poor with you, . . . but you will not always have me." This assumption also provides a good explanation for the interlocking form of Mark 14:8. The text, in this reading, would originally have included no reference

---

[24]März, "Traditionsgeschichte," 107.
[25]Brown, *John*, 1.451; Schnackenburg, *John*, 2.465–66.
[26]März, "Traditionsgeschichte," 104.
[27]On the generic features see above.
[28]On this methodical principle see Richter, *Exegese*, 161. The reference to the Passion *is* pre-Markan, but not absolutely originally, since the creation of a larger narrative context is a sign of expansion.

to the Passion.[29] At any rate, the connection with the Passion story was made before Mark, as demonstrated by the linguistic form of Mark 14:8[30] and by the fact that John, too, is familiar with this reference (and makes the reference to the Passion the point of the narrative). The story in Luke 10:38–42 has during the course of tradition found its way into the narrative strand that John picks up. The figure of Martha was originally not bound up with the story of the anointing. From another story with a similar theme comes the remark in John that "[Mary] wiped his feet with her hair" (John 12:3), which is certainly appropriate in Luke 7:38, but not in John 12:3.

The relationship between Mark 14:3–9; John 12:1–8, and Luke 7:36–38 has been evaluated differently in New Testament research. According to some scholars, the mention of the anointing of Jesus' feet in Luke 7:38 has no constitutive significance for the narrative and can easily be detached from it. It is therefore regarded as a later interpolation.[31] Others judge Luke 7:36–50 to be the version closer to the historical event.[32]

In addition, tradition-critical analysis introduces considerations of historical probability.[33] We have to note in the tradition an effort to make Judas appear in a bad light. This is especially apparent in John. The tradition knows that Judas kept the common purse (John 13:29), and so he could have been the one who protested against the conduct of the woman (John 12:4). In the course of the tradition, this detail was lost.

Analysis shows the confluence of traditions and the establishment of a larger narrative context as trends that were effective in the handing down of traditions. The tradition had already been subject to contamination, that is, manifold influences on the versions of the text. Thus Luke 10:38–42 influences the story of the anointing that John takes over. John is influenced by the scene of the anointing of Jesus' feet and the drying with the hair from Luke 7:38. Regardless of whether Luke 7:36–50, along with an account of the anointing of Jesus for death, is seen as the original version, or whether Mark 14:3–8 is considered the original, contamination has occurred. The trend toward establishing a larger narrative context by linkage with the Passion story is continued with particular clarity in John.

---

[29]According to Brown, *John*, 1.454, there is no indication that the narrative was once presented without the reference to the Passion story.

[30]Cf. März, "Traditionsgeschichte," 101, with reference to Jeremias.

[31]Ibid., 105.

[32]Bibliography in ibid.

[33]Cf. Brown, *John*, 1.453–54; Brown, ibid., 451–52, maintains that the Johannine version is older.

3.2 ROM 1:3–4: CONFESSION OF FAITH

The address of the letter to the Romans in 1:1–7 is obviously expanded in vv. 3–4 with a statement on the content of the gospel represented by Paul. A series of observations suggests that in vv. 3–4 Paul is using a formula derived from tradition. In what follows, this will be proved by using the criteria listed for the reconstruction of traditional material.[34]

3.2.1 The Reconstruction of the Pre-Pauline Formula of Faith

The beginning of the letter to the Romans strikes us as overburdened by the fact that "gospel" in v. 1 is more closely defined by a relative clause in v. 2 and then by an indication of its contents. The participial construction in vv. 3b, 4a could be detached without undermining the structure of the preface.[35] Since vv. 3b, 4a cause an interruption in the text, and since the context is resumed in v. 5, vv. 3b, 4a can be detached.

A series of words and phrases from this formula is not otherwise used in Paul: υἱὸς Δαυίδ is found only in the Gospel tradition and in the epistolary literature not coming from Paul (2 Tim 2:8; cf. also Rev 5:5; 22:16); γίνεσθαι ἐκ is found only in Gal 4:4 (likewise a traditional formula); ὁρίζειν is found nowhere else in Paul. Πνεῦμα ἁγιωσύνης (a Hebraic genitive, corresponding to the "spirit of holiness," which is attested to in Qumran) is otherwise not found in Paul, although πνεῦμα and πνεῦμα ἅγιον are used very often. Since Paul often uses the contrast σάρξ/πνεῦμα, it is possible that he inserted κατὰ σάρκα as the opposite of the traditional πνεῦμα ἁγιωσύνης. Ἐν δυνάμει is often found in Paul (eleven times).

"This statistical fact shows that with the exception of the expression ἐν δυνάμει all the other words and phrases are unusual for Paul or not to be found in his letters."[36] Ἐν δυνάμει and perhaps κατὰ σάρκα can be considered editorial touches.

Parallelism can also be looked on as a characteristic of confessional or literary formulas.[37] Dropping the definite article before words occurs in many traditional pieces,[38] and stylization also betrays the archaic character of texts.[39]

---

[34]From the extensive literature on the subject we may cite: Zimmermann, *Methodenlehre*, 193–203; Käsemann, *Romans;* Schlier, *Römerbrief;* Wilckens, *Römer.* In our presentation only the central problems of Rom 1:3–4 can be addressed.

[35]Zimmermann, *Methodenlehre*, 194.

[36]Ibid., 195; Wilckens, *Römer,* 57–58, takes a similar view.

[37]Schlier, *Römerbrief,* 24; Wilckens, *Römer,* 56–57.

[38]Zimmermann, *Methodenlehre*, 199.

[39]Schlier, *Römerbrief,* 24.

From the standpoint of the content of this confession of faith, the setting up of Jesus as the Son of God is foreign to Paul, just as tracing the descent of the earthly Jesus is not a Pauline theme (with the sole exception of Rom 9:5). Parallels in content to this passage can be noted in various other realms of tradition: the Son of David Christology (Matt 1:1, 20); the enthronement as messianic king in Acts 13:32–33 and Heb 1:5; 5:5. The statement about the resurrection and the messianic Christology are also linked in 2 Tim 2:8.

The formula in Rom 1:3–4 is also not congruent with Paul, but it is attested to by other domains of tradition. This allows us to infer that we have traditional material here. The original formula may have run:[40] (Paul's introduction: περὶ τοῦ υἱοῦ αὐτοῦ) τοῦ γενομένου ἐκ σπέρματος Δαυίδ (perhaps Pauline: κατὰ σάρκα) τοῦ ὁρισθέντος υἱοῦ θεοῦ κατὰ πνεῦμα ἁγιωσύνης ἐξ ἀναστάσεως νεκρῶν.

3.2.2 The Meaning of the Traditional Confessional Formula

Rom 1:3–4 offers a primitive Christology: the resurrection is proclaimed in a rereading of Old Testament texts, especially 2 Sam 7; Ps 2 and 110, as the enthronement of Christ as messianic king. In the process, "a first stage of the way of Christ, looking to the earthly Son of David, is distinguished from a second, subsequent stage, looking to the Son of God enthroned in a heavenly eschatological position of power. . . . "[41]

A paraphrase of the text might go like this:[42] ". . . born from the seed of David according to his earthly existence, installed (enthroned, *not* revealed) as messianic king (in the sense of the Old Testament conceptions, cf. 2 Sam 7; Ps 2 and 110), in power (in God's realm of Light) according to the spirit of holiness (genitive of quality) since/through the resurrection (from) the dead."

John 7:39 and Phil 2:5–11 represent a similar notion of a way of Christ with different stages, as does Mark, in the narrative form of the messianic secret.

---

[40]The reconstructions diverge.

[41]Wilckens, *Römer,* 60. Wilckens sees the beginning of the confessional tradition documented in 2 Tim 2:8; Rom 1:3–4 could be considered the next step in this tradition. Zimmermann, *Methodenlehre,* 201–2, takes Rom 1:3–4 to be a combination of two brief formulas that were originally used separately.

[42]Since the individual elements are disputed with respect to their traditional origin, they are all paraphrased.

3.2.3 Origin and Sitz im Leben of the Formula

This formula is fundamentally characterized by Old Testament modes of thought. Messianic Christology points to Jewish-Christian circles as the bearers of the tradition. Presumably the Sitz im Leben is the area in which Jesus Christ was recognized as messianic king. This does not necessarily have to be the liturgy[43] or a baptismal confession of faith.[44] It makes more sense to assume that the Sitz im Leben is the area in which the question of Jesus as Messiah was especially significant: the confrontation between Christians and Jews on the messianic dignity of Jesus.

---

[43]Zimmermann, *Methodenlehre*, 202.
[44]Michel, *Römer*, 31.

§14
Redaction Criticism

THE NEW TESTAMENT TEXTS HAVE GONE THROUGH A RATHER LONG genesis before reaching their definitive form. Complex traditions were adopted and joined together in a unity. The final version of the texts goes back to an "editor," who undertook a recasting of the texts.

The analysis of the New Testament scriptures by redaction criticism and redaction history tries to reconstruct the process of editing and the role played by the editor.

The reader has to determine in particular how the text has acquired its final shape, what materials were available to the editor; from what standpoint he chose this material, revised, and organized it; what elements he contributed; which audience he was aiming at; what means he used for guiding the reader; and, in general, what factors influenced him in his editing.

Through the editor the text comes to have a shape which the later reader will face. The text in its final form is also an object of synchronic analysis.[1]

INTRODUCTORY LITERATURE: PERRIN, *Redaction*, discusses redaction criticism, beginning with William Wrede. FRANKEMÖLLE, "Evangelist," provides an especially thoroughgoing critical reflection on the problems connected with editing in the light of a synchronic approach and communications theory.[2]

---

[1]Problems on this score are dealt with in Part 3.
[2]Frankemölle, "Evangelist"; quoted from the reprint in *Handlungsanweisungen*, 50–79. Further literature: Berger, *Exegese*, 29–30; Conzelmann, Lindemann, *Interpreting*, 82–87; Fohrer, *Exegese AT*, 9; Perrin, *Redaction*; Rohde, *Rediscovering*; Strecker, Schnelle, *Einführung*, 9; Zimmermann, *Methodenlehre*, 4. The following studies were pioneering: Conzelmann, *Theology*; Marxsen, *Mark*; Bornkamm, Barth, Held, *Tradition*; Trilling, *Israel*.

1. THE MODEL OF TEXTUAL ORIGINS UNDERLYING REDACTION-CRITICAL ANALYSIS

In keeping with the proposed methodology the process of editing the New Testament scriptures will be discussed within the framework of the model of interaction and communication.[3] The general model of communication through texts is as follows:

Source of Information–Author–Text–Reader–Use of Information.[4]

According to Diagram 28, editing is to be taken as a "recoding" of texts derived from tradition as a source of information. Various factors influence this recoding:[5]

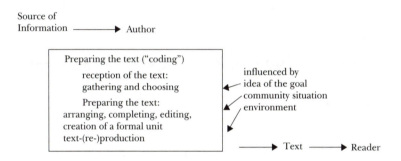

DIAGRAM 28: EDITING AS RECODING

One rule in effect not just for the Gospels but also (if not to the same extent) for all New Testament scriptures maintains that the editor is collector, writer, theologian, and "evangelist" all in one.[6] He has to gather and select the necessary material. He revises it stylistically and thematically. He takes care of the organization and arrangement of the material. He occasionally rounds off the material by adding shorter or longer texts.[7] Through this

---

[3]See Frankemölle, *Handlungsanweisungen*, 59, 75.

[4]See §3.

[5]On the model of revising/editing see above §4.

[6]This understanding, of course, developed only gradually. For early form criticism the evangelists were purely collectors of traditions.

[7]The actual method of work followed by the editor can be characterized more precisely, following Zimmermann, *Methodenlehre*, 226–34, by the following key words: stylistic improvements, elucidation of the text as given, omission of difficult expressions or sentences, transposition of images and pieces of tradition, shifts, addition and insertion of other pieces of tradition, completion through other pieces of tradition, composition of headings, connection of originally autonomous individual pieces.

work a new text comes into being, creating a formal unit.[8] The originally separate pieces are placed in a new context and thus are given an expanded sense.[9]

In doing his work the editor is influenced by many factors: by the peculiar nature (also the dignity) of the material handed down to him; by the viewpoints and conceptions of the goal that are in his mind; by the problems and religious needs of the church(es). The church community is not the only influence on the editor; he is also affected by an environment steeped in scriptural tradition: "The Old Testament, the Jewish and Hellenistic milieu, above all the primitive Christian, pre-Gospel and Gospel traditions, among other things, were for the evangelist—as far as the range of the material is concerned—much more formative than the community. . . ."[10]

2. PRACTICING REDACTION-CRITICAL ANALYSIS

The method of redaction criticism consists of an inferential procedure.

> Inferences about the editorial process can be made on the basis of
> linguistic-stylistic, semantic, and pragmatic peculiarities of a work, as well
> as from its genre. As for the individual pericopes, such conclusions are
> possible only in the light of the work as a whole.

The interferences concern the person of the editor and his manner of work (reception and handling of the text), the addressees and their world, the place and time of the work's coming into existence.

2.1 Inferences about the Editor and His Method of Work

Even when we are dealing with compositions assembled from various traditions, a text allows us to make inferences about its editor and his literary and theological achievement.

---

[8]Frankemölle, *Handlungsansweisungen,* 63. This was stressed above all by Güttgemanns, *Questions,* 184–88.

[9]The theology of the editor is not to be ascertained isolated from the tradition, but in it and with it: Dschulnigg, *Sprache* (see §8, n. 23, pp. 297–98). See also Frankemölle, *Handlungsanweisungen,* 66.

[10]Frankemölle, *Handlungsanweisungen,* 71.

2.1.1 The Person of the Editor

With regard to the person of the editor the indications in the text can be more or less clear: while Paul very often speaks about himself in his letters, the Gospels say hardly anything about their authors. Statements about the author occur in Luke 1:1–4 (at least about his procedure and intentions) and in the statements in the Gospel of John about the beloved disciple as a witness. An outline of the editor's intention and key theological concerns can be indirectly ascertained from the Gospels. Details about the authors can be found in the works of the apostolic fathers and church writers, especially Papias of Hieropolis, Irenaeus, and in the anti-Marcionite Gospel prologues. Of course, to what extent such testimony is based upon information independent of the Gospels has been disputed.[11] With pseudepigrapha we must use an inferential procedure in which, thanks to observations about the text, we can determine the situation presupposed in the letter, the rules of the community, the development of theological thought; then inferences can be made about the author.[12]

2.1.2 The Method of Work

As for the working method, the clearest indications are to be found when the editor explicitly presents it, as, for example, in Luke 1:1–4. Still, inferences can be drawn from other observations as to the editor's methods, namely, from the linguistic-stylistic character of the Gospel, from the main thrust of the content and the organization of the material, from the intended effect of the Gospel as a whole, and particularly clearly by means of synoptic comparison. Places where editors prefer to work are the beginning and the end of both individual sections and entire books.[13]

- The linguistic-stylistic character of a New Testament writing[14] reveals the editor's typical way of speaking and hence his way of working. When, for instance, in one of the Gospels a verse contains an especially large number of linguistic-stylistic features peculiar to an author, we have more reason to infer the editor's presence than we have in the case of other verses;[15] an atypical vocabulary, on the other hand, allows us to infer a contribution from tradition. An editor's favorite words are a particular key to redaction

---

[11]Cf. the introductory works.
[12]Cf., along with the introductory works, Laub, "Falsche."
[13]Berger, *Exegese*, 205.
[14]On vocabulary see §8.
[15]Strecke, Schnelle, *Einführung*, 11.

history. Linguistic indications, however, are not enough in themselves: editorial formations can be recognized only in connection with the viewpoints expressed by the content and in the light of the entire context.[16]

- The organization/composition of the material in a Gospel is likewise an important indication of the evangelist's theological interests.[17] Through the presentation and arrangement of his work he aims to impart a specific image of Jesus, as occurs, for example, through the gradual revelation of the nature of Jesus in the Gospel of Mark.[18] And so verses that are closely linked to the overall structure of the Gospel make us suspect that the editor has been at work.

- Each Gospel also has material high points. One can infer editorial interest on the part of the evangelist when themes that are important to him show up in individual passages, for example, the theory of the messianic secret in Mark, the theme of righteousness in Matthew, the kindness and humanity of Jesus in Luke. Such texts do not necessarily have to have been first shaped by the hand of the evangelist. Still, their frequency points to his interest in the subject.

- It is relatively easy to maintain the redaction-critical method when it concerns texts of which the one is a revision of the other, as can be shown by means of literary criticism. In such a case one must clearly define how the editor revised his material.[19]

- Texts that stand in a certain tension to the main lines of a work can be distinguished from the product of editing: they consist of traditional material.[20]

---

[16]On preference words see above §8. One has to agree with Dschulnigg, *Sprache*, 293–94, that in view of the thoroughgoing linguistic unity of, say, Mark's Gospel, purely linguistic observations are insufficient to infer redaction. Linguistic observations have to be supplemented by thematic-semantic ones. However, given an accumulation of linguistic and semantic peculiarities we must conclude that editing has occurred. On the problem of word counts see Friedrich, "Wortstatistik," 29–42.

[17]Strecker, Schnelle, *Einführung*, 111; Zimmermann, *Methodenlehre*, 225.

[18]On the messianic secret as a central theme of Mark's Gospel, cf. Egger, *Lehre*, 85–91 (see §11, n. 26).

[19]Thus the Synoptic Gospels are especially suitable for beginners in redaction historical analysis. With regard to the Two Source Theory, however, one must bear in mind that in some cases even in Matthew or Luke we have material that is older, from the standpoint of the history of tradition, than in their literary source, Mark.

[20]To be sure, these traditions, as Frankemölle rightly stresses in *Handlungsanweisungen*, 66, must not be removed from the editor's responsibility. His interest in the selection of the traditions at his disposal and in the decision to adopt certain traditions must be fully taken into account.

2.2 INFERENCES ABOUT THE ADDRESSEES

The author/editor is influenced by his communities, just as he himself wishes to influence them.[21] Of course, we know these communities only through the New Testament texts themselves. The communities, therefore, have only a mediated existence for the reader, as "interpreted and textual communities."[22]

To begin with, semantic analysis also permits us to draw conclusions about the situation of a community. If the editor says certain things with emphasis (key points of content), that must have something to do with the situation. To be sure, a great deal remains obscure on this matter.

Further clues about the addressees can be obtained with the help of pragmatic analysis. From the guidance which the author intends to give the reader we can make some inferences about the situation of the community. Of course, the situation is not simply the opposite image mirrored by the author's admonitions and statements.[23] The admonition to be faithful might serve, for example, to strengthen a community already striving for fidelity, or it could be a genuine warning to a neglectful community.

Other hints can be obtained from the content of a work, for instance, when certain problems are mentioned, say concerning relations between Jews and Christians, church discipline, etc.

In reconstructing the situation of the addressees, the Gospels, Acts, and the Epistles cannot be used in the same way, because it makes a difference whether an author wishes to hand down texts in order to keep alive the memory of Jesus or early church history, lest such "traditions" be lost, or whether the author wants to have a concrete influence on the behavior of a community. Thus the letters of Paul disclose a more concrete picture of the community than do the Gospels. Granted, the evangelists were also influenced by the situations in their communities, but those situations are not clearly embodied in the text. Because of this, the "communities of the Synoptics" cannot be defined as securely as Paul's communities. John, in contrast to the Synoptics, makes a few concrete references to the situation of his audience. According to John 9:22; 16:2 the disciples are under the threat of being excluded from the synagogue because they profess faith in Jesus. This allows us to infer a specific development in relations between Jews and Christians, which places the scene in A.D. 80–90.[24]

---

[21] In particular, Berger, *Exegese*, 202, views redaction history from the standpoint of the innovation striven for by the text.

[22] Frankemölle, *Handlungsanweisungen*, 67.

[23] See above all Berger, "Methode."

[24] Wengst, *Bedrängte*.

2.3 INFERENCES ABOUT THE PLACE AND TIME OF COMPOSITION

Even when they treat an earlier time, texts mirror the problems of the time in which the author is living. Hence, we can use texts to draw inferences not only as to the time they report about, but also about the time when the texts were composed.

The following problems are extremely important for the New Testament texts: (a) the destruction of Jerusalem; (b) the passage of the Christian message from the Jewish to the pagan world; (c) the development of church discipline; (d) the delay of the Parousia; and (e) (related to the history of the texts themselves) the question of literary dependency, among the Synoptics, for instance, or in the relation between 1 and 2 Thessalonians[25] or between Colossians and Ephesians.[26]

References to the historical circumstances mentioned above allow us to draw some inferences about the dating of the Scriptures:[27]

- When the destruction of Jerusalem is described in detail, the text was written after A.D. 70.

- When New Testament scriptures describe the church's turn to the Gentiles as a matter of course, this presupposes that the mission to the gentiles is already fully under way.

- From the presentation of the relation between Judaism and the Christian community (exclusion of Christians from the synagogue in John;[28] polemics against the Jews in Matthew) we can draw inferences about the time and place of editing.

In order to draw the correct conclusions, we have to review the extrabiblical information about the Jewish world. In addition, our study has to include some notion of the course of earliest church history. Beyond that we must draw upon the oldest evidence concerning the place and time of the composition of the Gospels.

[25] Cf Trilling, *Untersuchungen.*
[26] Cf. Schnackenburg, *Ephesians,* 26–30.
[27] On the dating: Wegner, *Symposion.*
[28] Wengst, *Bedrängte.*

SUMMARY AND WORKING SUGGESTIONS

Since the redaction-critical method has to draw conclusions from observations about the text, the working suggestions will indicate which observations, above and beyond literary criticism, are especially important for redaction-historical analysis and how conclusions can be drawn from these observations. To begin with, lists of peculiar linguistic and thematic features, as found in handbooks and introductions to the New Testament, will prove helpful.*

Analysis turns out to involve the following tasks:
With regard to editing:

*   Are there elements in this text that are typical of the vocabulary and characteristic language of the author in question?
*   How does the pericope fit into the overall context of the work and into the pragmatic intention of the work as a whole?

With regard to the author:

*   Are there direct references to the author?

With regard to the addressees and to the time and place of composition:

*   Gather direct references to the addressees.
*   Describe the intended effect of the work and draw conclusions about the situation of the community.
*   What attitude does the work betray toward the problems of Jews and Christians? Church discipline? The delay of the Parousia?
*   What conclusions can be drawn from this for the question of the time of composition?
*   List the community's problems spoken of in the text, and draw inferences as to the situation of the community for which the author is writing.
*   What data are provided by the oldest witnesses (Papias, Irenaeus, the anti-Marcionite prologues)? Can these statements be confirmed by the New Testament work in question?

---

* The following presentation is based on discussions in Egger, *Lehre*, 91–111. In particular, methodological specifications have been undertaken. For further literature cf. the commentaries.

3. EXAMPLE: MARK 3:7–12:
THE HIDDENNESS OF JESUS

The pericope Mark 3:7–12 belongs to the so-called summary reports.[29] This text plays an important role in the structure and arrangement of Mark's Gospel. In several proposed classifications, the text is seen as an introduction to a major section of Mark[30] or as the conclusion to a major section.[31] In judging to what extent the text can be traced back to tradition or the editorial process, opinions differ, ranging from the view that the whole text is a tradition taken over by Mark to the view that the text is a pure editorial construction.[32] The analysis of tradition criticism and redaction criticism is based on observations about the linguistic-syntactic, semantic, and pragmatic structure, as well as textual genre.

3.1 LINGUISTIC-SYNTACTIC CHARACTER

The text displays a series of linguistic features typical of Mark. This is especially true of the explanatory clause, belatedly appended in v. 10a, and the clauses put together with the particles ἵνα, ἵνα μή, γάρ, ὥστε.[33] If we are to understand the text, it is important to note that ἐθεράπευσεν in v. 10 is added only as an explanation.

3.2 SEMANTIC STRUCTURE

The theme of the summary report has, it is true, often been declared to be the "Great Throng of People and the Cures," "A Multitude at the Seaside" (RSV)[34] or some such heading, but careful analysis shows that the theme is the hiddenness of Jesus.[35] There is no narrative of

---

[29]On the genre of "conflated account" see above §11.

[30]According to Schweizer, *Mark*, on this passage, Mark 3:7–12 is the introduction of the section Mark 3:7–6:61; likewise according to de la Potterie, "Compositione"; according to Pesch, *Markus*, on this passage, the section introduces Mark 3:7–6:29.

[31]Thus in Gnilka, *Markusevangelium*, on this passage.

[32]Pesch, *Markus* I, 201, takes the text to be a (secondary, of course) formation derived from tradition, which has been shaped on the basis of already existent miracle stories; Keck, "Mark 3:7–12," takes verses 3:7, 8a, 9–10 to be traditional, with the rest traceable back to editing; Egger, *Lehre*, 100–101 takes the text to be purely a product of editing.

[33]On the linguistic peculiarities see Gnilka, *Markusevangelium*, on this passage. He takes the text, even from the linguistic standpoint, to be Mark's; Pesch, *Markus*, thinks that essential parts of the vocabulary point to pre-Markan tradition. Pesch bases his case on word counts, which show that the words in question also appear in pieces from tradition.

[34]Gnilka, *Markusevangelium*, on this passage; Pesch, *Markus*, on this passage: the rush to Jesus the healer and exorcist.

[35]Egger, *Lehre*, 93–95.

exorcism; Jesus simply bids the demons to be silent. The cures are mentioned in a subordinate clause explaining the need to prepare a boat. Getting the boat ready denotes a certain distance between Jesus and the crowd. The exact theme of the text is the press of the people and Jesus' withdrawal/command of silence. Thus, stylistic and thematic data yield the following structure of the text:

I. (vv. 7–8)

    (A) Jesus withdraws
    (B) the crowd follows

II. (vv. 9–12 in chiastic structure)

    (A) Jesus seeks distance, has a boat prepared
    (B) because of the press of the people who wish to touch him
    (B) because of the cry of the spirits
    (A) Jesus gives the command to be silent.

On the issue of tradition or redaction, these observations on the theme of the text show a close link between this text and the theme of the hiddenness of Jesus, along with the characteristically Markan idea of the messianic secret. This text too gives expression to the dialectic of revelation and concealment, a fact that speaks for its editorial character.[36]

3.3 FUNCTION OF THE TEXT AND PRAGMATIC PURPOSE

The summary report clearly has a narrative function in the Gospel as a whole. The text is in many respects a summary of the foregoing, picking up many motifs from the preceding narrative: cures in Mark 1:23ff., 34; confession formulas in Mark 1:24, 34; withdrawal of Jesus in 1:38, 45. At the same time the pericope is also a summarizing preview of what follows. There is an especially close connection with Mark 5:1–20 and 5:21–34. This linking of a short text with the surrounding context points to the editorial formation of the text. As narrative, this section also pursues further the line of revelation history which Mark promotes especially in the theory of the messianic secret: the hardening of the Pharisees and the incomprehension of the crowd are contrasted with the initiation of the disciples into the mystery of Jesus.[37]

---

[36]Because of these observations the text cannot automatically be viewed as a generalizing introduction to a tradition miracle cycle.

[37]For details see Egger, *Lehre,* 109–10.

From a pragmatic standpoint, this text corresponds to the pragmatic intention which Mark pursues through his entire work. He wants to lead the reader to understand the nature of Jesus as the Messiah and the Son of God.[38] And so in this respect, the text also answers to Mark's editorial interests.

3.4 THE GENESIS OF THE TEXT

The vocabulary used in this section unmistakably shows the text to be a generalization of individual stories. Word counts point up the connection between this text and the story of the healing of the woman with the hemorrhage (Mark 5:21, 24–34): Both passages use words that do not otherwise occur in the Gospels, or only once: θλίβω, συνθλίβω, μάστιξ, ἐπιπίπτειν.[39] Only in Mark 3:10 and 5:28 do people touch Jesus, otherwise it is always Jesus who touches them. And so we have sufficient explanation that the summary report generalizes an individual story. The same holds true for Mark 5:1–20. The vocabulary largely agrees: πνεύματα ἀκάθαρτα (Mark 3:11; 5:2), κράζειν (Mark 3:11; 5:5, 7), προσπίπτειν, προσκυνεῖν, (3:11; 5:6), υἱὸς θεοῦ (3:11; 5:7). But the particular stories are not generalized in such a way that the themes of those stories are extended to a summary of cures and exorcisms, but to a summary on the hiddenness of Jesus. Mark organizes and interrelates the individual motifs by joining them together in a manner that gives rise to the tension between "revelation and hiddenness." The idea of revelation is advanced by the motifs of the gathering of the people and the cry of the demons. The idea of hiddenness is advanced in particular by the motifs of the boat and the command to silence. And this summary corresponds linguistically-syntactically, semantically, and pragmatically to the peculiar nature of Mark. Thus we must also assume that it goes back to Mark and not to tradition.

The syntactic, semantic, and pragmatic structures that have been defined thus suggest the idea that Mark 3:7–12 is an editorial formation by Mark.

---

[38]Cf. the arc of tension between 1:1 and 8:27–29 and 15:39, which are central passages from a narrative standpoint too.

[39]Frequency: θλίβω: Matthew once, Mark once, Luke never, John never; συνθλίβω: only in Mark 5:24, 31; μάστιξ: Matthew never; in Mark only here and Mark 5:29, 34, Luke once, John never, Acts once; ἐπιπίπτειν: Matthew nine times, Mark eleven times, Luke thirteen times, John once, Acts once.

Part 5 ▨

Reading Historically

IN READING TEXTS HISTORICALLY THE POINT AT ISSUE IS THE ANCHOR-
ing of textual statements in history. The relation between the text
and the event expressed in it has to be clarified. This relationship
of text and event, along with the question of the ties between the
Old Testament and the New Testament, and between the Word of
God and human existence, is one of the central problems of biblical
hermeneutics.[1] The point we are addressing is the process of turning
events into speech (and writing) and the interpretations developed
in the course of this.[2] Historical inquiry is characterized by the
conviction that history and historical events are relevant to faith.[3]

---

[1]Ricoeur, "Préface à Bultmann," in *Conflict,* 381–401, esp. 386–88.
[2]Schnackenburg, "Geschichtliche."
[3]Cf. above all Käsemann, "Problem"; also in idem, *Essays,* 15–47, which posed
anew the question that had been repressed by kerygma theology.

§15
Inquiring into History

THE MERE FACT THAT AN EVENT OR A SAYING HAS BEEN HANDED DOWN does not allow us to conclude that this event actually happened or that the saying came from the person into whose mouth it has been placed. From this suspicion, to which all narratives and traditions are subject, the New Testament scriptures are not exempt. The question to what extent we can sketch a historically appropriate picture of events with the help of the New Testament texts is what the inquiry into historical events seeks to answer.

> The inquiry into historical events asks of the New Testament texts (that are primarily meant to be testimonials to faith) what really happened in the events reported in it.

In New Testament exegesis our inquiry must reckon with the peculiar nature of the New Testament scriptures as testimonials to faith. These texts were not composed as records and are not primarily interested in history. These scriptures are concerned with proclaiming Jesus Christ; indeed, they want to bring the reader to faith. So the picture of Jesus is likewise presented in the light of the Easter faith. Given this character, the New Testament texts do not provide all the information a historian would like. Still, a historically validated picture of Jesus and of the history of the early church *can* be outlined.

What actually happened? is a question that was foreign to the tradition-bearers and writers of the first age.[1] The inquiry into the historical facts has, it is true, evolved particularly in the quest for the the historical Jesus and the *ipsissima verba* and *facta* of Jesus, but it affects all the phenomena of primitive Christianity.

INTRODUCTORY LITERATURE: KÄSEMANN, "Problem," laid the foundation for a new search for the historical Jesus, and summarized that search ten years later in "Alleys." POLKOW, "Method," discusses the criteria that have been

---

[1]On the emergence of the historical question, cf. Kümmel, *Neue Testament;* idem, *Jahre.* On the use of criteria, cf. Lambiasi, *L'autenticità,* 21–134.

used by scholars to establish authentic Jesus materials. KERTELGE, *Rückfrage;* PERRIN, *Search.* The articles collected in this volume, especially those by LENTZEN-DEIS and MUßNER, familiarize the reader with the most important methodological problems.[2]

Historical inquiry differs from the approaches of literary criticism, traditions criticism, and redaction criticism in that the focus is no longer on the development of the text, but on its relation to historical reality. The student now asks, "How do we manage, in a methodologically correct way, to leap from the text back into history?"[3]

1. THE MODEL OF THE TEXT IN THE INQUIRY INTO THE HISTORICAL FACTS

The inquiry into the historical facts reads the New Testament texts not as testimonials to faith but as sources. Scientific history considers sources to be "texts, objects, or facts from which knowledge of the past can be gained."[4] We must distinguish between remains, i.e., "all the source material that has been left over in an immediate sense—in other words, without the intervention of an intermediary reporting for the purpose of historical knowledge" (tools, buildings, institutions) and traditions, i.e., "everything that has been left over from the events, reviewed and interpreted by human understanding."[5] Remains show no connection between the things that have been left over; on the other hand, they are not burdened by the biases of representation. Traditions offer events in a context, but selectively and evaluated.[6]

2. THE CONDUCT OF INQUIRY

The factuality of the material reported can be demonstrated neither through source criticism alone nor through genre and redaction criticism alone. All these methods help to grasp the peculiar nature of the texts, but in each case they get only to the text, not to the event.[7]

---

[2]From the extensive literature we may cite studies that give a bird's eye view of the problems concerning criteria: Kertelge, *Rückfrage;* Lentzen-Deis, "Kriterien"; Mußner, "Methodologie"; Dupont, *Jésus;* Lambiasi, *L'autenticità;* Latourelle, *Gesù.*

[3]Mußner, "Methodologie," 122.

[4]Kirn, quoted in von Brandt, *Werkzeug,* 58.

[5]Von Brandt, *Werkzeug,* 66, 71.

[6]Ibid., 67, 72–73.

[7]Although a particular method was developed for inquiry concerning Jesus, this method has not yet gained admission to the books on methodology. This is an autonomous method, as Hahn stresses in "Jesus," esp. 27 with reference to Dibelius, *ThR,* 214: Thus we have "entered a field that lies outside the work of form criticism."

> To establish the historicity of events, texts have to be read in the light of certain criteria to see how much historically reliable information they contain.

Along with the religious nature of New Testament texts, we have to consider the fact that they are ancient texts in which many temporal and environmental factors are at work.[8]

Scholars have elaborated a series of criteria that can be enlisted for examining the historical reliability of texts. Of course, the use of a single criterion is hardly sufficient; only a summary view of the various criteria allows us to make a fairly sure judgment. These criteria are:

- The criterion of the age of the sources

"Whenever possible, one should take one's starting point from old, safe sources."[9] Thus the oldest sources, ascertained by literary criticism and form and genre criticism, are as a rule historically more reliable than later texts produced by editors. Texts that from their linguistic form suggest a Palestinian origin bring us closer to the *ipsissimum verbum Jesu*.[10]

- The criterion of multiple attestation

This criterion is recognized in historical research and in many other fields (criminology, for example). It holds that events actually occurred and that sayings go back to Jesus when there is multiple attestation for them, that is, when they are attested in several mutually independent sources, such as Mark, the sayings sources, Paul, etc.[11] On the other hand, the independence of the sources in the New Testament presents a problem (Synoptic questions, the relation of John to the Synoptics). Multiple attestation is also present when a theme is attested in different genres, i.e., in accounts of miracles, parables, logia. This criterion is based on the consideration that facts or words that are reported by several independent sources or have found expression in several genres can hardly be completely invented. This criterion is especially important for determining the ways Jesus acted, and for narratives.[12] "By itself practically no narrative about Jesus can be defended as historical. One has to refer to the logia tradition. . . ."[13] An example of the

---

[8]Lentzen-Deis, "Kriterien," 95.

[9]Ibid., 94.

[10]Lambiasi, *L'autenticità*, 175; cf. in particular the studies of Jeremias, such as *Theology NT.*

[11]Latourelle, *Gesù*, 249–52; Lambiasi, *L'autenticità*, 141–53.

[12]Mußner, "Methodologie," 135.

[13]Lentzen-Deis, "Kriterien," 101.

application of this criterion is inferring that the theme of God's love for sinners was an object of Jesus' preaching and activity.[14] This motif is attested in a parable (the Prodigal Son, Luke 15:11–31), in a dispute (Matt 21:28–31: "The harlots and tax collectors go into the kingdom of God before you"), in the account of a miracle (Mark 2:1–2), in the story of a calling (Mark 2:13–17). Since this theme is attested in various genres and various ancient sources as well, it should probably be viewed as an authentic part of Jesus' kerygma.

- • The criterion of no analogy[15]

A deed or saying of Jesus is authentic when it can not be traced back either to ideas otherwise current in the Jewish world or to the first Christian community.[16] This criterion is based on the reflection that the community is inclined to place in Jesus' mouth words that correspond to its own interests. The criterion of no analogy (no discoverable reason) is therefore based on proving the difference between Jesus' words and behavior and the sayings/behavior of contemporary Judaism and the first Christian community. The disadvantage of this criterion is that by using it one can gather only a minimal amount of data. One example of the use of this criterion is proof of the unique authority of Jesus as expressed in these words, "But I say to you,"[17] and in the calling of the disciples.[18]

- • The criterion of continuity and coherence[19]

Under certain conditions, we can take as our point of departure the Jesus material, as determined by the criteria of multiple attestation and no analogy, and argue from it to further authentic Jesus material. This is possible because when words or deeds of Jesus are closely tied with authentic material (defined as such on the basis of these criteria and of literary-critical, genre-critical, or other connections), then they can also be looked upon as authentic. This is also the context in which we must consider Jesus' environment. Jesus' environment influences his words and works. In some matters his activity coincides with what was usual then; in other areas his work and behavior were new. The findings of archaeology, Jewish studies, and so forth help us grasp the picture more precisely.

---

[14]On the following material see Lambiasi, *L'autenticità,* 145 (with reference to H. K. McArthur; W. Trilling).

[15]Lentzen-Deis, "Kriterien," 97–99; Lambiasi, *L'autenticità,* 155–164.

[16]Latourelle, *Gesù,* 252.

[17]See above n. 3.

[18]See below.

[19]Lentzen-Deis, "Kriterien," 100; Lambiasi, *L'autenticità,* 164–73.

• The criterion of the sufficient reason

A fact or circumstance should be viewed as historical when, unless we assume it as factual, another series of circumstances cannot be explained.[20]

The general rule is that the criteria of historicity can be employed to sketch a certain broad framework and something like an overall picture of the historical Jesus.[21] In some cases proof cannot be established by means of these criteria. In such cases non-provability need not be equated with non-factuality. The path from the text to the event presupposes a vast knowledge of Jesus' environment.

SUMMARY OF THE WORKING STEPS AND POINTERS

Inquiry into the historical facts is always based on consideration of several texts. Thus, the first step in the inquiry is the gathering of texts that have to do with the same fact, the same behavior, or a similar saying. The solution of these problems, however, is possible only after grappling with the relevant secondary literature.

1. Age of the Sources

First we have to determine (with the help of redaction criticism, literary criticism, and genre criticism) which text dealing with a given theme is the oldest.

2. Multiple Attestation

In which mutually independent sources is the deed/saying attested? In which textual genres is the behavior in question or a similar pronouncement attested?

3. Non-analogousness

What position is taken by parallel texts from the Jewish environment or from the Christian communities to the deed or saying to be studied?

4. Continuity and Coherence

How does a saying or deed of Jesus fit into his environment and into the overall framework of his activity?

5. Criterion of the Sufficient Reason

To what extent can the genesis of the text be explained without assuming the historicity of the material recorded?

---

[20]Lambiasi, *L'autenticità*, 191–94.
[21]Cf. the works on Jesus of Nazareth and the presentations of New Testament theology.

3. EXAMPLE: THE MOTIF OF FOLLOWING

Use of the criteria of historicity shows that the saying "Follow me," which Jesus used to call certain persons to emulate him, belongs to the authentic Jesus material. In the following pages the criteria of historicity will be applied not to an individual text, but to the motif of "following."[22] The conceptual meaning of the motif has to be worked out by means of a statistical survey, differentiation on the basis of textual genre, and consideration of the themes bound up with "following."

3.1 USE OF THE WORD "FOLLOW" IN THE NEW TESTAMENT

The verb ἀκολουθεῖν is used 90 times in the New Testament; beyond that, ὀπίσω ἔρχεσθαι, to come after, to go behind, is used 35 times in a similar sense. The term appears almost exclusively in the Gospels (4 times in Acts, once in 1 Cor, 6 times in Rev); in the same way the term "disciples" in 225 of 271 cases is applied to those who follow the earthly Jesus. This usage shows that the New Testament has reserved the word "follow" for describing the earthly activity of Jesus. In addition, the imperative "follow me" is one of the more characteristic features of Jesus' way of speaking.[23] The word can mean physically walking behind a person, but in most cases it is used in the New Testament as a technical term and refers to the disciples' continual accompaniment of Jesus.[24]

3.2 GROUPS OF TEXTS

Two groups of texts in particular deal with following: calling narratives and sayings about following. Calling narratives (Mark 1:16–20; Mark 2:14–15; Mark 10:17–22) tell about a real action and have a stereotypical structure. In the beginning there is a short narrative introduction with key words, "pass by, see, call." Next appears the call to follow, with the words, "Follow me/behind me." Then with the key words "leave behind and follow," the answering (or in Mark 10:22, the non-answering) of the call is narrated.[25] In these narratives the authority of Jesus and the unconditional obedience of those

---

[22]These sorts of problems concerning historicity are dealt with above all by Riesner, *Jesus*, 408–40 (with bibliography); cf. also Egger, *Nachfolge*, 86–89, 98–107. The motif of following is often mentioned as an example of using the criterion of non-analogousness: de la Potterie, "Impostare"; Lambiasi, *L'autenticità*, 221–24.

[23]Schürmann, "Christus."

[24]For details see Egger, "Nachfolge," 216–17.

[25]On the elements of genre relevant here see Lambiasi, *L'autenticità*, 222.

called are clearly stressed. The paraenetic intention of the texts is obvious. A special kind of revision is found in Luke 5:11, where the motif of following is linked with a miracle story,[26] and in John 1:35–51, where the way to following is shown as a way to faith and fellowship with Jesus.[27]

The logia about following (Luke 9:57–62) in each case offer a saying directed at someone willing to follow; here only a narrative introduction is used. The theme of these texts is the radical conditions of following.

3.3. CHARACTERISTIC FEATURES OF "FOLLOWING" AND THE "CIRCLE OF DISCIPLES"

Jesus gathers a circle of disciples around him, whose composition is strikingly non-homogeneous (Galilean fishermen, former tax collectors, erstwhile zealots).[28] The characteristic features of this circle of disciples are the calling of the disciples by Jesus, personal ties to Jesus, service to Jesus, participation in the itinerant life and work of Jesus, and communal living in a circle of disciples.[29]

3.4 USE OF THE CRITERIA OF HISTORICITY

The criteria of multiple attestation and non-analogousness are particularly applicable to the theme of "following" (less so to the individual texts).

The theme of following can be found, as has been mentioned, in several text types: in a calling story (Mark 1:16–20), in the context of a miracle story (Luke 5:11), in the Johannine revision of calling as a way to faith (John 1:35–51), in logia (Luke 9:57–62).

Application of the criteria of non-analogousness is especially effective in this context. The difference between Jesus and the primitive Christian community can be seen in the fact that the word "follow" is used only in the Gospels, that following, therefore, was seen as something typical of the time of Jesus' earthly life. This linguistic usage shows that the primitive Christians already viewed the pre-Easter circle of disciples as a unique, unrepeatable fellowship.[30] Still more significant in the question of calling and the circle of disciples is the difference between Jesus and the Jewish world.[31]

---

[26] Pesch, *Fischfang.*

[27] Hahn, "John 1,35–51," 172–90.

[28] Riesner, *Jesus,* 408–14.

[29] Ibid., 414–19; Egger, "Nachfolge," 219–22.

[30] Riesner, *Jesus,* 421–22; de la Potterie, "Impostare," 457, also calls attention to this difference from early Christianity.

[31] The following differences have been worked out with particular clarity in Riesner, *Jesus,* 415–19.

According to the Synoptic miracle narratives, Jesus takes the initiative, whereas with the rabbis a disciple sought out a teacher for himself. Jesus' disciples and rabbinical disciples are further differentiated by the fact that for disciples of the rabbis introduction to the law was the central interest, and it was considered desirable to acquire knowledge of the law from more than one rabbi. Jesus binds the disciples to himself for a lifelong apprenticeship (cf. Matt 23:8–10). Being a disciple of Jesus—this is one more feature distinguishing it from studying with a rabbi—is marked by homelessness, which was not demanded by the scribes.[32]

Thus, Jesus' call to follow him belongs to the authentic Jesus material. In the texts dealing with it (narratives, logia) the reader's view is directed to the authority of Jesus and the claims he makes.

---

[32]On the particularly "offensive" saying about calling in Matt 8:21–22 see Hengel, *Leader.*

Part 6 🌑

Reading Hermeneutically

NEW TESTAMENT SCHOLARSHIP HAS THE RESPONSIBILITY OF LEADING us to a deeper understanding of the word of God as presented in the historically bound form of the New Testament. Its task is to grasp the theological content of the New Testament and to allow its message to contemporary men and women be heard."[1] In hermeneutical reflection we must clarify what it means to understand the biblical text and to grasp its meaning for today. Just as reflection on one's reading is an important prerequisite for correct reading,[2] so hermeneutical reflection is indispensable for correct understanding.

INTRODUCTORY LITERATURE: PALMER, *Hermeneutics*, discusses the basis of modern hermeneutics in Schleiermacher, Dilthey, Heidegger, and Gadamer. ROBINSON, COBB, *Hermeneutics*, provide essays on hermeneutics in theology particularly in the New Testament. ACHTEMEIER, *Hermeneutic*, discusses the New Hermeneutic as applied to the New Testament. CORETH, *Hermeneutik*, and STUHLMACHER, *Gospel*. Recent textbooks on the New Testament also offer reflections on interpretation and hermeneutics.[3]

The understanding of biblical texts has to reckon with a double peculiarity. The biblical texts come from the distant past. The texts are alien[4] to the reader because of their language, inner logic, and rootedness in a remote historical context. The reader finds herself in a different context of understanding. The conditions of her life are different, and her intellectual attitudes differ from those of the first readers. This temporal and cultural distance can be an obstacle to understanding. At the same time, however, such a distance offers a positive potential since with certain texts only distance in time will reveal their full sense and significance. The subjectivity with which all reading and understanding begin is likewise

---

[1]Zimmermann, *Methodenlehre*, 17.

[2]See §1. Reflection on reading is nothing but special hermeneutics. Reflection on reading now has to be incorporated into the understanding.

[3]Fohrer, *Exegese AT,* 148–71; Strecker, Schnelle, *Einführung,* 122–51 (with a presentation of several hermeneutical outlines). Berger, *Exegese,* 242–69, sees the unity of the various methods in the hermeneutical concept of pragmatic history.

[4]The historical critical method further strengthens this alienness.

at once a help and a hindrance to understanding what is being read. To be sure, we also need to reflect on the prior understanding which every reader brings to a text, since a naive reception of a text makes understanding it more difficult, or actually prevents it from being understood.

The second peculiarity of the text consists in the fact that with Holy Scripture we are dealing with texts that for the Christian reader have normative validity as the "Word of God." Reading the Bible as the "Word of God" presupposes faith in revelation and the readiness to accept this Word as a guideline for the interpretation and shaping of one's own life.

This doubly problematic situation assigns to hermeneutical reading the tasks of exposition and actualization. "Exposition" ascertains the meaning which the text had in its original environment, in other words, what the author wished to say to his contemporary audience.

"Actualization" presents the meaning which the text has as a text of the past and as the Word of God in today's concrete social, ecclesiastical, and personal setting. This sort of "bringing the message home" can take place in many ways, but it is also governed by certain criteria, and these criteria can be the object of scholarly methodical reflection.

"Mediation" is the presentation of the meaning of the text and/or its claims in preaching, catechesis, reading aloud, etc. Specific forms of mediation are not the focus of this methodology.

§16
Interpretation of Texts

THE INTERPRETATION OF A TEXT[1] AIMS TO ASCERTAIN THE MEANING which the text had in its original situation.

1. A COMMUNICATIONS THEORY MODEL OF INTERPRETATION

Alongside the manifold viewpoints of hermeneutical efforts, interpretation can also be handled within the framework of a communications theory approach. The interpreter, who through her work becomes a witness to a communication event from distant time, is a reader who reflects on the text and its rootedness in the process of communication, and imparts her understanding of all this to today's men and women.

1.1 INTERPRETATION AND A VIEW OF THE "SUBJECT MATTER"

It is essential for interpretation that the text's subject matter should come into view. To begin with, understanding takes its point of departure from the statements of the text and strives "to understand—as far as possible—the statements of the text in precisely the same way in which the hearer or reader back then must have understood them."[2] But that, of course, does not mean that interpretation is finished.

An appropriate understanding of a text is arrived at only when the interpreter has caught sight of the "subject matter" which the author and his first audience had been concerned with.

---

[1]Fohrer, *Exegese AT,* 148–56; Mußner, *Hermeneutik;* Stuhlmacher, *Verstehen;* idem, *Methoden,* 11–55.
[2]Fohrer, *Exegese AT,* 150.

I can understand a person speaking to me only if I look at what she is saying to me, if I let her show me the subject matter and "examine her vision and interpretation, personally looking at it."[3] This is because understanding does not mean duplicating what the author said at one time, but understanding the subject matter itself.[4] It would be inadequate to listen only to the word of the author since the "subject matter" might have more meaning than the author succeeded in presenting, including a more enduring meaning. In this sense interpretation reconstructs what had been an only partially successful communication event.[5] Thus, under certain circumstances one can understand a train of thought better than the author could have,[6] or one could also grasp the surplus meaning (in Jesus' activity, say) which could not find expression in the texts.[7] From the perspective of the subject matter, it might also be possible to distance oneself from the viewpoint peculiar to the author and to attempt a new, up-to-date, and concrete interpretation of the subject matter itself, though naturally always measuring oneself against the writer who made possible the first view of the subject.[8]

Certain basic structures are typical of this subject-oriented understanding.[9] In keeping with the "horizon structure," the content of any one part must be comprehended only in the totality of a meaningful context. The individual section acquires its meaning from the whole, and the whole from the individual section. Individual statements and texts in the Bible must therefore be understood in a larger context of meaning, and individual pericopes have to be read in the light of the text as a whole. Because of its circular structure, understanding is a spiral-shaped, forward-moving process that starts out from a prior understanding, but has to open up to the subject matter itself and evolve into an understanding of it.

Thus, understanding of the biblical texts can succeed only if the reader is open to new insights. The dialectical structure of understanding means that while understanding is possible only if one looks at the subject matter, there is no subject matter without linguistic mediation. The upshot of this for dealing with biblical texts is that in the final analysis the issue is not "understanding the text" but "understanding the subject matter by means of biblical

---

[3]Coreth, *Hermeneutik*, 64.
[4]Ibid., 67.
[5]Niederwimmer, "Unmittelbarkeit."
[6]Betti, *Allgemeine*, 601; Coreth, *Hermeneutik*, 135–36.
[7]Schnackenburg, "Geschichtliche."
[8]Coreth, *Hermeneutik*, 132–33.
[9]The following hermeneutical reflections follow ibid., 115–18, almost verbatim. The applications for work on the biblical texts have been added.

texts." Interpretation in this sense will then approximate a theology of the Bible.[10]

"Short cuts" to understanding as a way to the "subject matter" are possible within the church as a fellowship of tradition and understanding.

1.2 INTERPRETATION AS OBJECTIFICATION AND COMMUNICATING THE UNDERSTANDING OF THE TEXT

In interpretation, work on the text as a historical document in a sense comes to fulfillment.

Interpretation is understood as objectification of the understanding of the text that has been arrived at through analysis. This objectification, however, is open to new understanding.

In analysis many paths were paved through the text. In interpretation the results of taking these paths are gathered. Hence interpretation is a summary of the insights into the text which the interpreter was capable of at a given point in time. The shortest form of interpretation is preparation of a good translation.[11] In the step that is usually labeled "interpretation" the findings are brought together in a coherent presentation. What is needed here is a "concise presentation of [the text's] ideas, their arrangement and sequence."[12]

The interpreter, who has become a witness to a communication event from the distant past, then becomes the mediator for the readers of today by presenting to them what happened then, what the "matter" was, what "message" the author sent through the text to the addressees, and to what kind of thinking and acting the author wished to lead them.[13]

Interpreting means presenting the meaning available in a communication event from the past as a meaning available to men and women of our time.

---

[10]Strecker, *Problem.*

[11]As such, translation is possible only as the conclusion of scholarly work on the texts. However, since familiarity with translation problems is necessary at the very beginning of scholarly work, the problems in this area have already been treated in §7.

[12]Fohrer, *Exegese AT,* 158.

[13]In particular these are the findings of linguistic-syntactic, semantic, pragmatic, and genre-critical analysis, as well as of the reconstruction of the genesis of the text.

"Interpretation is not an end in itself, but is aimed at addressees—readers or listeners—and therefore it is dependent on the circumstances among which it takes place."[14]

2. EXECUTING INTERPRETATION

Interpretation of the text presupposes analysis of the text and tries to offer the reader help in understanding the text.

> The methodical problem of interpretation consists of shaping the interpretation in a way suitable to the text and to the audience.

Interpretation can be done in different ways. In order to make the text comprehensible to today's reader, the interpreter must first present its content, formal peculiarities, narrative and argumentative modes, and intended effect. But since today's readers no longer possess the information which the first readers had at their disposal (knowledge of the social environment, etc.), the interpreter must also introduce knowledge of things which the text takes for granted, but with which not everyone is now familiar. Just how much supplementary information on these matters will be needed depends upon the presuppositions which the intended reader brings to the interpretation. Since we are talking about events and occurrences from the past, narration is an appropriate form of interpretation.

Interpretation encompasses both the comprehensive exegesis of biblical texts as well as exegesis of individual passages, which consists of the explanation of important theological terms in the text and in the clarification of factual questions.[15]

The form in which the results of analysis are coordinated and the interpretation of a text presented is manifold: continuous commentary,[16] surveys of biblical theology, scholarly monographs, guides to understanding the text (e.g., for the exegetical preparation of sermons).

Since the interpretation of biblical texts seeks to make the text of the Bible understandable to men and women of today as the Word of God, still more paths of interpretation must be taken, apart from the more theoretical approach based on analysis of the text.

---

[14]Schlingmann, *Methoden,* 9.
[15]Fohrer, *Exegese AT,* 149–51.
[16]Lohfink, "Kommentar"; Panier, "Commentaire"; idem, "Kommentar."

§17
Actualization of Texts

DEALING WITH HOLY SCRIPTURES CONCLUDES ONLY WHEN WE HAVE attained an existential understanding of Scripture, that is, when Scripture has become the "Word of God" and the "source of spiritual life."[1] The text is then no longer read with that distance peculiar to historical reading, but as an "up-to-date" text that makes its claim on readers by giving them orientation, direction, and impulses for our time, and helps them to interpret and cope with their own lives and the tasks of our time. In encountering the text the interpreter should experience "(1) who he or she is in confrontation with the texts, and (2) who he and she could be in confrontation with them."[2]

An "actualizing" reading seeks orientation in constructing life and impetus in coping with it in the biblical text. The biblical text which comes from the past is heard by a reader who is moved by the questions of our time and who seeks in the Bible an answer to the questions of life and direction for conduct.

The actualizing of Scripture takes place in many ways: in preaching, instruction, personal reading of the Bible. Scholarly exegesis hardly reflects the meaning of a text for the present day. "On the strength of its systematic principles [scholarly exegesis] first of all distances the texts from the present, and hitherto has not felt any responsibility to take or rather to prepare the next step, the new actualization of the texts."[3] This de facto renunciation[4] of an opportunity of course runs counter to the widespread effort to read a biblical text "simply," without the instruments of scholarly exegesis,

---

[1] Second Vatican Council, Dogmatic Constitution "Dei Verbum," n. 21.
[2] Luz, *Matthew*, 96.
[3] Barth, Schramm, *Bibel*, 9. Similarly, Luz, *Matthew*, 96: "For manifold reasons, historical-critical interpretation until recently has fulfilled the second aspect of its double task only insufficiently (meaning, to make the interpreter conscious of her own prior understanding and to teach her something about herself)."
[4] There are, however, some works that offer longer or shorter indications of the meaning of a text for one's life, e.g., Kremer, *Österevangelien;* idem, *Lazarus.*

and to apply it to life.[5] It is above all in practical work on the Bible that one today hears demands for the actualization of Scripture. Only when the gap between academic analysis of Scripture and everyday problems—that is, between the scholar's carrel and the existential struggle in the streets—has been overcome, will the study of sacred Scripture have reached its goal.[6]

INTRODUCTORY LITERATURE: WINK, *Bible Study*, and idem, *Transformation*, provides guides for contemporary appropriation of biblical texts. Aids to practical Bible work offer, along with instructions, all sorts of reflections on the relation of the biblical text to life. On the connection between exegesis and existential appropriation, see above all BARTH, SCHRAMM, *Bibel*.[7]

For Christians, who acknowledge the biblical text as the normative Word of God, there is no dispensing with a continuation of scholarly work in the direction of a "translation" of the declarations of faith and their implicit claims into the variable speech and mental world of our time.[8]

1. MODELS OF READING AND UNDERSTANDING FOR ACTUALIZING READING OF SCRIPTURE

If the biblical text is to become the source of guidance for existence and action for our time, it will require not only knowledge of the biblical texts, but also reflection on today's men and women, i.e., an awareness of the hermeneutical situation.[9]

> The text can help construe and shape today's changed world situation only if the new experiences of the world, society, and the church (as documented by, among other things, current levels of knowledge in the natural sciences, psychology, and sociology) are worked into the process of understanding.

---

[5]Cf. Kremer, *Buch*.

[6]Wink, *Bible Study*, 17–18; cf. also Barth, Schramm, *Bibel*, 14–18.

[7]Barth, Schramm, *Bibel*; Wink, *Bibelauslegung*; idem, *Bible Study*. The practical step of actualization is discussed in more recent books on methodology using different terms: Fohrer, *Exegese AT*, 156–71: "theological criticism"; Berger, *Exegese*, 242–68: "hermeneutics of pragmatic history"; Strecker, Schnelle, *Einführung*, 121–51: "hermeneutics." In practical Bible work this step is especially important, and so in books on methodology there is a great deal of reflection about the nature of this particular step.

[8]Cf. Strecker, Schnelle, *Einführung*, 123 and 150; Barth, Schramm, *Bibel*, 48.

[9]Gadamer, *Problema*, 82.

To understand Scripture, therefore, a "dialogic structure" is essential.[10] Text and exegete become partners in dialogue, although partners of a quite special kind since the supremacy of scriptural authority must be preserved.[11] Certain rules are in effect for this dialogue. The text demands to be taken seriously as a text that has a message to communicate; that may be a text from the past but it is a message that aims to address the world of today. Every actualization finds its justification in this, and so begins by listening to the text, in order to hear it, and in it, ultimately, the "Word of God" concerning our life. According to the doctrine of inspiration, rightly understood, in the final analysis God himself addresses the reader through the text, in order to impart his Word to the reader. The "Word of God" in the full sense, then, is not the text by itself, but God's message that speaks through it even today.[12]

The following models of actualizing reading admittedly derive from practical Bible work, but they can stand up to hermeneutical scrutiny.[13] In these models, actualization is essentially understood as amplification of the text: The reader expands her understanding of the text by enriching it with new elements. Actualization, therefore, consists in reading biblical text in a new context, which can also be made up of connections which the text did not and could not have had at the time it came into being. In individual cases such "amplification" can be carried out in different ways.

1.1 CONSIDERATION OF A LIVING CHURCH TRADITION

The first kind of amplification is typical of the Catholic and Orthodox understanding of Scripture, but it also applies to practical reading in many Protestant churches.[14]

For Catholic reading the constitutive factor is consideration of a biblical and an extrabiblical context.

> Biblical texts are rooted in a process of churchly reception and transmission.

The Constitution on Revelation "Dei Verbum" of the Second Vatican Council, n. 12, summarizes the pertinent notion here: "Since

---

[10]Coreth, *Hermeneutik*, 101–2, 116–17.
[11]Cf. the critical remarks of Berger in *Exegese*, 243 and 251.
[12]Kremer, *Buch*, 361.
[13]On hermeneutics cf. above all Gadamer, *Truth;* idem, *Problema;* Betti, *Allgemeine;* Coreth, *Hermeneutik*.
[14]Kremer, *Buch*, 51.

Sacred Scripture must be read and interpreted in the spirit in which it was written; proper investigation of the sense of the holy texts requires that we pay no less careful attention to the content and the unity of all the Scriptures with an eye to the living tradition of the whole Church and to the analogy of the model of a hermeneutics based on pragmatic history, according to which tradition actually first makes understanding possible."[15] The model corresponds above all to church tradition, which presents us with the Bible as the "Word of God," which can be read and understood correctly only in the light of the Holy Spirit. In particular this means:

- the individual text is read in the context of the whole of Scripture

- texts are read with a view to other faith statements and the living tradition of the entire church (the so-called *analogia fidei*), with creeds, liturgical texts, and church decisions taken as points of orientation even for personal reading and scholarly exegesis

- texts are read in the context of the liturgy

- texts are read in the light of the life history and life experience of a person, a community, the church as well as in the light of the pragmatic history of the text.

Medieval theologians summarized their procedure of the fourfold sense of Scripture, oriented to this conception, in a mnemonic verse:

> Littera gesta docet, quod credas allegoria,
> moralis quid agas, quo tendas, anagogia.

> The letter/literal sense teaches the facts,
> "allegory" what you should believe,
> the moral sense, what you should do,
> "anagogy" (edification), whither you should strive.

This procedure too is an amplification inasmuch as it places a biblical text in a multiple context: the context of faith, life, and life experience, as well as hope.[16] True enough, some proponents of this mode of interpretation have discredited it by splitting hairs; but as seen in its best representatives, it is of extraordinary depth and far from all triviality. "With the fourfold interpretation the revela-

---

[15]Cf. Berger, *Exegese*.
[16]The standard work on the fourfold sense is de Lubac, *Exégèse*. A summary presentation of the theory of the fourfold sense can be found in Stuhlmacher, *Verstehen*, 83–84.

tory content of Scripture is, instead, expanded to all imaginable realms of experience and life."[17]

1.2 CONSIDERATION OF FUNCTIONAL HISTORY

Amplification on the basis of the history of the text's effect is related to the expansion of the understanding of the text.[18]

"The history of interpretation and the pragmatic effect of the Bible remind us of the abundance of potential meaning present in biblical texts. It recalls the fact that biblical texts do not simply have a fixed, closed-off sense, but are full of possibilities."[19]

The biblical texts have gone through varied reception. They have had not only a hermeneutical history in written texts, such as commentaries, etc., but also a functional history in the doings and sufferings of the church.[20] Church history has already been defined as the story of how the church has dealt with the Word of God.[21] Functional history shows how texts have suddenly come back to life and had an effect on people. In this sense the saints are above all a living commentary on the Gospel. For today's reader a look at the functional history of the Bible can impart new insights to the meaning of the text. This view of hermeneutic and pragmatic history "aims at helping introduce the biblical texts into the present." The experiences which Christians have had with the text in other situations are an important corrective for reading today.[22]

1.3 CONSIDERING THE READER'S EXPERIENCE

1.3.1 Considering Emotional Aspects

The method proposed by Walter Wink for work on the Bible seeks to help the reader appropriate biblical texts in a subjective-emotional sense. This sort of actualization has more to do with the reader's subjective problems. Wink ties in reflections on the historical

---

[17]Stuhlmacher, *Verstehen*, 83.

[18]On pragmatic history: Wrege, *Wirkungsgeschichte*, esp. pp. 11–31 (fundamental material); Berger, *Exegese*, 35–37.

[19]Luz, *Matthew*, 81. The pragmatic history of Mark 10:17–31 in the case of Francis of Assisi is presented in Egger, *Nachfolge*, 237–84; on the influence of the biblical texts on Francis of Assisi see Egger, *Alternative*.

[20]Cf. Luz, *Matthew*, 79–82; Wrege, *Wirkungsgeschichte*.

[21]Ebeling, *Auslegung*.

[22]Luz, *Matthew*, 82.

critical method[23] with a plea for the use of psychological methods in work on the Bible. As elements of interaction with texts, especially in group work, Wink suggests, along with discussion of the biblical text, amplification and practical exercises. For his most important practical tool Wink calls upon a catalogue of questions through which the participants can gain insights.

In the discussion of biblical texts the accruing problems are addressed by means of the historical-critical method. The method proposed by Wink takes the text as a text and the reader as a subject with equal seriousness; it passes over neither the reader's distance from nor closeness to the text. At the same time it gives directions for grasping the distance of the text and subjectively appropriating the text. This method gets down to business with the conviction that "something exists subjectively only when it is bound up with an emotion."[24]

A dialogue can succeed only when both partners in it are experienced and aware. Wink's method, which assigns a very large role in reading to personal experience, can help to overcome "a lack of awareness and experience on our side of the dialogue."[25]

1.3.2 Questions Put to the Text

This second model of reflective actualization in Diagram 29 builds on the model of Bible work proposed by Carlos Mesters.[26] This model starts from the assumption that today's men and women are seeking an answer to their questions. As a Christian, the believer here turns to, among other things, Holy Scripture.

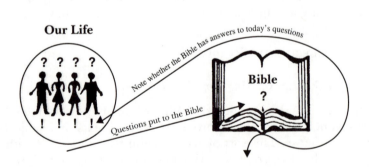

DIAGRAM 29: MODEL OF THE RELATION BETWEEN
LIFE QUESTIONS AND THE BIBLICAL TEXT

---

[23] Especially in his book *Transformation*.
[24] Quotation from Paul MacLean in Wink, *Bible Study*, 109.
[25] Thus Barth and Schramm in *Bibel*, 74, in connection with the presentation of Wink's concern.
[26] The model is taken from Mesters, *Incontrici*, n. 1, 30.

Despite its simplicity this model clearly shows the fundamental hermeneutical notion: actualization of texts takes place through a broadening of horizons and presupposes an awareness of one's own situation as well as an awareness of the foreignness of the text. The graphic presentation shows the process of understanding as a widening of one's horizon. The people who move in the wheel of life have to confront the problems of life, that are intellectual, emotive, and practical. A first prerequisite for receiving guidance for existence and action from the Bible is the consciousness of the conditions of one's own life and of one's own situation.[27] This awareness of one's own situation means that the exegete must make the reader aware not only of her own theological or denominational standpoint,[28] but also of the problems of today's world, and that must occur in such a way that the most important aspects of a problem area come into view. There is of course a danger that the exegete "can describe the problems of today's world only at second hand and not without amateurish abridgement." Nevertheless, the exegete must take a first step in what is intrinsically an interdisciplinary process by posing modern questions to the texts without doing them violence.[29]

Christians look to, among others, Scripture for the solution of certain problems, by putting questions to Scripture. Scripture, it is true, is a peculiar sort of dialogue partner since it is "capable of providing information only in a limited way."[30] Thus the questions put to the Bible should not be formulated too narrowly and must also be suited to it.[31] Scripture does not exist to offer a fundamental solution for every problem. Yet Scripture does give us a kind of map by which to orient ourselves. The reader questions the text and looks to see whether the text can provide an answer. Because of the temporal and cultural distance between the Bible and today's problems, we must often look for a perspective that allows us to interrelate biblical pronouncements and today's problems in a meaningful way.[32] Thus a conversation develops between reader and text. This method meets the demand that a method be worked out which questions not only the text but, today, also the subject of understanding.[33]

---

[27]Methodologically speaking, Mesters takes this into account by recounting in each case a concrete incident that calls attention to today's problems.

[28]Fohrer in particular stresses this in *Exegese AT,* 158–59, 166.

[29]Steck, *World,* 15–16.

[30]Fohrer, *Exegese AT,* 158. Cf. also the remarks on reading above in §1.

[31]Fohrer, *Exegese AT,* 160–61.

[32]Cf. Steck, *World,* 15–16.

[33]Barth, Schramm, *Bibel,* 48.

2. EXECUTING ACTUALIZATION

The actualizing of texts is subjective insofar as the reader is expressly drawn into the process of understanding.

> A method of actualization corresponding to the text and to the present-day situation must give directions concerning how to bring together the text and the reader's experience (i.e., familiarity with biblical text based on careful exegesis, and reflective knowledge about the situation and living conditions of today's men and women).

In the following section methods will be mentioned that match the models of the text and reading already presented. The difficulty of scholarly actualization is the fact that the actualization of texts belongs to the so-called creative forms of dealing with texts. Actualization cannot occur "wildly," as if every use of it were automatically in keeping with Scripture. Still, one cannot *plan* a fruitful encounter or guarantee the gaining of new insights or the success of actualization. Nevertheless, we can construct a framework conducive to a fruitful encounter with the Bible. And every actualization must be accompanied by the critical question to what extent the new insights are in harmony with what Scripture says.

2.1 SUMMARY VIEW OF BIBLICAL TEXTS AND CURRENT PROBLEMS

One initial procedure for actualization in the sense already presented might be the following: Taking a biblical text with a specific subject, first gather key words on the problems of today's world. The problems named in the key words then have to be explained, so that we are not treating them pre-scientifically while treating the text of the Bible with scientific rigor. Of course, dealing with today's problems is often possible only in an abbreviated fashion. The ideal way would be interdisciplinary dialogue.

As an example of such an approach to the text consider this: In actualizing the Passion story the idea would be to reflect on the story of the pain suffered by people in general. Or, with the question of "Law and Gospel," we would think about the problem of freedom, authority, and obligation in modern society. A few key words may also be cited, for instance, for the reading of Philippians. If we interpret the text as a letter in which Paul lets the community share in his experience of suffering and of Christ, and passes on to it the meaning which he has discovered in imprisonment, then the key

words, summarizing present-day issues, could be: the meaning of
life, the voice of the persecuted, forms of communication suitable
for the gospel.[34]

2.2 COMPARISON OF THE TEXT WITH ITS EFFECTS

Many important people evidently derive impulses for action from
the Bible. A look at the life and work (and possibly writings) of such
men and women can give us new insights into the meaning of
the text.

- What words in Scripture gave the impetus to the life and
  work of the man or woman in question?

- How were certain biblical sayings understood, and what
  effect did they have?

2.3 SEEKING THE FOURFOLD SENSE

In a modern version attention to the fourfold sense offers a model
of reading that comprises many individual steps of scholarly
actualization.

The individual steps:

(a) In attending to the literal sense (*littera*) the text is read
as a text from the past. Such reading is an indispensable prerequisite
for further commerce with the Scriptures. In scholarly work on
texts the synchronic and diachronic methods are to be employed in
this step.

(b) The vision of faith (which is how the misleading *allegoria*
should be translated) seeks to view the event, or the word in the
context of Scripture as a whole, in terms of faith (in keeping with
the so-called *analogia fidei*) and the liturgical life of the church
(without for that reason trying to find every conceivable statement
in the one biblical text). This step, which might be called the
"theological" and "christological" amplification of the text, is what
the survey of pragmatic history strives to take, that is, the history of
interpretation and dogma as well as functional history in the real
sense. In the Christian form of the fourfold sense it is crucial that
the second step is not a moral application (which one could employ
for every text, including fairy tales and so forth), but a christological
reading. Such a reading, which finds in the text a testimony to
"Christ and his Body," then becomes the basis for the further steps.

---

[34]Egger, *Galaterbrief,* 47–51.

(c) Directions for living (*sensus moralis*) can be gathered not only from the paraenetic parts of Scripture, but also from many other texts of Scripture that can help to interpret and shape our lives. The text then becomes a mirror in which a person can see herself. Then we have a confrontation between the text and the modern individual.

(d) In the directional sense (*anagogia*) the reader discovers pointers toward the consummation of history and her own life. The biblical text is questioned about its meaning, in particular against the background of contemporary problems of meaning and the future.

2.4 ACTUALIZATION BY MEANS OF STRUCTURALIST MODELS

Some structuralist models can be applied without much effort to the actualization of texts. As an example we may present the application of the actantial model to miracle accounts.[35]

Instructions

In this text the following persons are mentioned:

----------------------   ----------------------   ----------------------

To elaborate what develops between the persons with whom the story deals, one can use the following grid:

Giver	Gift	Recipient
----------------------	----------------------	----------------------
Helper	Seeker	Opponent
----------------------	----------------------	----------------------

At which place in this scheme would you insert the persons mentioned in the text? Describe how the persons in the text stand in relation to each other?

Where can you (should you/do you want to) insert yourself? Justify this position.

---

[35] From Egger, *Programm*, 35.

2.5 PSYCHOLOGICAL METHODS OF ACTUALIZATION

2.5.1 Emotional Appropriation of Texts

The method of biblical work proposed by Walter Wink primarily gives directions for emotional appropriation of texts.

In order to promote the reader's understanding, "all the associations, thoughts, feelings, and questions that emerge in the encounter with a text as an expression of its taking effect must as far as possible be heard and be recognized. This means not just the historical-critical responses, and, in fact, it might be better for them not to come first, since otherwise the others fall silent."[36]

In this method one works through questions. To match the three steps Wink sets up three groups of questions:[37]

(a) Questions that open up access to the peculiar nature of the text, in keeping with the historical-critical method, such as: What was Jesus reproached for? Why was Jesus not supposed to have dealings with sinners?

In this step the text should come into its own. The historical-critical method "preserves the right of the text to be different from what we want, even to be offensive."[38] The encounter with the text, of course, does not take place through a paper read by the group leader, but by means of the questions prepared by him (which presupposes a good preparation).

(b) Questions for amplification: Who is the Pharisee, the sinner in us? In "amplification" the idea is to "acclimatize ourselves to history."[39] The text should, as far as possible, stand full of life before our eyes, with the historical and literary facts serving as check points to protect us from speculation.[40] Then the subject who reads has to experience the resonance of the text. The questions for this step are, for example, in Mark 2:1–12: "Who is the paralytic in you?"[41] For Mark 2:13–17: "Who is the Pharisee and sinner in us?"[42]

(c) Pointers for an exercise: Write (engage in) a dialogue with the Pharisee in you. Through practical exercises, with the help of music, rhythmic movement, painting, modeling, the writing of

---

[36]Barth, Schramm, *Bibel*, 75.
[37]Wink, *Transformation*, 54–60. The questions are formulated for Mark 2:13–17.
[38]Wink, *Bible Study*, 39. Here Wink differs from various efforts to actualize biblical texts without considering the original meaning of the text, in that he helps the text to come into its own.
[39]Ibid., 39.
[40]Wink, *Transformation*, 54.
[41]Ibid., 44.
[42]Wink, *Bible Study*, 129.

dialogues, and the exchange of experiences in small groups, the text should have a deep influence on the reader.

An example of this more individualized confrontation with a text is the following:[43] Before reading Matt 7:1–5; Luke 6:37–38, 41–42, the participants are challenged to write down the name of an "enemy" (a person they hate or dislike or are vexed with) and to note in the form of key words everything they cannot stand about the person in question. Then the list is put aside. After the biblical text has been discussed, the participants are to consider how many of the things they wrote down apply to themselves.

2.5.2 Depth-Psychological Interpretation of Texts

The application of insights from depth psychology, especially in the wake of C. G. Jung's theory of archetypes, has led to a so-called depth-psychological interpretation of texts.[44] In this interpretation biblical texts are viewed in their function as auxiliary forces in a process of spiritual maturation, a function which dreams and fairy tales, etc. can also exercise. Thus the biblical texts serve as a kind of mirror in which the reader can make out the stages of the process of human maturation. "The method makes it possible to identify with different persons and events in a text and to perceive them as aspects, whether accepted or rejected, of one's own psyche. In the imagination a biblical saying is transposed into an I-statement."[45] This method which serves the unfolding of the personality makes use of specific rules.[46]

The biblical text undoubtedly has such a function and can serve the reader as a mirror.[47] An exclusive use of this method, however, goes against the grain of the biblical texts. The historical-critical method's interest in what actually happened is closely bound up with the peculiar nature of the Christian message as a whole, so that ignoring the issues raised by historical criticism would be questionable.[48] The suspension of the historical in essential areas[49] can be useful as a therapeutic procedure. But if the use of biblical texts is to do justice to the material, then the christological connectedness of the texts (such as the childhood narrative) has to be worked out before amplification.

---

[43]Wink, *Bible Study*, 53.
[44]Most recently, Drewermann, *Exegese;* Kassel, *Auslegung.*
[45]Kassel, "Urbilder," 105–12, esp. 110.
[46]Cf. the summarizing of the canonical rule in Drewermann, *Exegese*, 376–83.
[47]Cf. the "sensus moralis" according to the fourfold sense.
[48]Cf. Schroedel, "Bibel."
[49]Drewermann, *Exegese* 1.381.

We should not ignore the contribution which depth-psychological interpretation can make to biblical texts. This method directs our view toward important components of human understanding, to the significance of feelings. And that is something that work on biblical texts really cannot do without. Some methods of actualization that can be applied without adopting the theory of archetypes, such as free association, directed association, amplification, spontaneous and directed identification, etc. are dealt with in the introductions to books on practical biblical work.[50]

2.6 RULES FOR SPIRITUAL READING OF SCRIPTURE

In many aids to reading and discussing the Bible abridged rules are given for the spiritual reading of Scripture. These rules contain a whole host of approaches from traditional and recent exegesis. "Spiritual reading of Scripture" does not mean, as people often suppose, a kind of reading oriented purely toward edification, but a reading within the church, which has been given the promise of the Holy Spirit (John 16:13).

2.7 SACRED SCRIPTURE IN THE LITURGY

In liturgical use biblical texts are put into the context of other biblical and liturgical texts, as well as of the celebrations and the celebrating community. By means of this, and in the light of hermeneutics the text undergoes interpretation and actualization. "He (Christ) is present in his Word, since he himself speaks when the Sacred Scriptures are read in the church."[51]

---

[50]Cf. the books on the methodology of practical Bible work.
[51]Second Vatican Council, Constitution on the Liturgy, n. 7. Cf. also "Schriftgebrauch und -sinn in gottesdienstlichen Feiern," *Concilium* 11 (1975), n. 2.

Helps for the Study of the New Testament 🏵

Editions and Translations of the Biblical Texts

Biblia Hebraica Stuttgartensia. 4th ed. Ed. K Elliger and W. Rudolph. Stuttgart: Deutsche Bibelgesellschaft, 1990.

Septuaginta: Vetus Testamentum graecum, auctoritate Societatis litterarum Göttingensis editum. Göttingen: Vandenhoeck & Ruprecht, 1939–1993.

Septuaginta: Id est Vetus Testamentum Graece iuxta LXX interpretes. Ed. A. Rahlfs. 2 vols. in 1. Stuttgart: Deutsche Bibelgesellschaft, 1979.

The Greek New Testament. 4th ed. London: United Bible Societies, 1993. (UBS 4th ed.) Available in the same binding: *A Concise Greek-English Dictionary of the New Testament*, prepared by Barclay M. Newman. London: United Bible Societies, 1971.

Novum Testamentum Graece. 27th ed. Stuttgart: Deutsche Bibelgesellschaft, 1993. (Nestle-Aland 27th ed.)

Greek-English New Testament. Stuttgart: Deutsche Bibelstiftung, 1994. (RSV 2d ed. and Nestle-Aland 27th ed. on facing pages.)

Nova Vulgata Bibliorum Sacrorum editio. Ed. typica altera. Vatican City: Libreria Editrice Vaticana, 1986.

Biblia Sacra juxta vulgatam versionem. Editio minor. Stuttgart: Deutsche Bibelgesellschaft, 1990.

The HarperCollins Study Bible: New Revised Standard Version, with the Apocryphal/Deuterocanonical Books. San Francisco: Harper-Collins, 1993.

The New Oxford Annotated Bible with the Apocryphal/Deuterocanonical Books. New York: Oxford University Press, 1991. (NRSV)

Synopses

Synopsis quattuor evangeliorum locis parallelis evangeliorum apocryphorum et patrum adhibitis. Ed. Kurt Aland. 15th ed. Stuttgart:

Deutsche Bibelgesellschaft, 1996. (Greek text only: Nestle-Aland 27th ed./UBS 4th ed.)

Synopsis of the Four Gospels. 10th ed. Stuttgart: Württembergische Bibelanstalt, 1993. (A Greek-English ed. of the *Synopsis quattuor evangeliorum.* Nestle-Aland 26th ed./UBS 3d ed. and RSV 2d ed.)

Gospel Parallels: A Comparison of the Synoptic Gospels: With Alternative Readings from the Manuscripts and Noncanonical Parallels. Ed. Burton H. Throckmorton, Jr. 5th ed. Nashville: Nelson, 1992. (NRSV text arranged according to the Huck-Lietzmann Synopsis, 9th ed., 1936.)

New Gospel Parallels. Designed and edited by Robert W. Funk. Foundations and Facets. Sonoma, Calif.: Polebridge Press, 1985. (RSV. A new edition based on the Scholars Version is in preparation; so far only Mark has been published.)

Kloppenborg, John S. *Q Parallels: Synopsis, Critical Notes, and Concordance.* Foundations and Facets. Sonoma, Calif.: Polebridge Press, 1988.

Concordances

Even-Shoshan, Avraham. *Konkordantsyah hadashah le-Torah, Neviim, u-Khetuvim / A New Concordance of the Bible.* Jerusalem: Kiryat Sefer, 1977–.

Lisowski, G., and L. Rost. *Konkordanz zum hebräischen Alten Testament, nach dem von Paul Kahle in der Biblia Hebraica edidit R. Kittel besorgten masoretischen Text.* 2d ed. Stuttgart: Württembergische Bibelanstalt, 1958.

Wigram, George V. *The Englishman's Hebrew Concordance of the Old Testament: Coded with Strong's Concordance Numbers.* Reprint. Peabody, Mass.: Hendrickson, 1996.

A Concordance to the Septuagint and the Other Greek Versions of the Old Testament (Including the Apocryphal Books). Ed. Edwin Hatch and Henry Redpath. Grand Rapids, Mich.: Baker, 1987.

Vollständige Konkordanz zum griechischen Neuen Testament: Unter Zugrundelegung aller modernen kritischen Textausgaben und des Textus receptus. Arbeiten zur neutestamentlichen Textforschung 4. Berlin; New York: W. de Gruyter, 1975–1983.

Computer-Konkordanz zum Novum Testamentum Graece von Nestle-Aland, 26. Auflage, und zum Greek New Testament, 3rd ed. 3d ed. Berlin; New York: W. de Gruyter, 1987.

Analytical Concordance of the Greek New Testament. Ed. P. Clapp, B. Friberg, and T. Friberg. 2 vols. Grand Rapids: Baker, 1991.

Kohlenberger, John R. *The Exhaustive Concordance to the Greek New Testament.* Grand Rapids, Mich.: Zondervan, 1995.

Wigram, George V. *The Englishman's Greek Concordance of the New Testament: Coded with Strong's Concordance Numbers.* Peabody, Mass.: Hendrickson, 1996.

Neirynck, F. *New Testament Vocabulary: A Companion Volume to the Concordance.* Bibliotheca Ephemeridum theologicarum Lovaniensium 65. Leuven: University Press/Peeters, 1984.

Morgenthaler, Robert. *Statistik des neutestamentlichen Wortschatzes.* 4th (unchanged) ed. Zurich: Gotthelf, 1992.

Morgenthaler, Robert. *Statistik des neutestamentlichen Wortschatzes: Beiheft zur 3. Auflage.* Zurich: Gotthelf, 1982.

Kohlenberger, John R. *The NRSV Concordance Unabridged: Including the Apocryphal/Deuterocanonical Books.* Grand Rapids, Mich.: Zondervan, 1991.

Editions and Translations of Extrabiblical Texts

New Testament Apocrypha. Ed. E. Hennecke and Wilhelm Schneemelcher; English translation ed. R. McL. Wilson. 2 vols. Rev. ed. Louisville: Westminster/John Knox, 1991–1992.

The Apocryphal New Testament: A Collection of Apocryphal Christian Literature in an English Translation. Ed. J.K. Elliott. New York: Oxford University Press, 1993.

The Old Testament Pseudepigrapha. Ed. by James H. Charlesworth. 2 vols. Garden City, N.Y.: Doubleday, 1983–1985.

The Dead Sea Scrolls in English. 4th ed. Baltimore: Penguin Books, 1995.

The Dead Sea Scrolls Translated: The Qumran Texts in English. Ed. Florentino García Martínez; translated into English by Wilfred G.E. Watson. 2d ed. Grand Rapids: Eerdmans, 1996.

Die Texte aus Qumran: Hebräisch und deutsch mit masoretischer Punktation. Trans. and ed. Eduard Lohse. 4th ed. Munich: Kösel, 1986.

The Temple Scroll: An Introduction, Translation, and Commentary. Ed. Johann Maier. JSOT Supplement Series 34. Sheffield: JSOT Press, 1985.

The Apostolic Fathers. 2d ed. Trans. J. B. Lightfoot and J. R. Harmer. Ed. and rev. Michael W. Holmes. Grand Rapids, Mich.: Baker, 1989.

The Apostolic Fathers. Loeb Classical Library. Cambridge: Harvard University Press, 1976–1985.

Philonis Alexandrini opera quae supersunt. Ed. L. Cohn and P. Wendland. 7 vols. in 8. Berlin: W. de Gruyter, 1962–1963.

Philo. Trans. F. H. Colson and G. H. Whitaker. 10 vols. Loeb Classical Library. Cambridge: Harvard University Press, 1927–1962.

Philo Supplement I: Questions and Answers on Genesis. Trans. R. Marcus. Loeb Classical Library. Cambridge: Harvard University Press, 1953.

Philo Supplement II: Questions and Answers on Exodus. Trans. R. Marcus. Loeb Classical Library. Cambridge: Harvard University Press, 1953.

The Works of Philo. Trans. C. D. Yonge. 1 vol. Peabody, Mass.: Hendrickson, 1993.

Flavii Iosephi opera. Ed. Benedictus Niese. 7 vols. 2d ed. Berlin: Weidmann, 1955.

Flavii Iosephi opera omnia. Ed. Samuel A. Naber. 6 vols. Leipzig: Teubner, 1888–1896.

Josephus. Ed. H. Thackeray, R. Marcus, A. Wikgren, and L. Feldman. 10 vols. Loeb Classical Library. Cambridge: Harvard University Press, 1966–1969.

The Works of Josephus. Trans. William Whiston. 1 vol. Peabody, Mass.: Hendrickson, 1987.

Philostratus, the Athenian. *The Life of Apollonius of Tyana, the Epistles of Apollonius and the Treatise of Eusebius.* Trans. F. C. Conybeare. 2 vols. Loeb Classical Library. Cambridge, Mass.: Harvard University Press, 1969.

Language Helps

Bauer, Walter. *A Greek-English Lexicon of the New Testament and Other Early Christian Literature.* 2d ed. Ed. W. F. Arndt, F. W. Gingrich, and F. W. Danker. Chicago: University of Chicago Press, 1979.

Greek-English Lexicon of the New Testament Based on Semantic Domains. Ed. J. P. Louw and E. A. Nida. 2d ed. New York: United Bible Societies, 1989.

Blass, Friedrich. *A Greek Grammar of the New Testament and Other Early Christian Literature.* Ed. A. Debrunner. Trans. and ed. R. W. Funk. Chicago: University of Chicago Press, 1961.

Rienecker, Fritz. *A Linguistic Key to the New Testament.* Trans. Cleon Rogers. Grand Rapids: Zondervan, 1976–1980.

Zerwick, Max. *Biblical Greek Illustrated by Examples.* Trans. Joseph Smith. Rome: Pontifical Biblical Institute, 1963.

Zerwick, Max. *A Grammatical Analysis of the Greek New Testament.* Trans. Mary Grosvenor. 3d ed. in 1 vol. Rome: Biblical Institute Press, 1988.

Lexicons

Theological Lexicon of the Old Testament. Ed. Ernst Jenni and Claus
   Westermann. Trans. Mark Biddle. 3 vols. Peabody, Mass.:
   Hendrickson, 1997.
Theological Dictionary of the New Testament. Ed. Gerhard Kittel and
   G. Friedrich. Trans. G. Bromiley. Grand Rapids, Mich.:
   Eerdmans 1964–1976.
Exegetical Dictionary of the New Testament. Ed. Horst Balz and Gerhard
   Schneider. 3 vols. Grand Rapids, Mich.: Eerdmans, 1990–
   1993.
Spicq, Ceslas. *Theological Lexicon of the New Testament*. Trans. and
   ed. James D. Ernest. 3 vols. Peabody, Mass.: Hendrickson,
   1994.
The New International Dictionary of New Testament Theology. Ed. Colin
   Brown. 4 vols. Grand Rapids, Mich.: Zondervan, 1986.
Léon-Dufour, Xavier. *Dictionary of the New Testament*. Trans. Terrence
   Prendergast. San Francisco: Harper & Row, 1980.
Odelain, O., and R. Séguineau. *Dictionary of Proper Names and Places
   in the Bible*. Trans. Matthew J. O'Connell. Garden City, N.J.:
   Doubleday, 1981.

Important English-Language Commentary Series
on the New Testament

The New Jerome Biblical Commentary. Ed. R. E. Brown, J. A. Fitzmyer,
   and R. E. Murphy. 1 vol. Englewood Cliffs, N.J.: Prentice-
   Hall, 1990.
The New Interpreter's Bible. Nashville: Abingdon Press, 1994–.
Hermeneia. Minneapolis: Fortress, 1971–.
International Critical Commentary. Edinburgh: T. & T. Clark, 1895–.
Word Biblical Commentary. Waco: Word, 1982–.
Anchor Bible. New York: Doubleday, 1964–.
New International Greek Testament Commentary. Grand Rapids:
   Eerdmans, 1978–.
New International Commentary on the New Testament. Grand Rap-
   ids: Eerdmans, 1951–.
Black's New Testament Commentary. Peabody, Mass.: Hendrickson,
   1960–.
New International Biblical Commentary. Peabody, Mass.: Hendrick-
   son, 1988–.

Bibliographical Tools

Danker, Frederick W. *Multipurpose Tools for Bible Study*. Revised and expanded edition. Minneapolis: Fortress, 1993.

Scholer, David M. *A Basic Bibliographic Guide for New Testament Exegesis*. 2d ed. Grand Rapids: Eerdmans, 1973.

Fitzmyer, Joseph. *An Introductory Bibliography for the Study of Scripture*. 3d ed. Subsidia Biblica 3. Rome: Pontifical Biblical Institute, 1990.

New Testament Abstracts. Cambridge, Mass.: Weston School of Theology, 1956–.

General Biblical Reference

The Anchor Bible Dictionary. Ed. David Noel Freedman. New York: Doubleday, 1992.

Index of Modern Authors

Index of Ancient Sources 🎴